Cameras in the C

Cameras in the Courtroom

Television and the Pursuit of Justice

MARJORIE COHN AND DAVID DOW

ROWMAN & LITTLEFIELD PUBLISHERS, INC.
Lanham • Boulder • New York • Oxford

ROWMAN & LITTLEFIELD PUBLISHERS, INC.

Published in the United States of America
by Rowman & Littlefield Publishers, Inc.
A Member of the Rowman & Littlefield Publishing Group
4720 Boston Way, Lanham, Maryland 20706
www.rowmanlittlefield.com

P.O. Box 317, Oxford OX2 9RU, United Kingdom

Published by special arrangement with McFarland & Company, Inc., Publishers, Box
611, Jefferson, North Carolina, 28640. Copyright © 1998 Marjorie Cohn and David
Dow. Queries regarding rights and permissions should be addressed to McFarland.

First Rowman & Littlefield edition 2002

British Library Cataloguing in Publication Information Available

The McFarland & Company, Inc., edition of this book was previously catalogued by the
Library of Congress as follows:

Cohn, Marjorie, 1948–
    Cameras in the courtroom : television and the pursuit of justice / by Marjorie Cohn
and David Dow.
        p.   cm.
    Includes bibliographical references and index.
    1. Conduct of court proceedings—United States. 2. Television
Broadcasting of news—Law and legislation—United States. I. Dow,
David, 1937–   . II. Title.
KF8725.C63   1998
347.73'12—dc21
                                                                    98-16132
ISBN 0-7425-2023-4

Printed in the United States of America
♾™ The paper used in this publication meets the minimum requirements of American
National Standard for Information Sciences—Permanence of Paper for Printed Library
Materials, ANSI/NISO Z39.48-1992.

To Jerry,
my inspiration

To Nancy,
with love and gratitude

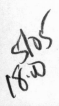

Acknowledgments

We are grateful to many for their contributions to this book—to our interview subjects, who generously shared their wisdom and experience; to Court TV, which supplied most of the photographs in the book and gave us the run of their facilities during a research visit; to Jerry Wallingford, for his invaluable contributions to the manuscript; to our inspirational spouses, Nancy Edwards Dow and Jerry Wallingford, who patiently shared their lives with computers, fax machines, untidy stacks of documents and long phone conversations as we collaborated on this work from our respective homes, 120 miles apart. Nancy and Jerry, we promise to make it up to you. We also heartily thank Marlene Stanger and David Wallingford, our dedicated assistants, without whose help this book could not have been written. Marjorie's cousin, Charles Davidson, gave generously of his time to design the cover, and photographer Miguel Pizarro donated the photograph of the authors. And we thank Marjorie's sons—Victor and Nicolas, and their dad, Pedro López—as well as David's children—Mary and Mark—for their unconditional love and support in this and all our endeavors. We want to express our appreciation to each other for being flexible and reasonable as this book evolved; through that process, we developed a great mutual respect.

Finally, we are grateful for the Bill of Rights, which guarantees a defendant the right to a fair trial while granting the public access to the criminal justice system. It is these two rights that set the stage for this book.

Table of Contents

Preface to the Paperback Edition

Cameras in the Courtroom: Television and the Pursuit of Justice was conceived in the final days of the 1995 O. J. Simpson murder trial and born into its aftershocks. Courts and cameras made for a volatile subject mix in those days. Americans' long audio-visual immersion in their justice system—or a unique, disturbing version thereof—stirred national soul-searching, head-shaking and lawmaking. The governor of the Simpson saga's host state pushed (unsuccessfully) to ban cameras from California courtrooms altogether. Federal court officials put the brakes on tentative steps toward allowing them. The authors poured in revisions, reflecting the fast-moving developments, right up to the to-press date of the 1998 edition of *Cameras in the Courtroom*.

Today's environment is changed but, surprisingly, no less dynamic. Major national and international events have a way of crashing through courthouse doors, stirring up judicial fallout.

Weeks after Americans cast their votes for president in the 2000 election, they watched Florida jurists grapple with a disputed outcome on network television.

Allowing the telecasts from the chambers of the Florida Supreme Court and lower jurisdictions aroused almost no debate. The contested presidential ballots had been cast in a state that had virtually pioneered cameras in the courtroom. The controversy arose when the fate of the presidency was propelled to the U.S. Supreme Court, which had *never* admitted a television camera. Appealing for an exception, C-SPAN Chairman Brian Lamb wrote Chief Justice William Rehnquist: "We respectfully suggest that televised coverage . . . would be an immense public service and would help the country understand and accept the outcome of the election." CNN attorney Floyd Abrams added: "There has never been a case where the public's right to observe judicial proceedings has been more important than this one."

The justices were unmoved. In his response, the chief justice said: "a majority of the Court remains of the view that we should adhere to our present practice of allowing public attendance and print media coverage of argument sessions, but not allow camera or audio coverage." The Court did, however, make one unprecedented concession. It released audiotapes of its two hearings immediately after they ended.

For the first time, millions of Americans heard the actual voices of the

xii   PREFACE TO THE PAPERBACK EDITION

nation's most powerful jurists probing lawyers on issues that would ultimately figure in the five-to-four ruling that sent Republican George W. Bush to the White House over the protests of his rival, Democrat Al Gore. The networks played the tapes over stock photos of the justices and computer-generated mock-ups of the Court. Though it was at best a jury-rigged form of television, NBC anchor Tom Brokaw found the exercise "thrilling." A network producer called it "historic."

Would it portend a gradual easing of the high court's rigid camera rules? There's no evidence of it so far. In fact, the next time the federal court system found itself in the international spotlight, with the camera issue at center stage, the response was doctrinaire rigidity.

The case involved Zacarias Moussaoui, a French citizen of Moroccan descent accused of conspiracy in the September 11, 2001, terrorist attacks on the Pentagon and New York's World Trade Center. Court TV urged U.S. District Judge Leonie Brinkema to exempt Moussaoui's trial in Alexandria, Virginia, from the ban on cameras in federal courtrooms. Writing in *The New York Times,* the cable network's president, Henry Schleiff, argued that televising the trial would "show the rest of the world—including our adversaries—the quality of justice that America applies even to its enemies." The defendant's lawyers endorsed the application, asserting that television would offer "an added layer of protection" for a fair trial. The Justice Department opposed the motion. And Judge Brinkema ultimately ruled against the applicants, citing security concerns. Any benefits from televising the trial, she said, would be "heavily outweighed by the significant dangers worldwide broadcasting . . . would pose to the orderly and secure administration of justice."

But Brinkema's courtroom would not be a camera-free zone. In a move reminiscent of another terrorism case—the 1997 Oklahoma City bombing trial of Timothy McVeigh—Congress approved closed-circuit telecasts, beamed to remote sites where relatives of the September 11 victims could follow the proceedings in *U.S. v. Moussaoui.*

Meanwhile, the Pentagon, assigned to hold military tribunals for accused terrorists, barred all television coverage of the proceedings except its own, or at least a fictional Hollywood version facilitated by military image makers. Pentagon brass cooperated with several entertainment shows, including the popular CBS series *JAG,* in preparing installments on mock tribunals. As *The New York Times* reported: "The Pentagon was eager to oblige, because, in the wake of Sept. 11, the military sees what television analysts call 'militainment' as one of the most effective ways to get its message across, free of the filters of a critical press corps."

In Congress, however, there has been a bipartisan move in recent years to open federal courtrooms to the same kind of discretionary camera policy that now prevails in a large majority of state courts. The successful audiocasts of the Supreme Court arguments in *Bush v. Gore* appeared to add an extra push to the so-called sunshine-in-the-courtroom movement. Sponsors have included such prominent senators as Patrick Leahy of Vermont, Charles Schumer of New York, and Charles Grassley of Iowa.

Across the country, the anticamera backlash unleashed by the Simpson murder trial appears to have dissipated, even in California, where, perhaps understandably, it was most prolonged. Six years after the Simpson verdict and not thirty paces from the courtroom where it was rendered, Superior Court Judge Larry Paul Fidler was preparing for a televised trial of Sara Jane Olson, another high-profile defendant, when the former 1970s radical accepted a plea agreement. Olson was accused of planting bombs under two police cars to avenge the deaths of six members of the Symbionese Liberation Army in a 1975 shoot-out with police.

Shortly before her 2002 retirement (the Olson case would have been her last big trial), Los Angeles County courts spokeswoman Jerrianne Hayslett told us, "I'm definitely seeing a more open approach to cameras in the courtroom." Why? "Several reasons," she said, including "the distance from the Simpson trial—it's beginning to fade. And we're getting new judges all the time. The new ones don't have that as part of their history." Added Hayslett: "While there are still areas of contention, there is a more reasoned discussion, based on added experiences." The judges' media committee even commissioned an educational video on courtroom camera coverage, produced by members of the local broadcast news community.

And the last two hold-out states—South Dakota and Mississippi—edged into the television age. Both now allow TV access to arguments before their state supreme courts. The change in Mississippi was largely inspired by a favorable reception to the telecasts from Florida courts in the disputed 2000 presidential race. Mississippi's court of appeals also feeds out coverage of its proceedings over the Internet and makes CD-ROMs available for broadcast. Nevertheless, camera coverage remains a sensitive issue in that state. Just months before the Mississippi Supreme Court appointed a committee to study the merits of allowing cameras in trial courts, it reprimanded Justice Court Judge Pat Carr for allowing still photo and television coverage of a murder arraignment and two other proceedings in his courtroom. Besides the reprimand, Carr was ordered to pay court costs of $100.

The relaxing of post-Simpson anti-camera tensions has even engendered benefits for the entertainment industry. For weeks, camera crews were allowed to shadow prosecutors in the San Diego County District Attorney's office as they interviewed witnesses and prepared for trial. The prosecutors became stars in a new prime-time television series—a "drama-mentary," as producer Dick Wolf called it—with the title of *Crime & Punishment*.

A crime drama played out in one San Diego courtroom rivaled the Simpson trial for sheer prurient interest. The area's television viewers were glued to no fewer than six channels carrying gavel-to-gavel coverage of the preliminary hearing of David Westerfield, accused of abducting seven-year-old Danielle van Dam from her bedroom in an affluent suburb and killing her. What could have been a one-day hearing became a three-day mini-trial as attorneys on both sides played to the camera in an effort to influence prospective jurors who might be tuned in.

The victim's parents, who wouldn't likely have been called to testify in an untelevised preliminary hearing, were grilled about their swinging sexual life-style and their alcohol and marijuana use the night Danielle disappeared. The wall-to-wall coverage of the Westerfield hearing in place of regular programming prompted an uprising of basketball fans angry at the preemption of NCAA tournament first round games.

Any benefit that could have inured from the gag order issued by Superior Court Judge H. Ronald Domnitz, who found a "clear and present danger of substantial prejudice" from pretrial publicity, was overwhelmed by saturation TV coverage of the hearing itself and the snippets of salacious testimony repeatedly aired on evening newscasts. Few trials have been better candidates for a change of venue due to prejudicial pretrial publicity.

Ironically, as camera access to U.S. courts was expanding, the nation's specialist in courtroom broadcasting cut back its coverage. Faced with a chronic ratings problem in prime time, Court TV switched strategy. Instead of relying chiefly on the "hot" trials of the daytime hours to provide the grist of nighttime programming, the network decided to fill prime time with a mix of original, court and crime-related series and reruns of popular criminal justice shows, including *NYPD Blue*, *COPS*, and *Homicide: Life on the Streets*. It even commissioned movies with justice-related themes. The result has been a big surge in evening ratings since the changeover in 1999 under Schleiff, who succeeded Erik Sorenson as chief executive. While declining to discuss profits, spokeswoman Betsy Vorce says the revised format "has been very successful." Court TV has graduated from a midlevel cable channel, available in about thirty million homes, to a basic cable fixture in nearly seventy million homes. Daytime fare still consists largely of the trial coverage and analysis that has been the network's mainstay. As this book went to press, Court TV's cameras had recorded nearly 800 legal proceedings since the outlet signed on in 1991.

Court TV won critical acclaim for broadcasting segments of the first Bosnian war crimes trial in The Hague—that of Duko Tadic—in 1996. Since then, an even larger war crimes proceeding has sometimes filled American television screens tuned to C-SPAN—the trial of long-time Yugoslav President Slobodan Miloevic, accused of genocide, war crimes and crimes against humanity. But nowhere have the TV audiences been more attentive—and reactive—than in Miloevic's home country, where some Serb loyalists regard the former strongman as a hero and Albanian survivors view him as a butcher responsible for thousands of deaths. Miloevic's use of the proceedings to put NATO leaders on trial for their bombing of Yugoslavia led President George W. Bush to call for disbanding the very tribunal the U.S. government was instrumental in establishing. The Hague court's television camera has been more than a recorder of history; it's been a vehicle of national catharsis, arousing and soothing the painful passions of a tragic decade.

This book began as an unlikely project inspired by the unlikeliest of trials, the nearly nine-month-long Simpson affair. A criminal defense lawyer and a journalist, wearing their time-honored and often conflicting interests like badges of honor, decided to collaborate on a book that could only lead to differing conclusions. What broadcast journalist did not revel in the parodic defense of the Simpson courtroom camera by Court TV's Floyd Abrams? "The camera pleads absolutely a hundred percent not guilty," he declared. And what true-blue criminal defense attorney did not smile approvingly as Judge William Howard pulled the plug on national television coverage from his country courtroom in South Carolina's Susan Smith case, in the interest of a fair trial for a double murder defendant who'd drowned her own children?

These conflicting instincts have tended to polarize the debate over cameras in the courtroom. Journalists feel strongly they should be able to report the news as they see fit. Many attorneys, criminal defense lawyers in particular, fear that once cameras are allowed into courtrooms, they will change the very proceedings they aim to depict, to the detriment of a fair trial for their clients.

At first, the contradictions in our respective positions seemed irreconcilable as we confronted the timeless tension between the public's right to know and the defendant's right to a fair trial. We engaged in a dialectical ballet of sorts, passing sections of the manuscript back and forth for comment and rewrite, standing fast or compromising, as we honed our views. We soon realized that one solution does not fit all situations, when an issue is as complex as cameras in the courtroom. Yet, relatively little that wasn't pure advocacy had been written about the subject. Although we differed in experience and instinct, we heartily agreed on the need for illumination. So we set out to write a book that explored a wide range of viewpoints.

In dozens of interviews with judges, attorneys, jurors, witnesses, scholars and journalists, we found almost no one *without* an opinion. We often discovered viewpoints in unlikely places. James Towery, past president of the California State Bar—an organization that for most of its existence had opposed cameras in courtrooms—turned out to be an unabashed fan of Court TV and advocate of television in most judicial settings. Nina Totenberg, the widely respected legal affairs correspondent for National Public Radio, reminded us that not all journalists walk in lockstep either. "After more than twenty-five years of covering the courts, I have concluded it's a rotten idea to have television there," Totenberg told a national meeting of defense lawyers. Paradoxically, we found that defense attorney Leslie Abramson, who had been paid for her legal commentary on ABC, was a vocal opponent of injecting cameras—ABC's or anyone else's—into the legal process.

Despite polarization in the immediate aftermath of the Simpson criminal case, we have since encountered a large middle ground of people who think cameras belong in some, but not all, courtrooms—who think television can be a force for education, accountability, and justice in some cases and an impediment to justice in others. As research for *Cameras in the Courtroom* progressed, we increasingly found our own views falling into this middle ground. If there is a central message to our book, it is that the decision to admit or not admit a camera into a courtroom should be a reasoned process, a calm, objective counterpoint to the passion that often accompanies the high-profile cases broadcasters seek to televise. Like the search for justice, decision making on the camera issue should be a product of open minds, hard questions, and clear reasoning. In our final chapter we suggest guidelines for decision makers, invite the federal court system to adopt the flexible approach of its state counterparts, and point toward the likely future of televised judicial proceedings. We also advocate the televising of Supreme Court proceedings, where the public's right to see the judicial system in action is most significant.

Some of the sources whose views and knowledge contributed to this book have moved on to other pursuits. Life, inside and outside the courtroom, is a dynamic process. That's what continues to make cameras in the courtroom a good news story. It is evolving, perhaps breaking out anew as these words are set into type. We hope our book will be instructive and thought provoking not only to judges, lawyers and journalists, but to a wider audience as well. For what is at stake in the issues treated here affects every person who cares about justice in the television age.

Marjorie Cohn

David Dow

Preface

This book began as an unlikely project inspired by the unlikeliest of trials. A criminal defense lawyer and a journalist, wearing their time-honored and often conflicting interests like badges of honor, decided to collaborate on a book that could only lead to differing conclusions. The work was born in the closing days of the O. J. Simpson murder trial as courtroom camera, the observer, emerged as courtroom camera, the defendant. By the time the trial ended, in acquittal and an orgy of finger-pointing, Defendant Camera was on trial in courtrooms, state legislatures and meeting halls across the country.

In this atmosphere of post–Simpson recrimination, it was tempting to hunker down defensively and self-righteously in solidarity with our professional flag wavers. What broadcast journalist did not revel in Court TV attorney Floyd Abrams' parodic defense of the Simpson courtroom camera when he said, "The camera pleads absolutely a hundred percent not guilty"? And what true blue criminal defense attorney did not smile admiringly as Judge William Howard pulled the plug on national television coverage from his country courtroom in South Carolina's Susan Smith case, in the interest of a fair trial for a double murder defendant accused of killing her own children?

These conflicting instincts have led inexorably to a polarization of views about cameras in the courtroom. Journalists feel strongly they should be able to report the news as they see fit. Many criminal defense attorneys fear that once cameras are allowed into courtrooms, they will change the very proceedings they aim to depict, to the detriment of their clients.

At first, the contradictions in our respective positions seemed irreconcilable as we confronted the timeless tension between the public's right to know and the defendant's right to a fair trial. We engaged in a dialectical ballet of sorts, passing sections of the manuscript back and forth for comment and rewrite, standing fast or compromising, as we honed our views. We soon realized that one solution does not fit all problems, when an issue is as complex as cameras in the courtroom. Yet, relatively little that wasn't pure advocacy had been written about the subject. Although we differed in experience and instinct, we heartily agreed on the need for illumination. So we set out to write a book that explored a wide range of viewpoints.

1

2   PREFACE

In dozens of interviews with judges, attorneys, jurors, witnesses, scholars and journalists, we found almost no one *without* a view. We often discovered viewpoints in unlikely places. James Towery, then-president of the California State Bar, an organization that for most of its existence had opposed cameras in courtrooms, turned out to be an unabashed fan of Court TV and advocate of television in most judicial settings. Nina Totenberg, the widely respected legal affairs correspondent for National Public Radio and ABC's *Nightline*, reminded us that not all journalists walk in lockstep either. "After more than 25 years of covering the courts, I have concluded it's a rotten idea to have television there," Totenberg told a national meeting of defense lawyers.[1] Paradoxically, we found that defense attorney Leslie Abramson, who had been paid for her legal commentary on ABC, was a vocal opponent of injecting cameras—ABC's or anyone else's—into the legal process.

Despite polarization in the immediate aftermath of the Simpson criminal case, we encountered a vast middle ground of people who think cameras belong in some, but not all, courtrooms—who think television can be a force for education, accountability and justice in some cases and an impediment to justice in others. As research for this book progressed, we increasingly found our own views falling into this middle ground. If there is a central message to our book, it is that the decision to admit or not admit a camera to a courtroom should be a reasoned process, a calm, objective counterpoint to the passion that often accompanies the cases broadcasters seek to televise. Like the search for justice, decision-making on the camera issue should be a product of open minds, hard questions and clear reasoning. In our final chapter, we suggest guidelines for decision-makers, invite the federal court system to adopt the flexible approach of its state counterparts, and point toward the likely future of televised judicial proceedings.

Perhaps the most difficult task was keeping pace with our subject matter. Chapters had to be amended right up to the moment the printers took over. Court TV underwent a change of ownership and management. Indiana signed on as the 48th state to allow at least limited courtroom camera coverage. Tennessee revised its laws. And the federal courts, while remaining anti-camera at their core, again cracked open the door for limited experimentation. Yet each time we were forced back to the keyboard, we were reminded of the dynamic landscape we had chosen to portray. The issue of cameras in the courtroom is, at its heart, a good news story. We hope this book will be instructive and thought-provoking to judges, lawyers and journalists, but to a wider audience as well. For what is at stake in the issues treated here affects every person who cares about justice in the television age.

Chapter One

The Simpson Legacy

> The day may come when television will have become so
> commonplace an affair in the daily life of the average person
> as to dissipate all reasonable likelihood that its use in court-
> rooms may disparage the judicial process.—*Estes v. Texas
> (1965)* (Harlan, J., concurring)[1]

The Controversy

Perched above the seat of Juror Number 98 in Department 103 of the Los
Angeles County Superior Court was the silent, remotely-operated "eye on the
wall." Much of the time it was trained on the figure in the witness chair, panning back and forth to the interrogating lawyer. Occasionally, it trolled the
small, congested courtroom to focus on the defendant or a lawyer or someone
occupying one of the 48 seats assigned to select members of the press corps,
friends and family of the defendant and victims and "the public."

Because of this lone television camera, millions of people throughout the
world followed every detail of O. J. Simpson's murder trial. It was the theater
of the century. Never before has a defendant so truly received his right to a
"public trial" guaranteed by the Constitution of the United States. And never
has the public had greater access to a U.S. courtroom.

Americans were hooked. Millions stayed glued to Court TV or other television outlets providing "O. J. updates." In the Los Angeles suburb of Tarzana,
a dentist kept a television set mounted in front of his dental chair tuned to the
Simpson trial to distract patients from the discomfort of the procedures he
performed. The Simpson trial replaced soap operas as viewing fare during break
time for nurses at a hospital. Yet, Simpson-vision appeared to be a love-hate
relationship. A CBS News poll more than half-way through the trial found
74 percent of Americans thinking it "a bad idea" to televise trials, a nearly complete reversal from the findings of a Roper poll 12 years earlier.

The Simpson case has crystallized debate over televised trials like no other
event in the camera's decades-long march to acceptability in the courtrooms
of 48 states. Among the questions being raised: Has this electronic miracle

revealed the wheels of justice … or driven them? Does it give viewers the real picture of the American justice system or a distorted view restricted to "mega-trials"? Will the expectations of jurors in criminal cases be unrealistically raised as a result of the vast resources expended in the Simpson trial? Does the courtroom camera change the very nature of trials—the behavior of judges, juries, witnesses, and defendants—and prolong them? And finally, post–Simpson, what is the future of the courtroom camera itself?

The debate over these questions ranges from the academic to the hyperbolic: "Television has turned the Simpson trial into a throwback to the Roman Colosseum," wrote Los Angeles attorney Charles Lindner, during the throes of the criminal trial, "a gladiatorial contest surrounded by profiteering charlatans. Television has paraded gossip writers, fortune-tellers, mind readers, fashion critics and, most recently, dog psychiatrists before its audience. Before the trial is over, a dancing bear will undoubtedly cross the screen."[2]

Countered Steven Brill, founder of Court TV, the Courtroom Television Network: "We need cameras in the courts as the antidote to all the garbage that has polluted reporting of these serious and seriously-distorted events."[3]

The camera became an issue at several junctures in the Simpson trial, most notably in November 1994, when Judge Lance Ito angrily threatened to eject it after false news reports on DNA evidence and some accidental shots of jurors by a hallway camera. Simpson's lawyers argued the camera should be barred from pretrial proceedings but retained for the trial itself, so long as that did not force Ito to sequester the jury. Attorney Robert Shapiro offered the defense reasoning:

> We would suggest that cameras be allowed in the courtroom because we believe that the evidence or lack of evidence will show that Mr. Simpson is not guilty of these crimes. And for Mr. Simpson to have a life after this case with his children will require the American public to have an understanding that his acquittal was based on evidence that was presented in a courtroom, not based on evidence that was in some way manipulated by lawyers, not based on evidence that was excluded based on legal technicalities.
>
> And since just about everyone in the world has an opinion on this case without hearing any evidence, we favor the fact that when Mr. Simpson, if he is acquitted, returns to society, that the public has a true perspective on what the real state of the evidence was in this case.[4]

Shapiro's argument and those of media attorneys carried the day. The camera stayed in the Simpson courtroom, not only for the remainder of the pretrial proceedings, but for the trial itself.

But across the country, in Union, South Carolina, the televised Simpson extravaganza triggered different repercussions. Judge William Howard weighed accused murderer Susan Smith's right to a fair trial and the public's right to know and decided the camera had to go. Much of the world had vilified

Smith, who confessed to drowning her two young sons by driving her car into a lake with the boys strapped in car seats. Citing the Simpson case, her lawyers urged Judge Howard to avoid a "media circus" by barring the courtroom camera. The judge had his own reservations, worrying about "community hostility" toward witnesses in the small town environment.[5] The camera was ordered out of court. "I did not realize until the cameras were gone," said defense attorney David Bruck, "how paralyzing they were and how much they increase the level of tension." In the semi-rural setting, "they gave the sense that we were all on display in a tiny boxing ring in a stadium of unimaginable dimensions, with millions of people watching."[6]

The Simpson trial also cast a long shadow over another high-visibility case 400 miles north of the Simpson courtroom. Sonoma County Superior Court Judge Lawrence Antolini refused to admit cameras into the trial of Richard Allen Davis, accused and eventually convicted of the abduction and murder of 12-year-old Polly Klaas in Petaluma. "Nothing like the O. J. Simpson case is going to happen in my courtroom," was Antolini's tart promise to prospective jurors. "I am not concerned about being discussed at the dinner table," he said, "but what I am concerned about is running an orderly case." Antolini turned aside the appeal of a media attorney who argued that the Simpson case "has been a circus, but not because there's a camera there."[7]

On the same day that Judge Antolini barred television coverage from his California courtroom, a judge in Corpus Christi, Texas, denied a request by

Court TV and the Spanish language network Univision to provide live coverage of the trial of Yolanda Saldivar, the 34-year-old woman accused of murdering the *Tejano* music star known as Selena. Both the prosecution and defense concurred in the ruling by state District Judge Mike Westergren. The Simpson case, said the judge, was "a factor" in his decision.

The sentiments of those judges were widely echoed by their brethren on the bench. Constitutional law scholar Erwin Chemerinsky of the University of Southern California frequently lectures to groups of judges around the country, including the federal judges whose courtrooms are among the last holdouts against cameras. "I think the federal judiciary was on the verge of cameras in the courtroom until the Simpson case came along," Chemerinsky remarked after a lecture at the height of the trial. "[Now] I think it's going to be a long time before cameras are allowed in federal court.... I can not possibly overstate the number of judges who've come up to me and talked about how much the Simpson case is an embarrassment and how they blame it on the cameras." In fact, a federal experiment with courtroom cameras was curtailed during the televised pretrial proceedings of the Simpson murder case, only to be revived on a very limited scale 18 months later.

Chemerinsky sees it as a classic case of blaming the messenger. And he is by no means alone in his defense of courtroom cameras. In an interview with CBS News during the Simpson trial, Professor John Langbein of Yale Law School was lavish in his praise of televised trial coverage. "These cameras are an absolute godsend," said Langbein, "because the public has been educated to think that criminal trials are what they saw on Perry Mason and it ain't true. What it's showing people is the way the system really works."

But is the Simpson case typical of the criminal justice system? Few defendants possess O. J. Simpson's vast resources to employ a legal "dream team" and the finest experts and investigators money can buy. Few trials extend beyond eight months and cost taxpayers more than $7 million. Though DNA evidence is increasingly used in criminal cases, it remains the exception rather than the rule. Prosecutors in the Simpson case tested blood and other evidence at not one, but *three* different DNA laboratories.

The very length of the Simpson trial did, however, expose television viewers to a huge assortment of everyday courtroom issues and legal building blocks common to even the most mundane cases. "Constitutional rights," "due process" and the "Fourth Amendment" have become household terms. "I think more people have learned about the legal system from the Simpson case than any other single event in American history," says USC's Chemerinsky. "And I think that's a very good thing."

Two years later, British viewers would receive an education in U.S. jurisprudence by watching telecasts of the Louise Woodward case, the trial of a 19-year-old English *au pair* convicted of murder (ultimately reduced to manslaughter) in the death of a Massachusetts infant. Britain's *Sky News* reported that an audience of more than 6 million followed the courtroom saga, boosting the channel's ratings by up to 1,000 percent at key trial moments.

If televising such trials is a force for public education, Court TV, which signed on in 1991, has done much of the educating. The Simpson case was the 380th trial the network had televised to what became 28 million cable subscribers during the Simpson saga. One of Court TV's early fans was David Harris, a legal scholar who wrote in the *Arizona Law Review* that "it is one thing to be aware of the presumption of innocence; it is quite another to watch the system do the best that human institutions can to be fair to an individual accused of the most horrible acts imaginable."[8]

Many think a "public" trial in the 1990s requires television and radio coverage because of the small number of courtroom seats allocated to the public (just eight for non-media members of the general public in the Simpson case). In the early days of an America typified by small communities, trials were often held in town squares to facilitate public viewing. But in today's urbanized nation of 260 million citizens, most have never witnessed a trial firsthand. "I think people know less about the judiciary and the legal system than other branches of government," opines Professor Chemerinsky. Broadcast coverage, he says, may be the only readily-available check citizens have over the judiciary. "If people see that there was a fair trial," he notes, "confidence in the judiciary is inspired. If people see that there wasn't a fair trial, then people can take remedial steps and react in the appropriate way."

That line of thinking has some deep and distinguished roots. Supreme Court Justice Louis Brandeis wrote in 1933: "Publicity is justly commended as a remedy for social and industrial diseases. Sunlight is said to be the best of disinfectants; electric light the most efficient policeman."[9]

The high court affirmed that thinking 47 years later in its landmark *Richmond Newspapers* decision guaranteeing public access to trials. "To work effectively," said the justices, "it is important that society's criminal process 'satisfy the appearance of justice,' ... and the appearance of justice can best be provided by allowing people to observe it."[10]

Does the Camera Change the Process?

In this book we will examine a key assertion of many criminal defense lawyers: that television alters and distorts the trial process, to the detriment of their clients. Some claim the camera's presence may discourage witnesses from testifying. Professor Chemerinsky, however, maintains that loss of witnesses is a possibility in any highly-publicized trial, with or without cameras. "Yet," he says, "we would never allow a completely closed trial simply because some witnesses don't want to come forward and testify because it's a public trial. I don't think the argument is any different about cameras in the courtroom."

On the other hand, although televised testimony may turn away some potential witnesses, Defense Attorney Jill Lansing worries that the courtroom camera attracts volunteers with more interest in television exposure than in contributing to the evidence. Lansing, who defended Lyle Menendez in his first California murder trial, relates that one "less than honest" person who testified for the prosecution was fired after his employer viewed the flaws in his televised testimony.

Many expressed concern during the Simpson trial that some witnesses stepped forward for their moment of televised fame. A Simpson juror shares that concern. Francine Florio-Bunten, who was dismissed more than four months into the trial, feels that O. J. Simpson houseguest Brian (Kato) Kaelin "seemed almost too enthralled with the whole thing."

However, Florio-Bunten insists the courtroom camera did not affect her performance as a juror. If she had remained to render a decision, she insists it would not have been influenced by its palatability in a community that had seen the same testimony, by television, that she had seen in the courtroom. "The only thing I thought about was *I* was going to have to live with the decision," she says. "That's it. Not anybody else. Me."

Florio-Bunten became so comfortable with life under the camera that she adapted it to her own needs. To remain close to her husband, who watched part of the proceedings from a sick bed during her sequestered days, she devised a system of signals. A cough, precisely at 3 p.m., loud enough to be caught by courtroom microphones, was her daily greeting to him. Sometimes the pre-arranged greeting was a rousing sneeze.

While allowing the camera to remain in the Simpson courtroom, even Judge Lance Ito had some publicly-stated concerns about its impact on the trial's principals. "My experience," he told lawyers, "is that individuals coming into this courtroom and taking this witness seat and having cameras six feet away is pretty intimidating. You look at this array of photographic equipment, that's intimidating. This camera pointing at the witness stand here is intimidating."

Ito added: "When I listen to counsel argue in this courtroom, I see the nervousness in their eyes, especially with counsel that I'm familiar with. I've seen counsel come into this courtroom and speak on this case that I've known for 20 years who I can tell are nervous and I can tell that their performance is affected by this eye here."[11]

Still, Ito did not exercise his discretion under rule 980 (b) of the California Rules of Court to refuse, limit or terminate film or electronic media coverage "in the interests of justice to protect the rights of the parties and the dignity of the court, or to assure the orderly conduct of the proceedings."

The most frequently-used rebuttal to Ito's concerns is the findings in studies from more than half of the 48 states (all but Mississippi and South Dakota) that currently allow cameras in the courtroom. Virtually all concluded the courtroom behavior of judges and attorneys was not significantly altered.

Although cameras are barred from almost all federal courts, it is not due to hard evidence that they would disrupt or alter courtroom behavior. In fact, a three-year experiment by the federal Judicial Conference involving cameras in civil proceedings in select trial and appellate courts ended with a recommendation that federal courts permit televised proceedings.

Some believe cameras may, indeed, change courtroom behavior—for the better. They argue that the lens is a check on the excesses of autocratic judges and forces lawyers to sharply hone their arguments, lest they embarrass themselves before a television audience that may include their peers and potential clients.

Television coverage was widely blamed for extending the length of the Simpson case. With a camera present, critics assert, lawyers embellished arguments, waged unnecessary debates, prolonged the examination of witnesses and tended to "perform" for the camera. But some trials have droned on longer than the Simpson criminal trial—without cameras—among them, California's Charles Manson case and the "Hillside Strangler" trial, albeit each had more victims and evidence than the Simpson case.

The vast public exposure to the Simpson trial, with its parade of experts and high tech evidence-processing, does seem to have changed expectations in other courtrooms. There have been anecdotal reports of juries disappointed by a lack of DNA evidence. In one case, jurors voted to acquit because the police failed to test hairs in a ski mask worn by a robbery defendant. And a woman declared during deliberations in a Berkeley, California, robbery trial that she wouldn't convict the defendant or any other African-American because she thought O. J. Simpson had been set up.[12]

The View Through the Lens—A Truer Picture?

The images created by television are dramatic. David Halberstam, describing the impact of television on the civil rights movement in his book, *The Fifties,* wrote:

> Film was so powerful that a reporter was well advised to get out of the way and let the pictures do the talking. Certainly, that was true in Little Rock. The images were so forceful that they told their own truths and needed virtually no narration. It was hard for people watching at home not to take sides: There they were, sitting in their living rooms in front of their own television sets watching orderly black children behaving with great dignity, trying to obtain nothing more than a decent education, the most elemental of American birthrights, yet being assaulted by a vicious mob of poor whites.[13]

Television correspondent Daniel Schorr described the televising of the integration process in Little Rock as "a national evening seance."[14]

And certainly, many televised pictures from the O. J. Simpson trial spoke powerfully for themselves—the prosecution's failed glove demonstration, the images of victim Ronald Goldman's grieving family as autopsy photographs were displayed, the testimony of witnesses to Detective Mark Fuhrman's use of racial epithets, Fuhrman's assertion of his Fifth Amendment rights against self-incrimination.

Supporters argue that part of the power of courtroom television images is that they present unfiltered truth. No intermediary exists between the events and the viewer's eye except a precautionary seven-second delay and the "kill" switch on the judge's desk. Unlike the print media, television conveys the actual event, not a reporter's interpretation of it. There is little room for human distortion.

But some see distortion of another sort—what is *not* seen by the cameras: the kind of mundane, run-of-the-mill cases that fill the dockets of most American courtrooms and consume the lion's share of tax money expended on the justice system. Karen Jo Koonan, a trial consultant with the National Jury Project, bemoans that fact and its implications for public policy-making. "People are forming impressions based on what they see in the O. J. Simpson case or the Menendez brothers case," she says, "and the policy decisions are going to be made based on that when 99.9 percent of the cases have nothing to do with the experience in those cases." Koonan wishes for the legal equivalent of C-SPAN,[15] focusing on the random, everyday courtroom diet of cases. "The 'interesting' cases," says Koonan, "don't reflect the reality for most people coming into contact with the legal system."

Live, gavel-to-gavel coverage of a trial such as the O. J. Simpson case also creates a "second trial"—a public view of the proceedings that may differ significantly from that of jurors. For instance, television viewers of the Simpson criminal case saw police Detective Mark Fuhrman invoke his Fifth Amendment right against self-incrimination after his own recorded words discredited his assertion that he had not used the racial epithet *nigger* in the preceding ten years. Jurors were not in court for that episode, and they were not told about it.[16]

In earlier proceedings, television audiences heard of more than a dozen incidents pointing to Simpson's alleged abuse of his murdered ex-wife that were barred from jurors because of the age of the incidents, their lack of relevance, or violation of the hearsay rule. One incident involved a call to a battered women's shelter by a woman identifying herself as "Nicole" less than a week before the murder of Nicole Brown Simpson. The caller expressed concern for her life and told of threats by her "prominent" ex-husband.

Thus jurors returned to a community which viewed a different trial on television than they had witnessed in the courtroom. Their verdict was subject to criticism, in part based on the collective impact of images they never saw and words they never heard. In fact, some jurors from the first trial of Erik and Lyle

Menendez on charges of killing their parents still complain of harassment from people who watched the proceedings on television and feel there should have been convictions rather than the mistrials that resulted when both juries failed to agree on verdicts.

But is that a cause for yanking cameras from courtrooms? After all, accounts of Fuhrman invoking the Fifth, his racial slurs and hate-mongering, and the excluded incidents involving spousal abuse allegations were all covered extensively by non-broadcast entities, as well—newspapers, magazines and wire services. Still, there is no denying the peculiar power of the camera. Surveys repeatedly indicate that more than half of all Americans receive virtually all of their news from television.

Weighing in the Camera

Ultimately the debate over cameras in the courtroom boils down to a constitutional balancing act that tantalizes and torments legal scholars—the right of public access, on one side, and a defendant's right to a fair trial, on the other. This free press–fair trial controversy is, in the words of the U. S. Supreme Court, "almost as old as the Republic."[17]

The clash between the First and Sixth Amendments to the Constitution bedeviled Supreme Court Justice Hugo Black in 1941: "Free speech and fair trials" he wrote, "are two of the most cherished policies of our civilization, and it would be a trying task to choose between them."[18]

Thirty-one years later, a similar constitutional conflict haunted John Brown, chief judge of the 5th U.S. Circuit Court of Appeals. He called it a "civil libertarians' nightmare."[19]

Criminal defense attorneys often argue that "fair trial" rights should take precedence over "public access" when it comes to cameras in court. California attorneys Angela E. Oh and Michael Yamamoto note that it is, after all, "the defendant's image [that] is selectively emblazoned across television screens presenting a visual target upon which the anger and repugnance of the public often builds."[20]

Conversely, pro-camera advocates believe public access rights should be fulfilled in a meaningful way. But the debate has sent them scrambling for fresh ammunition. Court TV founder Steven Brill finds it in the incident, cited earlier, which nearly caused the judge to expel the camera from the Simpson criminal trial—the erroneous report about an incriminating DNA test. "To be sure, what we must worry about most is the defendant's rights, not public education," says Brill. But "it was because of the camera in the courtroom that Judge Lance Ito was so effectively able to refute the KNBC report of a completed DNA test of one of Mr. Simpson's socks. The defendant [whose lawyers did not oppose cameras at the hearing] has to have been helped by that."[21]

But the trial prompted even participants who had favored or acquiesced to courtroom television to re-examine their views. Some became opponents. At least one, defense attorney Gerald Uelmen, turned against cameras during the trial; then, in its aftermath, turned part way back. During his critical period, the former Santa Clara Law School dean told an audience: "The unprecedented public scrutiny of this case has intruded to alter the roles and behavior of all the participants in many ways, some subtle, some not so subtle." Of witnesses, he said: "We may never be able to sort out all the ways their credibility was enhanced or diminished by their celebrity."[22] Others said the trial was an aberration—a distorted laboratory for examining the effects of cameras in the courtroom.

Some legal analysts are convinced that the camera in the Simpson trial altered the behavior of a higher court in at least one instance. Jerome Wallingford, an appellate expert and adjunct law professor at San Diego's Thomas Jefferson School of Law, cites the unusual action of the state appeals court in barring Judge Ito's proposed jury instruction, after Mark Fuhrman had invoked his Fifth Amendment rights. "Appellate courts do not want to review the trial until it's over," observes Wallingford. "If they start second-guessing the judge's evidentiary and instructional rulings during trial, they'll be besieged by writs in the future. There's no doubt in my mind the California Court of Appeal would never have given Judge Ito's ruling a second thought had the case not been televised and drawn such massive public attention."

The uproar over television coverage of the Simpson trial has spawned the inevitable cries for more study of the subject. Trial consultant Lois Heaney of the National Jury Project contends that most of the studies that led 48 states to allow televised trials were incomplete, from a scientific point of view. The studies largely concluded that cameras did not alter the behavior of trial participants. But no "double blind" studies have been conducted. Respondents can not truly say what would have happened without the presence of a camera. They merely responded anecdotally that the camera did not change their performance. However, Heaney thinks much of that could be self-serving, because jurors want to feel good about decisions they have rendered and witnesses want to feel good about testimony they have given. The same applies to trial lawyers and judges. In other words, says Heaney, they have "a self-reporting bias." We will examine the studies in a subsequent chapter.

No state has ever revoked the general right to have cameras in court once it has been legislated. But lawmakers, initially at least, seized on the Simpson spectacle as a rallying cry for shaking up the justice system. As the Simpson proceedings steamed toward their seventh month amid speculation of a possible hung jury, the California Senate Judiciary Committee held a day-long hearing on "Jury Reform" just a block from Judge Ito's courtroom. Among the "reforms" discussed at the hearing: proposals for less-than-unanimous verdicts in criminal trials and abolishing peremptory challenges during jury selection. And for a time after the trial, the messenger was under the gun. Competing measures to bar, and retain, cameras in California courtrooms clashed in the state legislature, then withered away. Ultimately, the state's Judicial Council modified the rules.

Whether by legislative act or exercise of judicial discretion, defense attorney Uelmen thinks cameras may face closed doors at the big, emotionally-charged trials of the future. "To find out what's really happening in the next trial of the century," he says, "the American public may have to start reading newspapers again."[23]

Lois Heaney, the veteran trial consultant, adds wryly: "The Simpson case could be the golden egg that spoiled it for the media...."

Chapter Two

Cameras Through the Years

There is no reliable record of the first appearance of a news camera in an American courtroom. But two things are clear: by the 1920s, still photographs of court proceedings were relatively common in the nation's newspapers, especially in tabloids; and from their earliest appearance, courtroom cameras evoked controversy.

As early as 1917, the Illinois Supreme Court advised the state's trial courts not to allow still or newsreel photography of trials. Eight years later, 45 judges, taking their cue from the Illinois Bar Association, voted to ban cameras from courtrooms and their immediate vicinity. And in 1927, a Baltimore judge issued contempt citations after a journalist ignored the court's order barring photography in his courtroom.

If today's mass broadcast coverage of mega-trials has its roots in any single event, it is in a trial that may have been as much a small-town publicity stunt as a search for justice. Even with a recent influx of industry, Dayton, Tennessee, today boasts of just 10,000 residents. But for nine days in 1925, the small county seat 40 miles north of Chattanooga basked in the world spotlight as the site of the so-called Scopes "monkey trial." It featured two of the greatest legal giants of their day, defense lawyer Clarence Darrow and three-time presidential candidate William Jennings Bryan. It became the first trial ever broadcast over radio. Chicago station WGN obtained exclusive broadcasting rights, after agreeing to wire up five loudspeakers in Dayton where local residents could follow the courtroom action. Clearly relishing the attention, Judge John Raulston declared, "My gavel will be heard around the world."[1] The judge also allowed newsreel and still cameras into the courtroom and occasionally complied with photographers' requests to "put your face a little more this way, Judge."[2] The defendant, a high school teacher named John Thomas Scopes, was convicted of violating a law against teaching the theory of evolution in classrooms where Biblical "creationism" was the only acceptable fare. The conviction, carrying a $100 fine, was eventually overturned because any fine over $50 had to be assessed by a jury, not a judge. That result, however, would be obscured by the bright afterglow of publicity and debate.

The Lindbergh "Circus"

Part of the debate involved the role of cameras in the courtroom. But the event that shaped legal attitudes on that subject for decades came ten years later, in another small town—Flemington, New Jersey. It was there that a German immigrant carpenter named Bruno Richard Hauptmann was brought to trial for the kidnap-murder of the infant son of Colonel Charles Lindbergh, the internationally famous aviator and American hero. Judge Thomas Trenchard placed tight restrictions on camera coverage, limiting the four still photographers allowed inside the courtroom to picture-taking during recesses and before and after court. But Sheriff John Curtiss made a gentlemen's agreement with five newsreel companies, allowing them to film the trial provided they showed no footage until after the verdict. One camera was discreetly placed inside a wall clock; another was mounted on the balcony railing and tucked under a large wooden box in a humorous attempt to conceal it. The "hidden" camera was impossible to miss. Efforts to augment the dim courtroom lighting by installing high-intensity bulbs in overhead fixtures helped boost temperatures in the gallery to uncomfortable levels.[3]

The trial would be widely denounced for its "carnival atmosphere." "The Flemington Circus—This Way to the Big Tent," screamed one newspaper headline. Another blared, "It's a Sideshow, a Jamboree...."[4] But careful hindsight indicates that the courtroom cameras contributed relatively little to the offensive spectacle. The court was often packed well beyond its capacity of 260. At one point 275 spectators and witnesses, and 135 journalists jammed the room. The case was a magnet for the elite of the writing and broadcast world, including Walter Winchell, Gabriel Heatter, Dorothy Kilgallen, Heywood Broun, Ford Madox Ford and Edna Ferber. There were also daily sightings of non-journalistic celebrities as the case assumed a chic role in New York society. Spectators were treated to the comings and goings of Ginger Rogers, Lynn Fontanne, Clifton Webb and Moss Hart from the entertainment world, former heavyweight boxing champion Jack Dempsey and society women such as Mrs. Ogden Livingston Mills, who arrived in a chauffeur-driven Rolls Royce. Comedian Jack Benny was a courtroom regular who once quipped of the defendant, "What Bruno needs is a second act."[5]

Some in the gallery read or worked crossword puzzles, prompting Ferber to hark back to scenes of the French Revolution. "We are like the knitting women," she wrote, "watching the heads fall at the foot of the guillotine."[6] Frequently, 71-year-old Judge Trenchard admonished the gallery for outbursts of laughter and even applause. The defendant himself had to be quieted after shouting to one witness, "Mister, Mister, you are lying." The next morning, his wife, Anna Hauptmann, was reprimanded when she, too, loudly accused a witness of lying.

The lawyers exercised only slightly more restraint. Running a daily gaunt-let of hundreds of reporters and photographers outside the courthouse, defense attorney Edward Reilly boasted that he would name four people who were the real kidnappers of the Lindbergh baby; but when pressed, he refused to do so.[7] At one point prosecutor David Wilentz told the press, "We are going to wrap that kidnap ladder around Hauptmann's neck," a reference to a lad-der thought to be the kidnapper's means of egress from the victim's second-story bedroom. In his closing argument, Wilentz several times referred to Hauptmann as an "animal," called him "Public Enemy Number One of this world," and sniped at him with venomous tirades:

> I think too much of my friends and my wife and my kids to be around him at all—I feel itchy, I feel oozy. I just couldn't stand being anywhere near him. I never walked into that jail even to get a confession from him.[8]

The atmosphere around the courthouse was no less carnivalesque. Venders did a brisk business in toy replicas of the kidnap ladder, bookends in the shape of the courthouse, and photographs of Lindbergh with a forged signature. One enterprising copyboy sold "certified locks of Baby Lindbergh's hair" at $5 a packet.[9] Weekend sightseers streamed into Flemington by the thousands and took Sunday tours of the empty courtroom. As the jury deliberated, a crowd gathered outside the courthouse and began chanting, "Kill Hauptmann! Kill the German."

Press coverage of the trial was excessive, frequently inflammatory and at times, downright irresponsible. Reporter Joseph Alsop of the *New York Her-ald Tribune* was under orders to file ten thousand words a day. Many of the trial's headlines screamed with pro-prosecution leanings: "Hauptmann shows signs of cracking," "Bruno Alibi Pierced," "Hauptmann's Case Crumbles." The *New York Post* described Hauptmann on the witness stand as "a thing lack-ing in human characteristics." The Hearst Corporation paid defense attorney Reilly's $25,000 retainer and signed Anna Hauptmann to a contract promis-ing that she would speak only to Hearst's *New York Evening Journal*. To ensure she kept her word, the paper assigned three female reporters to keep track of her, even staking out her rented room at night as she slept.[10]

But few of the accounts characterizing the Lindbergh trial as a "circus" or "Roman holiday" cited excesses of cameramen *inside* the courtroom. Wal-ter Lister, who covered the trial for the *Philadelphia Evening Bulletin*, recalled only one confirmed violation of the rules against taking pictures while court was in session, which involved a photo of the jury announcing its guilty ver-dict. In addition, the judge reprimanded the newsreel consortium for releas-ing some of its footage just before the trial ended, in violation of the pretrial agreement. And Joseph Costa, a founder of the National Press Photographers Association who covered the trial for the *New York Daily News*, noted:

It was not the action of photographers, *per se*, but the very nature of the entire story that created the conditions that prompted such a characterization ["Roman holiday"] and which was unfairly blamed on photographers.[11]

Still, Hauptmann had barely been sentenced to death before the highly agitated legal establishment swung into action.

Canon Fire at the Camera

The American Bar Association (ABA) appointed a special committee headed by former Minnesota Supreme Court Justice Oscar Hallam to conduct an exhaustive analysis of press coverage and other facets of the Lindbergh case. The committee came back with 16 recommendations, including a proposal that cameras be banned from courtrooms. A second committee, made up of members of the bar and the press, was then formed to work out standards governing publicity in criminal trials. While splitting largely along professional lines, this second panel recommended permitting cameras in court, but only with the approval of the judge and perhaps of counsel for both sides.

The ABA's House of Delegates proposed the committee keep meeting until all members could agree on the final draft of its report. But before that happened, the House of Delegates adopted on September 27, 1937, what was formally known as the Professional Ethics and Grievances Committee revised Canon 35. It called for a blanket ban on courtroom photography and radio broadcasting. The canon passed unanimously, virtually without debate. Canon 35—"Improper Publicizing of Court Proceedings"—read as follows:

> Proceedings in court should be conducted with fitting dignity and decorum. The taking of photographs in the courtroom during sessions of the court or recesses between sessions, and the broadcasting of court proceedings are calculated to detract from the essential dignity of the proceedings, degrade the court and create misconceptions with respect thereto in the mind of the public and should not be permitted.

In 1952, Canon 35 was amended to prohibit television cameras. Nine years later, the ABA went even further, extending its disapproval of cameras in court to appearances of judges in courtroom programs, such as simulated trials. In 1946, Congress stepped into the picture, forbidding radio and photographic coverage of criminal cases in federal courts. The Judicial Conference of the United States later adopted a resolution adding television to the list of proscribed media.

While lacking the force of law, the action of the American Bar Asssociation and its Canon 35 weighed heavily against the admission of cameras into courtrooms. By the 1950s, just four states—Oklahoma, Kansas, Texas and Colorado—had made moves toward even limited camera coverage of trials. Some believe Oklahoma was the first state to admit a television camera to a trial. Filming from a specially constructed booth in the rear of the courtroom, WKY-TV covered portions of the December 1953 trial of Billy Eugene Manley—the swearing-in of the jury, some of the testimony and the sentencing. A microphone hidden near the front of the courtroom recorded sound. Photo floodlights were placed in chandeliers to augment courtroom lighting. Judge A. P. Van Meter could discontinue the camera's operation at any time by pressing a small button at the bench. The films were shown, after editing, during newscasts.[12]

The first "live" telecast took place in neighboring Texas almost exactly two years later. Harry L. Washburn was tried and convicted of murder in the Waco courtroom of Judge D. W. Bartlett, who had experimented with still cameras in his court the previous summer. The defendant himself approved of the television coverage, saying: "Naw, let it go all over the world, I don't care."[13] Reviews were mixed. Judge W. H. Duckworth, chairman of the Conference of Chief Justices of the United States, said television made a "bullfight" out of the Waco trial, and "thwarted the very essence of justice."[14]

Retorted Judge Bartlett: "That's water off my back, just like a duck's. When Fulton used his first steamboat, he was jeered, but the steamboat is accepted now. They just don't understand—if they understood how this is being handled they wouldn't object."[15]

The local television station reportedly received hundreds of calls, all favorable except for a few persons who objected to the preemption of their favorite programs. Members of the Waco-McLennan County Bar Association who responded to a questionnaire strongly believed television was the least disturbing of the mass media covering the trial. They favored admitting TV to future trials if it was handled in the same manner as the Washburn trial, but noted that few courtrooms had a balcony such as the one from which television equipment operated unobtrusively in the Washburn case.[16]

Colorado held the first state hearing on the subject after Hugh Terry, general manager of KLZ Radio and Television (now KMGH), editorialized heavily to admit cameras to local courtrooms. A steady stream of witnesses, many from the media, appeared before the state supreme court during the week-long hearing beginning January 30, 1956. Justice O. Otto Moore, speaking for the court, concluded that Canon 35 should not be categorically enforced in Colorado. He said individual trial judges should have discretion to admit cameras to their courtrooms. "No limitations should be inflexibly applied to all cases," he said, "because every case involves different personalities and circumstances."[17] He dismissed the contention that opening courtrooms to cameras and microphones would induce abnormal behavior. Should judges or lawyers perform for the camera, he said, society should have a chance to witness that and act against the offending party. And he cited the power of broadcasting to educate citizens about the workings of the judiciary, which he called "the most misunderstood" branch of government.[18]

Cameras Become a Supreme Issue

Whatever small gains broadcasters made toward winning access to courtrooms were stopped in their tracks by a single high profile case of the 1960s. It involved Billie Sol Estes, a Texas financier and friend of President Lyndon B. Johnson. Estes was accused of inducing farmers to purchase fertilizer tanks and equipment that didn't exist and then providing mortgages on the fictitious property. A jury convicted him in a trial that lasted just three days in Tyler, Texas, after a barrage of pretrial publicity prompted a change of venue. The trial judge, exercising his discretion under Texas law, allowed television and photographic coverage of both a two-day pretrial hearing and the trial itself. But there was a major difference in the two proceedings. Twelve television cameramen and still photographers were admitted to the pretrial hearing. Cables snaked across the courtroom floor. Almost everyone conceded it was a disruptive scene. When the actual trial began, all of the photographers were restricted to a booth in the back of the courtroom, constructed and painted to blend in with the room's permanent decor.

Estes appealed his conviction, contending that the photographic and broadcast coverage had deprived him of a fair trial. The case eventually worked its way to the Supreme Court, which issued a five to four decision in 1965 that froze debate over cameras in the courtroom for more than a decade. The court overturned Estes' conviction, although Justice Tom Clark, writing for the majority, conceded that he could not provide empirical evidence that the camera coverage had prejudiced the case against Estes. But he declared at length that the mere presence of television cameras had a detrimental psychological impact on jurors, witnesses, the judge and defendant.[19] In his concurring opinion, Chief Justice Earl Warren, joined by Justices William Douglas and Arthur Goldberg, wrote:

> The prejudice of television may be so subtle that it escapes the ordinary methods of proof, but it would gradually erode our fundamental conception of trial. A defendant may be unable to prove that he was actually prejudiced by a televised trial, just as he may be unable to prove that the introduction of a coerced confession at his trial influenced the jury to convict him....[20]

Justice Potter Stewart dissented. He acknowledged there had been "confusion in the courtroom" during the pretrial hearing, but noted that nothing bearing on the defendant's guilt or innocence was discussed, only procedural

Here and on opposite page: Photos from the appendix of Chief Justice Earl Warren's concurring opinion in *Estes vs. Texas. Above:* September 1962: Cameras are focused on the petitioner at a hearing on a pretrial motion by the defense to exclude cameras from the courtroom. The hearing lasted two days, at the end of which the motion was denied. *Opposite top:* When the trial was held in October 1962, a booth had been built for the cameras. This photo shows the booth on the first day of the trial. *Opposite bottom:* By the second day of the trial, the booth had been modified as shown here. This is how the booth remained for the rest of the trial.

matters. He challenged the assertion that the presence of cameras influenced courtroom principals in subtle ways.

Almost lost in the 158 pages of painstakingly crafted legal language of *Estes v. Texas* were two short passages that virtually promised these were not the final words on cameras in the courtroom—passages of hope to broadcasters and photo-journalists:

—"Today's decision is *not* a blanket constitutional prohibition against the televising of state criminal trials," wrote Justice William Brennan in his dissent.[21]

—"When the advances in these arts permit reporting ... by television without their present hazards to a fair trial we will have another case." Those words were penned by Justice Clark, the author of the majority opinion.[22]

Indeed, there was to be "another case," though it took 16 more years to land on the desks of the Supreme Court justices. It was *Chandler v. Florida,*[23] a product of legal and social revolution.

For a while after *Estes,* the outlook for courtroom cameras turned even

bleaker. The Supreme Court followed its reversal in the case of the Texas wheeler-dealer by overturning the murder conviction of Ohio physician Sam Sheppard, ruling that his rights to a fair trial were damaged by the prejudicial impact of pretrial publicity on jurors and the local community. Although the Sheppard case did not deal specifically with television coverage, it nevertheless reinforced public sentiment against televised trials. In 1972, the American Bar Association's House of Delegates updated its Canon 35 with a new rule, only slightly less restrictive than the original. It allowed cameras in courtrooms, but only for specific non-news purposes, such as making a court record, presenting evidence or producing educational materials for students.

Meanwhile, the exploding technology of television was becoming more and more pervasive in its influence on the American psyche, even if legal officialdom was slow to embrace it. The controversial and costly war in Southeast Asia became known as the "television war," as network newscasts fed viewers a nightly diet of bloodshed and heartbreak featuring the satellited images of American sons and daughters. With hindsight, many would label the prime time offerings of the 1970s "The Golden Age of Television." In addition to entertainment programs, the nation sat mesmerized through hour after televised hour of the Senate Watergate hearings. Each episode provided a new excursion into the dark secrets of the Nixon White House, evoking a crescendo of cries for "new openness" in government.

Inevitably news organizations took up the cry and carried it to the courthouse steps. Florida was in the vanguard. In 1975, the Post-Newsweek stations in Florida petitioned the state supreme court to rescind its prohibition of television coverage in the courtroom. The petition was rejected in part, but the court authorized a modest experiment with cameras that was never carried out due to a lack of willing trial participants. Two years later, the court approved another one-year pilot program which allowed the electronic media to cover proceedings in all of Florida's state courts without the consent of the participants.

Within months, several million viewers in Florida and elsewhere were absorbed in the courtroom drama of *Florida v. Zamora*,[24] involving a 17-year-old boy accused of murdering an elderly neighbor two years earlier. The trial attracted international interest because of the unusual defense: "voluntary subliminal television intoxication." The defense contended that Ronny Zamora was so satiated with the massive amounts of crime and violence he'd seen on television that he didn't know right from wrong.

When the trial was over, Judge Paul Baker submitted a report to the Florida Supreme Court that seemed to allay the concerns raised by Justice Clark in the *Estes* decision 12 years earlier. Baker said the television equipment produced no distracting noises or flashes during the trial. He said he had met privately with jurors after the trial. Although some blamed the lone TV camera for minor distractions, none said it affected his or her ability to concentrate on testimony or instructions. The judge concluded that the public has a right to see how a judge conducts business, and television was a good way of doing that. Prosecutor Tom Headley was equally positive, noting "no distraction from the television and still cameras." Defense Counsel Ellis Rubin gushed to reporters that "televising of the Zamora trial is the greatest educational tool this country will ever have as to what goes on in a court of law ... I think it is a wonderful thing."[25]

The Supreme Court Revisited

Armed with favorable assessments from the Zamora trial and others, the Florida high court in 1979 permanently opened the state's courtrooms to television coverage, subject always to the discretion of the presiding judge.

Not everyone was happy with that. And Florida's accommodating attitude toward courtroom cameras had yet to be tested before the highest court in the land. Enter *Chandler v. Florida.* The case went to the U.S. Supreme Court after two Miami Beach policemen, Noel Chandler and Robert Granger, were convicted of burglary and other related crimes. The trial was televised in December 1977 as part of Florida's one-year pilot experiment with cameras in courts. Before trial, the defendants tried unsuccessfully to have the pilot program declared unconstitutional. During jury selection, the defense lawyers asked each potential juror if he or she could be fair and impartial despite the presence of a television camera in the courtroom. Each responded in the affirmative. Because of defense opposition to televising the trial, the judge limited camera coverage to one portion of the prosecution case and closing arguments.

Defense attorney Joel Hirschhorn argued to the Supreme Court that the use of the television camera had denied his clients a fair and impartial trial. But this time the Court said that the mere presence of a camera does not necessarily impair the trial process. The justices found no evidence that Officers Chandler and Granger had been prejudiced by the limited television coverage of their trial. In its unanimous decision, the Court ruled that the *Estes* decision, rendered 16 years earlier, did not imply a constitutional ban on still camera, radio and television coverage in all cases under all circumstances. On the contrary, the court affirmed the premise that "consistent with constitutional guarantees, a state may provide for radio, television and still photographic coverage of a criminal trial for public broadcast, *notwithstanding the objection of the accused.*"[26]

Interestingly, just three of the justices who had been involved in *Estes* remained on the court for the *Chandler* ruling. All three—Potter Stewart, Byron White and William Brennan—were *Estes* dissenters.

While the *Chandler* decision stopped short of declaring that cameras have a constitutional *right* to be in American courtrooms, it clearly gave state courts a green light for further experimentation with television and still camera coverage of trial proceedings. And as more and more states responded to this new "go" signal, the legal establishment bowed to reality. In 1982, the ABA House of Delegates approved still another new canon, replacing the 1972 prohibition on camera coverage for news purposes. The new Canon 3A(7) did not endorse news cameras in the courtroom, but allowed for their possible use at the discretion and under the supervision of a state's highest appellate court.

Encouraged by *Chandler* and the new ABA canon, state after state opened courtroom doors to cameras, subject to the discretion of the presiding judge. Forty-eight states now allow photography of at least some court proceedings. Nine restrict camera access to appellate or state supreme court sessions. Maryland, Maine and Delaware limit camera coverage to civil trials. Only still photos are permitted in Utah's trial courts.[27] By most accounts, trend-setting Florida has the most experience with cameras in courtrooms. One study estimates "thousands" of Florida trials have had television coverage. *Time* magazine reported during the 1979 murder trial of Theodore Bundy in Tallahassee that "people have become accustomed to the pervasiveness of TV," so much so that "two jurors were blasé enough to fall asleep—on camera."[28]

Federal courts remain largely untouched by developments at the state level, exemplifying the ambivalence that lingers over cameras in the courtroom. In 1991, the U.S. Judicial Conference commissioned a three-year experiment with cameras in civil trials in six federal court districts. Despite findings of "small or no effects of camera presence," the Conference renewed its ban of photography in federal courts, most likely a reaction to perceived excesses in the O. J. Simpson trial.

Technology and the Law

Cameras gained acceptance in state courts in part because of technical advances. The photographers who jockeyed for shots during recesses in the Lindbergh proceedings typically lugged large, cumbersome Speed Graphics which announced their shots with noisy "clicks" and required flash enhancement in murky courtroom lighting. The advent of the compact 35-millimeter news camera in the 1960s made still photography less obtrusive. Today, most judges require that still courtroom cameras be encased in "blimps"— padded housings that absorb the distinctive "ker-atch-a-tee" noise of a closing camera shutter. Photographers are typically assigned to fixed positions at the rear of the room, away from the normal line of sight of jurors. Flash is usually forbidden and unnecessary, given modern fast films that produce perfect pictures even in dusk-like conditions.

The newsreel photographers of the Scopes and Lindbergh era were equipped with heavy, 35-millimeter movie-style cameras. Changing the cast-metal film magazines was a noisy, clanging procedure. Television brought a more compact technology to court: 16-millimeter motion picture cameras that were smaller and less obtrusive. Changing film magazines could still be a noisy business. But portable battery packs at least eliminated the need to string electrical cables across the courtroom.

The mid–1970s brought the video revolution—and the technological developments that contributed most to television's acceptability in courtrooms. These advances gave judicial entrée to Court TV, the first full-time network devoted solely to coverage of court proceedings. Gone were the noisy film magazines and, in big cities, the two or three-person crews. The courtroom images didn't even need to be recorded in court. A technician could record the proceedings on a video tape recorder outside the courtroom, connected to the camera by a single cable. And now, occasionally, the camera operator isn't even in the courtroom. As in the O. J. Simpson case, the camera is a wall-mounted robot, responding to the commands of an operator at a remote console with a "joy stick" very much as in a modern video game. The equipment is virtually silent, though former Simpson juror Francine Florio-Bunten claims that during lulls in testimony, she could hear the faint whirr of the panning camera high above her head. She did not consider it a distraction, however.

But as the Simpson aftermath has proven, the new, relatively unobtrusive technology has not allayed concerns that courtroom cameras somehow compromise the conduct and outcome of trials. The debate continues, in a charged atmosphere reminiscent of the post–Lindbergh era. In upcoming chapters, we shall see that the familiar constitutional issues underpinning the debate are being dusted off for fresh battles. Justice Clark was prescient when he mused in the 1965 *Estes* decision, "…we will have another case."

Chapter Three

Is the Televised Trial a Fair Trial?

> I would not have cameras in the courtroom if I didn't have a
> rule that said they could be in there absent a showing of some
> prejudice or there being some basis to remove them.—Honor-
> able William Howard, presiding judge, Susan Smith trial

A Courtroom Without Cameras

When the Southern gentleman jurist was called to Union, South Carolina, from
Charleston to preside over the Susan Smith murder case, he confronted a question that has perplexed hundreds, perhaps thousands, of judges in the Television Age—can a televised trial be a fair trial?

South Carolina, like most states without outright camera prohibitions,
allows the trial judge wide discretion in deciding that issue. Initially, Judge
Howard worried he would be abusing his discretion if he banned television
coverage without a showing by the defense that TV exposure might inflict
some tangible harm on Smith's chances for a fair trial. But in the end his decision rested less on hard proof than on a common sense appraisal of the unique
circumstances of the case. The defendant's life was at stake. She stood accused
of drowning her two young children. The jurors all came from a small town
of only 10,000 inhabitants, many of whom had known Smith and her family
for years. The trial testimony would involve private, intimate details about people in Union. Defense witnesses might hesitate to bare their souls and blame
themselves for the tragedy that occurred when Smith drove her two young
sons into a lake and drowned them.

Recalls Judge Howard: "I just felt that there was too much chance that
some of those people [the jurors] could be back there thinking, 'I'm going to
have to atone for this decision whatever it may be,' and that these cameras
would be an extra burden in that regard." In other words, a televised trial

might well *not* be a fair trial. Howard banned the cameras. A brief but well-run and well-tried case followed in which the defendant was convicted and sentenced to life in prison.

The Simpson Show

Unlike Smith's lawyers, defense attorneys in the O. J. Simpson murder trial did not object to the camera's presence. They, in effect, said television coverage would prove Simpson's innocence to the viewing public and pave the way for a warm reception when he returned to private life after his acquittal. That is, they thought cameras in the Simpson courtroom would, if anything, enhance the defendant's chances of a fair trial.

It turned out to be history's most widely watched test of the cameras-and-fair trial issue. Though the jury acquitted Simpson, at least one of his attorneys emerged with mixed feelings about allowing TV coverage of the case. Gerald Uelmen, the bespectacled law professor-turned-defense attorney, was known as "Dean Uelmen" in the Simpson trial. Imported by Simpson's "Dream Team" from Northern California, the former Dean of Santa Clara University School of Law argued motions and technical evidentiary matters for the defense. Although he initially favored televising the trial, he began to question his position as the trial proceeded. "My concern," he says, "was that the cameras were impacting the behavior of the participants—the judge, the lawyers, and most significantly, the witnesses. We had witnesses who did not want to testify because they didn't want to be subjected to being on national television. We had other witnesses who gloried in it. Their testimony was like a gig. So from that perspective, I became convinced that while it's great theoretically to have this unobtrusive eye in the courtroom so the whole public can watch, when the eye itself becomes a presence affecting the proceeding, it really skews what's happening, and at that point it should be excluded."

But Uelmen ultimately emerged from the trial seeing benefits to television in some cases. He noted in the Simpson case that both sides gained important new witnesses, who stepped forward after watching the case on TV. Kathleen Bell, whose explosive testimony impeached Detective Mark Fuhrman, wrote to the defense team after she watched Fuhrman on television during the preliminary hearing. Likewise, witnesses who came to the trial and authenticated photographs taken of Simpson wearing gloves (allegedly the same brand as the murder gloves) had seen the case on television and thought they had relevant testimony for the prosecution.[1]

Thus, televising a trial may enhance its fairness in some cases and corrupt it in others. The decision to admit or exclude cameras must be determined on a case-by-case basis.

Court TV

Top: O. J. Simpson at his trial for murder. *Bottom:* Judge Lance Ito presiding at the O. J. Simpson criminal trial.

The Fair Trial Rights of the Accused

The concept of "fair trial rights," which is at the heart of the courtroom camera controversy, has been evolving for hundreds of years. Immediately after the American colonies wrested their independence from Britain, all of the states granted the right to a jury trial in their constitutions. Before the enactment of the Bill of Rights in 1787, the jury trial guarantee in criminal cases was the only right contained in all the state constitutions.[2] The jury was considered the conscience of the community, in whose hands resided the most awesome power—the license to take liberty or life from one of its countrymen.

Although the Constitution guarantees a fair trial as a matter of due process,[3] the basic elements of a fair trial are defined in the Sixth Amendment. It guarantees the accused in all criminal prosecutions "the right to a speedy and public trial, by an impartial jury of the State and district wherein the crime shall have been committed...." Chief Justice William Howard Taft, in *Tumey v. Ohio*,[4] defined the denial of due process as "every procedure which would offer a possible temptation to the average man ... to forget the burden of proof [beyond a reasonable doubt] required to convict the defendant, or which might lead him not to hold the balance nice, clear and true between the State and the accused...."[5]

In case after case, U.S. courts have affirmed the basic principle that a defendant's risk of losing his liberty or life demands nothing less than absolute fairness and equity. The Supreme Court has asserted that part and parcel of the fair trial guarantee is excluding extraneous influences that could divert the jury from the crucial task of determining guilt or innocence. In *Estes v. Texas*, the high court stated, "We have always held that the atmosphere essential to the preservation of a fair trial—the most fundamental of all freedoms—must be maintained at all costs."[6]

The Sixth Amendment also guarantees the accused in a criminal trial "the right ... to have compulsory process for obtaining witnesses in his favor..."; that is, the right to subpoena witnesses to testify in his behalf. The Supreme Court has further recognized a defendant's "constitutionally guaranteed access to evidence."[7] When the camera in the courtroom causes witnesses to be less forthcoming in their testimony, or prevents them from testifying at all, the defendant's right to a fair trial is in jeopardy.

The "Public" Trial

One of the key fair trial guarantees is the defendant's right to a *public* trial. That was especially important to our Founding Fathers, who were reacting against the despotism of the English "star chamber" proceeding, used by the crown to single out and railroad undesirables with no public accountability.

The goal of the public trial was to provide a tribunal "free of prejudice, passion, excitement and tyrannical power."[8]

Emanating from the Sixth Amendment to the Constitution, "the requirement of a public trial was to guarantee that the accused would be fairly dealt with and not unjustly condemned. History had proven that secret tribunals were effective instruments of oppression."[9] A public trial "has always been recognized as a safeguard against any attempt to employ our courts as instruments of persecution. The knowledge that every criminal trial is subject to contemporaneous review in the forum of public opinion is an effective restraint on possible abuse of judicial power."[10]

By maintaining trials open to the public, autocratic judges are less likely to deny legal protections to the accused. And many argue that a courtroom camera, by making the trial even more public, adds an extra level of insurance against judicial abuses. Rikki J. Klieman, the articulate, raven-haired anchor for Court TV, practiced as a criminal defense attorney for many years in Boston. In a post–Simpson verdict article in the *Chicago Tribune*, she wrote, "I blessed the camera when certain judges were kept honest rather than being arbitrary or capricious."[11] Klieman's comments are echoed by National Jury Project trial consultant Karen Jo Koonan, who thinks a camera in the courtroom "puts restraints on the judge in a way that is beneficial to the defendant. The judge is not going to be as arbitrary (as many judges are) in front of the camera, where he is going to have to justify his behavior to a larger audience. A lot of these judges get away with so much because no one pays any attention to them."

Conscious of the highly public nature of the Simpson trial, Judge Lance Ito made a very telling gesture. Defense attorneys pressed him to play the predominantly black jury 61 segments from Detective Mark Fuhrman's explosive taped interviews with a screenwriter, segments laced with racial slurs and ramblings about police violence and cover-ups. The judge eventually ruled that just two segments were presentable to jurors. But he allowed the defense to air publicly all 61 excerpts during the admissibility hearing outside the jury's presence. He wanted no one, including a huge television audience, to think anything was being covered up or concealed.[12]

Estes, Sheppard and Chandler

In its 1965 reversal of the swindling conviction of Texan Billie Sol Estes, the Court thought whatever support television gave to his "public trial" rights was far outweighed by damage inflicted upon his "due process" rights. Justice Clark wrote that the mere presence of the cameras in the courtroom had a harmful psychological impact on jurors, witnesses, attorneys, defendants and judges.[13] But the high court found no specific prejudice suffered by Estes as a result of the television camera.

A year later, the Supreme Court said that, if anything, the murder trial of Ohio physician Sam Sheppard had been too public. Though the issues in the *Sheppard v. Maxwell* case dealt largely with pervasive publicity of all types, and not the specific impact of courtroom television, the result was the same: the reversal of Sheppard's conviction for denial of due process. The Court reprimanded the trial judge for his inability to control the "carnival atmosphere" in and around the courtroom. It suggested a number of devices to protect defendants from inordinate publicity, including delay of the trial, a change of venue or sequestering the jury.[14] (See Chapter 10.)

But as noted in the preceding chapter, the Court's attitude shifted significantly in ensuing years. In 1981, it upheld the convictions of two Florida policemen in a partially televised trial, refusing to declare the presence of the camera an automatic violation of the defendants' rights to due process of law. However, the Court held that if the accused could demonstrate the broadcast of their trial would deny them due process by compromising the ability of the jury to judge them fairly, or adversely impact the trial participants, the court must exclude the camera.[15]

The Supreme Court had reversed Billie Sol Estes' conviction 16 years earlier without pointing to any discernible prejudice suffered by him as a result of the television cameras. In *Chandler*, the Court, with a substantially different makeup in personnel, shifted to the defendant the burden of proof to demonstrate prejudice—a nearly impossible burden to meet. This was a dramatic shift in the law of cameras in the courtroom. It exemplified the Burger Court's evisceration of many of the rights gained by criminal defendants from the Warren Court.[16]

Defense Attorneys Weigh In

A significant minority of attorneys and a large number of criminal defense attorneys think cameras negatively impact justice in the courtroom.[17] A 1981 study commissioned by the California Judicial Council revealed that only 13 percent of criminal defense attorneys favored electronic coverage of criminal proceedings.[18]

California lawyers Angela E. Oh and Michael Yamamoto believe that except in extraordinary circumstances, criminal defendants do not benefit from intense public scrutiny into the process of criminal justice. They explain, "We sometimes have legitimate defenses to mount which may actually lead to acquittals. However, thanks to television cameras and uninformed but 'insightful' analysis by non-participants in the process, the chances of prevailing on behalf of our clients are greatly reduced. Because most juries are not sequestered and because the commentators, who rarely lean in our favor, generally do not wait for both sides to be heard and all the evidence to be introduced before offering their conclusions, premature judgments as to the ultimate question of guilt or innocence are frequently encouraged."[19]

Jack T. Litman, a New York defense attorney who has led the battle to keep cameras out of New York courtrooms, thinks the veto power rests with the accused. He says, "If television cameras affect the role of a single participant, the accused has not received a fair trial. If television negatively affects a minority of jurors or witnesses, an unacceptable risk is presented. No defendant should be forced to have his trial televised."[20]

Many criminal defense attorneys feel that since the Constitution is designed to protect the accused from injustice, it is the accused who is in the best position to determine whether his or her right to a fair trial would be compromised by television coverage. In the Simpson case, the defendant decided initially, at least, that his fair trial rights would not be jeopardized by televising the trial. "We did not object to the presence of the camera," says defense attorney Uelmen, "and of course, once the cameras were there, from our position on the defense side, we didn't want to pull the plug halfway through, after the country had just seen the prosecution's case... Once we opened the door, it was impossible to close it at any appropriate point."

However, Oh and Yamamoto maintain, "the defendant should retain the right to object and to exclude television cameras [at any stage in a trial] if for no other reason but to preserve the presumption of innocence—an endangered American constitutional right."[21]

Defense attorney Leslie Abramson also worries about the presumption of innocence in televised trials. The tenacious advocate for Erik Menendez, who doubled as an ABC News legal commentator on the criminal justice system, criticized the cynicism of the media: "The message we're sending to the public is, 'everybody on trial is guilty but come on into court and we'll tell you about the constitution—wink—nod...,'and I think all of that absolutely undermines all of our notions of justice."[22]

The Defendant in the Eye of the Camera

During his nine-month trial, the camera spent considerable time focused on O. J. Simpson's face, trying to capture his reactions to the twists and turns of the volatile courtroom drama. Was that in itself a threat to his fair trial rights? Perhaps, says defense lawyer Jill Lansing, who represented Lyle Menendez. "Every time the camera zooms in on Mr. Simpson and his face, looking for every smile or frown or whatever, I feel, why should anyone have that extra pressure? But the jury's doing it [the same thing]. They just don't have zoom lenses in their eyes."

Some defendants perceive that they are prejudiced as a result of television coverage of their trials. Joel Steinberg, convicted in a televised New York trial of murdering his six-year-old daughter, felt closeup shots and camera angles portrayed him in an inaccurate, insensitive manner. He said, "I saw

Drawing by Levin, © 1979, The New Yorker Magazine, Inc.

"For heaven's sake, man, look ashamed. We're being televised."

very little coverage that fairly expressed my sentiments, my natural manner." He found it "unfavorable and unflattering." Steinberg thought the purpose of the coverage was "to bolster a negative image and the reason for that was the more sensationalism, the more [public] interest."[23]

Dr. Roberta Entner, a communications scholar from New York University, cites the suggestive nature of many defendant close-ups. After a lengthy analysis of televised courtroom proceedings in New York, Entner concluded, "Recurrent negative visuals can be unfair to the defendant. In my research, most defendants were photographed in unsympathetic poses. Showing the accused in the worst possible manner can encourage the audience's perception of guilt because the defendant looks guilty and the TV condemnation can never be undone to the accused who is eventually acquitted...."[24] Those were prophetic words. Although the Simpson defense favored televising the trial so that people would see justice had been done and that Simpson could lead a normal life after he was acquitted, he faced ridicule and scorn following his acquittal. Dean Uelmen calls it the "Rodney King Syndrome," in which the public feels "we saw it with our own eyes and we're in just as good a position as the jury to evaluate it."

Another member of Simpson's "Dream Team" was Alan Dershowitz, a Harvard law professor who watched the trial on television in Boston and faxed or e-mailed directions to the defense as the trial progressed. It was his job to protect the record in case of a conviction and appeal. Dershowitz appeared on *Larry King Live* in October 1994, in the midst of pretrial proceedings. Although he supported excluding the TV cameras from the courtroom at that point, he noted their value in helping the public to accept verdicts in high profile trials: "I think that justice is seen to be done when it's on television," says Dershowitz. "For example, William Kennedy Smith—I think if his case hadn't been on television, the American public would not have accepted the verdict. And, if Mike Tyson's case had been on television, I think more people would support his claims of innocence than now do." The logic is sympathetic to Tyson, a Dershowitz client. But it clearly did not apply to the Simpson murder trial aftermath.

The Televised Witness

Critics of televised trials contend that one of their greatest dangers is the power to influence what jurors see and hear about a case—in other words, the very body of evidence. Some would-be witnesses may decline to testify because they do not wish to be in the public eye. Others may flourish in the spotlight and color or slant their testimony to appear more dramatic before the television audience. Prosecution witnesses—police officers and forensic experts— testify frequently and are generally accustomed to public exposure. By contrast, defense witnesses are often inexperienced, and more likely to be intimidated by the knowledge that they are on television.[25]

Simpson attorney Barry Scheck shares Uelmen's concern that defense witnesses were lost because the trial was televised. "We had great difficulty getting witnesses to come forward because they simply didn't want to be a part of this, and I think it was a very, very disturbing phenomenon," Scheck told an interviewer.[26] Despite their concerns, however, their client won a speedy acquittal.

In 1988, Scheck figured prominently in another high profile case in which cameras became an issue—the Steinberg murder case. Scheck represented Steinberg's live-in girlfriend and co-defendant, Hedda Nussbaum. Though Nussbaum did take the stand for the prosecution, Scheck believes television coverage weighed heavily on her testimony. "It was hard enough for her to get up there in front of all these people in the courtroom," said Scheck. "But then to have the conscious awareness that all America could see her, I'm really sure put tremendous pressure on an already quite fragile woman."[27] Steinberg defense witness Marilyn Walton was so afraid her testimony would subject her to dangerous repercussions, that at one point she simply refused to talk anymore.[28]

Menendez attorney Lansing, convinced an important defense witness was lost because of the cameras in the first trial, felt it would have been much easier to try the case in a more private setting, because: "We were asking witnesses to tell us about situations they saw where there was mistreatment of children and about which they did nothing. It's very hard to get people to do that...."

Gregory K. McCall argues in the *Columbia Law Review*, "When the witness has a bona fide objection to the presence of cameras, and the judge nevertheless permits coverage to continue (as he has discretion to do in many states) the end result—prejudice to the defendant—is the same as in cases of outright intimidation."[29]

If the trial judge fails to control witness access to broadcasts of the trial, testimony may be compromised. The Supreme Court in the *Estes* case was concerned that witnesses might go home each night and watch the day's proceedings on television, despite a judge's admonition not to do so. "They could view and hear the testimony of preceding witnesses, and so shape their own testimony as to make its impact crucial."[30] And although Judge Ito instructed some witnesses not to watch broadcasts of prior testimony in the Simpson case, many admitted on the stand they had followed the testimony of witnesses testifying about the same subject matter.

Attorneys Playing to the Cameras

The Supreme Court warned in its *Estes* ruling that telecasting might impair the defendant's right to effective representation by counsel: "The distractions, intrusions into confidential attorney-client relationships and the temptation offered by television to play to the public audience might often have a direct effect ... upon the lawyers...." In fact, Estes' defense counsel insisted he could not concentrate on the case because he was distracted by the cameras.[31]

Susan Smith's attorney, David Bruck, argued to Judge Howard that cameras would distort the proper exercise of discretion by an elected prosecutor. Solicitor Thomas Pope pressed for the death penalty, thus forcing the case to a trial that could place him in the national television spotlight. If the court excluded cameras, Bruck said, Pope might be more amenable to a plea bargain for life in prison, since the lure of instant celebrity would be gone. Ultimately the case was not televised and there was no plea bargain. The jury convicted Smith and sentenced her to life in prison.

Judges Reacting to the Cameras

The job of the trial judge is to ensure that the defendant receives a fair trial. That difficult task requires his undivided attention.[32] To the extent that the judge's awareness of the presence of the cameras distracts her from that duty, the defendant may suffer. Justice Clark, in the *Estes* case, admitted: "Judges are human beings also and are subject to the same psychological reactions as laymen. Telecasting is particularly bad where the judge is elected.... The telecasting of a trial becomes a political weapon, which, along with other distractions inherent in broadcasting, diverts his attention from the task at hand—the fair trial of the accused."[33]

Indeed, John M. Thompson, a superior court judge in San Diego, never allows cameras in his courtroom. Why? "I'm protecting myself," he told a group of students. He wants to be able to level with the defendant he is sentencing; in front of a camera, he says he would have to "restrain myself and refer to someone's [criminal] record as just crappy," instead of scolding the accused in stronger terms.[34]

Simpson attorney Uelmen notes the amount of time Judge Ito spent managing the cameras: "I know he devoted a lot of time setting up the mechanics of how this was going to be covered—monitoring the monitor, and so on. There was a lot of extra work that the judge had to do just to manage the process of having cameras in the courtroom."

Ito had a "kill switch" at the bench which he used at times to cut the sound broadcast to the public. He constantly monitored the angle of the camera, making sure no juror was photographed, no autopsy photograph broadcast.

Chief Justice Earl Warren, concurring in the *Estes* case, criticized the trial judge for his unusual offer to the press. He had invited reporters to bring their television cameras into his chambers to take films of him reading one of his pretrial orders. "On this occasion, at least, the trial judge clearly took the initiative in placing himself before the television audience and in giving his order, and himself, the maximum possible publicity."[35]

The Impartial Jury and the Televised Trial

Historically, jurors were chosen specifically because they had background knowledge about the parties, the facts and the evidence in the case.[36] The modern jury must base its decision only on the evidence presented in court. Justice Oliver Wendell Holmes asserted, "The theory of our system is that the conclusions to be reached in a case will be induced only by evidence and argument in open court, and not by any outside influence, whether of private talk or public print."[37]

However, some exposure to the case will not automatically disqualify a juror. The issue is whether a person, despite any knowledge she may have about the case, can sit in judgment as an impartial juror.

Juror Accountability

Trial consultant Karen Jo Koonan maintains, "The more the cameras are in the courtroom the more the jury is going to be aware of its accountability to the community." She cites a question commonly asked of prospective jurors who have law enforcement officers in their families: How would you feel going back to your relatives after finding a defendant not guilty? Televised trials raise a similar concern on a larger scale. Will the juror feel responsible to explain her verdict to the entire community? Most states that permit televised trials reduce this pressure by prohibiting identifiable shots of jurors.

The Criminal Justice Section of the New York State Bar Association raised a slightly different concern in a 1994 memo to the House of Delegates that was sharply critical of courtroom cameras:

> Cameras in the courtroom signal the jury that the case is especially notorious, that its verdict will be highly publicized and that the jurors' decision will likely be scrutinized by their neighbors and friends. This not-so-subtle message influences jurors to accept general public perceptions of guilt—and thus vote to convict—and is far *less* likely to bolster jurors who harbor reasonable doubt.

However, that dynamic did not develop in the Simpson murder trial. Jurors quickly reached a verdict favorable to the defense. Critics dismissed it as the product of a largely black jury that knew it must return a verdict which would play well in their community. But three black jurors who wrote a book after the trial strongly denied that, claiming their decision was based strictly on the prosecution's failure to prove guilt beyond a reasonable doubt. They spent an entire chapter analyzing evidence that led the jury to its decision.[38]

It is also noteworthy that this jury was sequestered for nearly nine months. Isolated from the outside world with only fellow jurors as companions, the jury molded itself into a tightly knit community. By the time the case was over and deliberations began, there was little disagreement in this congenial group.

Although Timothy McVeigh's Denver trial for the Oklahoma City bombing was not televised, Judge Richard Matsch took extraordinary measures to protect the anonymity of the federal jury. He ordered a partition constructed in the courtroom to shield the identities of jurors from the press and public. The jury convicted McVeigh and sentenced him to death. After the verdict, the 11 jurors who attended a news conference enthusiastically said, "No," when asked whether they would have wanted [public] cameras in the courtroom. They referred to the profound responsibility and emotional difficulty they had had in deciding the case.[39] The dynamics of every case are different. It is altogether possible that the McVeigh jury would have reached the same decision with or without cameras in that courtroom.

Retrials and Future Jury Pools

Justice Clark in the *Estes* case warned that retrials could be jeopardized because potential jurors may have seen and heard the first trial when it was broadcast. Defense attorney Uelmen feels that attorneys on both sides in the Simpson case acted with that in mind: "We both tried this case with the cloud over our heads that this may not be the ultimate resolution of the case. There may be a need for another trial, if there was a hung jury or if there was a conviction and reversal, and all of the future jurors are out there watching. I think at times things were more directed to those future jurors." Likewise, trial consultant Lois Heaney, who helped select the Menendez juries in the first trial, expressed concern that the jury pool for the retrial may have been tainted by its exposure to television coverage of the first proceeding. A defense public opinion survey conducted between Menendez I and Menendez II revealed about 80 percent of all potential jurors in Los Angeles thought the brothers were guilty of first degree murder.[40]

Simpson prosecutor George "Woody" Clarke is concerned that in criminal cases, there might be evidence admitted in the first trial which may be excluded in the retrial. If jurors in the second trial had been exposed to evidence either from the first trial or information that was never presented to the jury at all, that may taint jurors in the retrial.

Many jurors in criminal cases tried post–Simpson have higher expectations of both sides. Some feel a case has not been properly presented if there is not exhaustive scientific evidence or lengthy examination of witnesses. Although the O. J. Simpson case was atypical in every way, it now serves as a model for many people who followed the trial on a daily basis for many months.

Striking the Balance

Although the defendant's right to a fair trial must be protected at all times, the United States Supreme Court has held that "The authors of the Bill of Rights did not undertake to assign priorities as between First Amendment and Sixth Amendment rights, ranking one as superior to the other."[41] The public's right of access to the courtroom, guaranteed by the First Amendment, may be curbed only where there is a compelling interest at stake. When a fair trial is jeopardized, that is a compelling interest. The determination of when fairness is threatened must be made on a case-by-case basis since every trial is unique. The next chapter will explore the tension between the right to a fair trial and the right of public access to the courtroom occasioned by the television camera. It will provide the parameters for the debate.

Chapter Four

Does a "Public Trial" Mean a Televised Trial?

> A trial is a public event. What transpires in the courtroom is public property. —Justice William O. Douglas, *Craig v. Harney*[1]

Justice Douglas knew his history. He knew, for instance, of the 1807 trial of Aaron Burr, the brilliant lawyer, former senator and vice-president accused of treason. Chief Justice John Marshall, sitting as trial judge, was so concerned about accommodating the aspiring masses, so determined that Burr's trial be "a public event," that he moved it from a small Virginia courtroom to the great hall of the state House of Delegates in Virginia.[2] A horde of spectators from Virginia and "far beyond" packed the Hall and overflowed into the rotunda. Historian Alf J. Mapp reports, the audience was so large "that sandboxes had been brought in to augment the brass cuspidors de rigueur in American public buildings of the period." Even a future military hero, Winfield Scott, was there, standing on a large box lock of a chamber door to see above the crowd.[3] By one account, Burr "had as his audience the whole nation. Crowds poured into the city as to a great public fair, and they were rewarded with superb theater,"[4] as Burr was eventually acquitted.

Today's concept of a public trial has dramatically changed. There were just eight seats available to the public in the small courtroom where O. J. Simpson was tried for murder. The rest were set aside for families and friends of the participants, members of the legal teams and representatives of the news media. "Public" seats were at such a premium that the superior court conducted a daily lottery, with as many as 400 persons casting lots with Deputy William Dinwiddie. He ran the drawing with a vigilant eye for scalpers who commanded up to $200 for a courtroom seat. A public trial? Hardly, by the historical standard of Justice Marshall. Yet the Simpson trial was available to a public audience that dwarfed the excited crowd at the Virginia House of Delegates, a throng of hundreds-of-millions—everyone within sight and hearing of a television set.

Technology has changed, and so has America, from a collection of colonial villages to a national village of more than a quarter-billion people. In today's America many argue that citizens cannot truly enjoy their right to an open, public trial without the assistance of television. In her argument to retain the camera in the Simpson courtroom, media advocate Kelli Sager contended, "The fundamental precept of access is that everyone who wants to should be able to have access to court proceedings, should be able to observe what is going on.... It is physically impossible to have everyone in the courtroom. But through television, anyone who wants to observe the proceedings may do so."[5]

Legal scholars Erwin Chemerinsky and Laurie Levenson, both frequent broadcast commentators on court issues, are even more emphatic: "A meaningful public trial in the 1990s *requires* that it be broadcast because few people realistically can attend court proceedings."[6]

Is a public trial, in the modern age, necessarily a televised trial? Scholars on both sides of that question point to the evolution of the "public trial."

Under English common law, all criminal proceedings were conducted in public, in order to ensure fairness, discourage perjury and misconduct of the participants, and prevent biased decisions.[7] Trials were "open-air meetings of the freemen who were bound to attend them."[8] The freemen were the landed gentry, the original jurors who were "called upon [by the king] to render judgment."[9] Thus, the English tradition of openness evolved not only as the right, but also the duty, of the public—that is, freemen—to attend criminal trials.

Sir Thomas Smith's description of the public character of the criminal trial was quoted by the United States Supreme Court more than 400 years later in *Richmond Newspapers, Inc. v. Virginia:* Aside from the written indictment, "all the rest is doone openlie in the presence of the Judges, the Justices, the enquest, the prisoner, *and so manie as will or can come so neare as to heare it,* and all depositions and witnesses given aloude, *that all men may heare from the mouth of the depositors and witnesses what is saide.*"[10]

In the United States, the right to a public trial was created for the benefit of the accused.[11] This is clearly enunciated in the Sixth Amendment: "In all criminal prosecutions, *the accused shall enjoy the right to a* speedy and *public trial....*" The Supreme Court has stated unequivocally that neither the press nor the public has a constitutional guarantee under the Sixth Amendment to attend criminal trials.[12]

Americans do, however, enjoy a First Amendment right to attend trials,[13] emanating from freedom of speech and of the press. But it also derives from the right to assemble, both as an independent right and as a catalyst to augment the free exercise of other First Amendment rights. It is well-established in our jurisprudence that the First Amendment provides the right to receive information and ideas as well as the right to freely express them.[14] And the right to publish necessarily implies the freedom to gather information.[15]

The public can only be denied its right of access where the judge spells out findings that support an overriding interest. Thus, where courtrooms have limited seating capacity, reasonable restrictions on attendance may be imposed, including preferential seating for the media.[16] In the event a courtroom cannot accommodate all members of "the public," the media are often considered "surrogates" for the public. The Supreme Court has held that the press is entitled to a greater degree of First Amendment protection than individual members of the public, when the media are "acting as the 'eyes and ears' of the public."[17] Justice Potter Stewart wrote that freedom of the press was included in the Bill of Rights "to create a fourth institution outside the Government as an additional check on the three official branches."[18]

Courts can place reasonable limits on media access as long as they don't try to regulate the *content* of the coverage.[19] Camera advocates argue that barring cameras does exactly that, because a direct telecast cannot be duplicated in written or oral descriptions.[20] The electronic media speak through their cameras. Thus, excluding cameras restricts freedom of speech under the First Amendment.[21] Proponents cite a federal court ruling: "Neither the courts nor any other branch of the government can be allowed to affect the content or tenor of the news by choreographing which news organizations have access to relevant information."[22] In other words, judges cannot edit or censor the content of broadcasts. But so far, the courts have not agreed that excluding broadcast equipment necessarily censors the content of the news. Restrictions on cameras in courtrooms regulate the *effects* of the televised broadcast, not its *content*.

Access of the public to criminal trials, while protected by the Constitution, can be limited. A judge may close the courtroom if the State demonstrates a "compelling governmental interest," but closure must be "narrowly tailored" to serve that interest.[23] The Supreme Court promulgated this rule in *Globe Newspaper Co. v. Superior Court*, in which a Massachusetts judge had closed a rape trial to the press and public during the testimony of the minor victims, under a statute mandating closure in every case involving a sex-offense victim under 18. The Court struck down the statute as unconstitutional because of its mandatory nature. Weighing factors such as the age and psychological maturity of the victim and the nature of the crime, the judge must decide, on a case-by-case basis, whether closing the courtroom is necessary to protect the well-being of the victim.[24]

Likewise, the courts have ruled against any blanket exclusion of the public from jury selection. The definitive word came from Chief Justice Warren Burger in the first *Press-Enterprise* decision. While recognizing a "compelling interest" for fairness in the jury selection process, Burger said there must be specific findings in a given case of a "substantial probability" that a fair trial will be prejudiced by an open proceeding. He required that a trial judge consider less drastic alternatives before closing jury selection to the public.[25]

The same principle applies to the inherent tension between the fair trial rights of the accused under the Sixth Amendment, and the rights of public access under the First Amendment. When those rights conflict, the contradiction must be resolved, case by case. The high court, in its *Nebraska Press Association* ruling, refused to declare one right superior to the other.[26] "The right to an open public trial is a shared right of the accused and the public," said the Court ten years later, "the common concern being the assurance of fairness."[27]

A Right to a Televised Trial?

The Defendant

Although a defendant has an undisputed right to a public trial, the courts have refused to carry that a step further and agree the accused has a right to a *televised* trial. In 1982, Wisconsin lawyer Gillam Kerley, charged with failure to register for the draft, sought permission to videotape his trial. The court rejected the request, ruling there was no constitutional right to tape a trial. And in affirming the court's ruling, the appellate court stated, "All we have in the case before us is a limitation on the manner of news coverage; the media can do everything but televise the trial."[28]

The court drew a distinction between the *denial* of public access to a trial—where the judge must apply a "strict scrutiny" test—and a *limitation* on public access, which is constitutionally permissible as long as the limitation is reasonable and neutral.[29]

A year later, another federal court made a similar ruling in the case of U.S. District Judge Alcee Hastings, who was charged with conspiracy and obstruction of justice in Florida. He argued that his Sixth Amendment right to a public trial entitled him to record and broadcast his trial. His claim was rejected.[30]

In making their requests, both Kerley and Hastings waived any possible prejudice that might have resulted from the presence of cameras in their courtrooms.[31] But the courts were not impressed. Appellate judges reviewing the *Kerley* case were blunt: "Even though many rights may be waived by a defendant, a criminal trial is not a game.... While strategic decisions often result in the waiver of some of the safeguards of a trial, it would be anomalous for a court to close its eyes in advance to what some believe to be impending unfairness and for the government to participate in a plan to hold a trial that could be regarded as unfair."

The court balanced the gains to be achieved from videotaping and broadcasting an "already public trial" against the "risks and uncertainties of the procedure," and denied Kerley's request.[32]

The Public and the Press

The *Kerley* ruling cited the Supreme Court's 1965 decision overturning the swindling conviction of Billie Sol Estes, who had been denied due process by camera coverage of his case. But the *Kerley* court carefully avoided contradicting the 1981 *Chandler* decision, which held that the mere presence of a television camera in a criminal trial does not necessarily violate a defendant's due process rights. *Chandler* had stopped short of saying there is a constitutional right to televise trials. Each state is free to decide the camera issue for itself but trials should not be televised where due process would be jeopardized.[33]

In other words, the Constitution doesn't necessarily *prohibit* cameras in courtrooms, but it does not *require* they be allowed in either. That standard has guided courts ever since and provided ammunition for both pro-camera advocates and a sweeping prohibition against cameras in federal courts. Even when both parties in General William Westmoreland's 1984 libel action against CBS agreed to television coverage, U.S. District Judge Pierre Leval barred cameras, and an appeals court backed him up, relying on the federal no-cameras rule. Except for those filling 70 "public" seats each day, Americans never saw, first-hand, a case involving a burning issue of the nation's most incendiary war—whether Westmoreland, as CBS News reported, presided over a systematic U.S. military effort to inflate U.S. successes in Vietnam and understate American losses.[34]

When rejecting camera coverage, courts typically frame their rulings as the product of a balancing act. In the *Hastings* case, the Eleventh Circuit Court of Appeals cited, on the positive side of the scale: fostering public confidence in the fairness of the justice system, serving as a public check on judicial abuses and promoting truth; and on the negative side: concern for court order and decorum and pursuit of a fair trial.[35] The appellate judges felt the negatives outweighed the positives in that case.

Correspondingly, federal appellate courts have consistently held there is no *right* to see trials on television. As the *Westmoreland* court put it: "There is a long leap ... between a public right under the First Amendment to attend trials and a public right under the First Amendment to see a given trial televised. It is a leap that is not supported by history. It is a leap that we are not yet prepared to take."[36]

But in 1996, a federal trial court in New York took that leap, citing advances in technology since *Estes* and *Westmoreland* were decided. In *Katzman v. Victoria's Secret*, Federal District Court Judge Robert Sweet wrote that the press has a presumptive right to televise trials and the public has the right to see them on television.[37] Echoing that view are Kelli Sager and Karen N. Frederiksen, Los Angeles lawyers who have represented news organizations in many high profile cases. Writing in the *Southern California Law Review*, they argue that in today's context, there *is* a constitutional right to televise criminal proceedings: "The expansive constitutional right of public access to court proceedings, coupled with more than two decades of experimentation and experience with electronic coverage of judicial proceedings, mandates a presumption in favor of allowing such coverage."[38] The only exceptions to that presumption, they argue, are "compelling justifications," and any restrictions on camera coverage should be narrowly tailored to fit the circumstances.[39]

For instance, Sager notes, there may be a compelling need to protect the identity of an undercover police informant or someone in the federal witness protection program. There may also be "rare" cases, she says, in which a fearful witness refuses to testify with a camera present or a jury pool could be tainted if certain pretrial proceedings were televised. But in each case, Sager stresses, the camera should be excluded only long enough to address the specific problem. The problem should not become an excuse for a blanket exclusion.

Some, however, think Sager and fellow First Amendment militants interpret the public's right of access too broadly; that they seem to be arguing, incorrectly, that the courts must accommodate every member of the public who wishes to watch a particular trial on a particular day. "If that were so," muses Los Angeles defense attorney Leslie Abramson, "O. J. Simpson's trial would have been held in the Los Angeles Coliseum and not in the Criminal Courts Building."[40]

Ironically, it was another Los Angeles lawyer, Robert Shapiro, who argued before Simpson's criminal trial that it "definitely should be" televised. He claimed the public had the "right to see the real evidence from the witness stand, and the only way that can be accomplished firsthand is either to have the trial in the Coliseum or on television."[41] Ultimately, it was the television camera that obviated the necessity to hold the trial in the Coliseum; every member of the public (with a TV set) who wanted to watch could simply turn on television.

Discrimination Against Television Media?

Sager and other camera advocates argue that the exclusion of television cameras from courtrooms violates the constitutional right of freedom of the press because it discriminates against the electronic media in favor of the print press. But the courts, so far, have not agreed. In his concurring opinion in *Estes v. Texas*, Justice Harlan contended that courts cannot "be said to discriminate where they permit the newspaper reporter access to the courtroom. The television and radio reporter has the same privilege. All are entitled to the same rights as the general public. The news reporter is not permitted to bring his typewriter or printing press."[42]

But many, including some print reporters, think Harlan's logic misses an important point: the unique contributions of television to an informed public.

Drawing from history, *Los Angeles Times* columnist Bill Boyarsky poignantly noted: "With radio [and no television], millions of Americans thrilled to the sound of [President Franklin] Roosevelt's voice without ever knowing how badly polio had disabled him." In arguing that Simpson's civil trial, too, should have been televised, Boyarsky bemoaned the role of the press as "filter" of the news for the public: "As one of the filters, I think that's too limited. We describe, but it's through our eyes. In these multimedia times, the reporters at the scene, equipped with only note pads and the power of observation, don't have the credibility of half a century ago, when we were the sole source of information.

"Nor should we be," wrote Boyarsky. "If there had been television, rather than journalistic filters, the media could not have made the dying Franklin Roosevelt seem healthy."[43]

In matters outside the courtroom, courts have decried differential treatment between print and broadcast media. New York City mayoral candidates Mario Cuomo and Edward Koch tried to exclude selected members of the media in 1977 by limiting access to their campaign headquarters to those who had received invitations. Ruling in *American Broadcasting Cos. v. Cuomo*, a federal court observed, "once there is a public function, public comment, and participation by some of the media, the First Amendment requires equal access to all of the media or the rights of the First Amendment would no longer be tenable."[44]

In 1981, a federal court in Georgia struck down a judge's order excluding television crews from a White House press pool. The court said the order violated the press and public's First Amendment right of access to White House events. It felt television coverage "provides a comprehensive visual element and an immediacy, or simultaneous aspect, not found in print media."[45]

Television camera access to the judicial branch raises similar concerns about the public's right to know. But in criminal cases, another crucial variable must be factored in—the defendant's right to a fair trial. The stakes are higher when someone is on trial for his liberty or his life.

At least one state appellate court has said the electronic press with its cameras must be afforded access to a criminal trial equal to that enjoyed by the print media with its pens, pencils and notepads. The Ohio Court of Appeals in *Cosmos Broadcasting v. Brown*, held that access may only be denied where the trial judge clearly states there is an issue at stake greater than the interest in promoting equal access.[46]

One such issue is the fair trial right of the accused. But deciding when the presence of cameras endangers a fair trial has always been a sticky proposition, as explored in chapter three.

Proving that a televised trial will be a flawed trial usually involves some speculation and crystal-balling. And it must be balanced against the rights of public access in the television age.

The Multi-Purposes of a Public Trial

Fairness

Chief Justice Burger wrote in the *Richmond Newspapers* case, "It is not unrealistic even in this day to believe that *public inclusion* affords citizens a form of legal education and hopefully promotes confidence in the *fair* administration of justice.'"[47]

The Court, in turn, has consistently affirmed that a public trial benefits the defendant. Where the public has a window into the courtroom, it is much more difficult for a tyrannical judge to eviscerate the fair trial rights of the accused. The question is whether a television camera provides an additional check on "abuse of judicial power."[48] Or does it pose another source of abuse? The answers vary widely, case to case, attorney to attorney. In her days as a criminal defense lawyer, Court TV's Rikki Klieman "always felt that the camera [in the courtroom] worked 100% to my advantage. I felt that it kept arbitrary and capricious judges honest. I felt that they would never do things in front of a camera that they might otherwise try to do." Klieman represented Christian Science parents accused of manslaughter for the death of their child after they opted for spiritual healing instead of medical care. When the judge sought to rule against the defense, she went into chambers rather than of ruling in open court in full view of the camera. "She wanted to go hide, and my feeling then, as now, was that the camera is the agent of the truth and ... the government is the one entity that wants to look for silence, because when you speak up in society against the tyranny of the government, then that is the time that you can achieve justice."

Another defense attorney, Jack Litman, is just as sure that keeping cameras out of a New York courtroom prevented an unfair trial for a high profile client. Robert Chambers was charged with killing a 19-year-old woman during a sexual encounter in Central Park. The case generated intense publicity. Litman argued that his client had already been convicted in the media. Television coverage, he insisted, would compound the problem by exposing the public to a steady stream of vilifying cinematic tidbits. "My view was that television would air the most salacious 30-second sound bite or what they believed was the most damning piece of evidence against Chambers," said Litman, "and of course [they would] leave out all the mitigating circumstances and all the favorable evidence for Chambers." In Litman's view, "the public pressure is generally a pressure to convict."[49] Chambers was acquitted after an untelevised trial.

Leslie Abramson acknowledges that the Founding Fathers didn't like secret trials because they were used by the British royalty as tools of oppression. But she insists, the founders "could not have imagined that public scrutiny might become so exaggerated and intrusive that it would create miscarriages of justice every bit as grotesque as those plotted in the Star Chamber."[50] She is adamant that televising the Menendez brothers' first trial, which ended in a hung jury, hurt them badly in their second trial. When interviewed on Court TV's *Cochran and Grace*, Abramson cited the defense's public opinion survey mentioned earlier, which showed that a majority of potential jurors in Los Angeles thought the defendants were guilty of first degree murder before the jury in the second trial was ever selected.

Abramson is convinced that Judge Stanley Weisberg felt empowered by the hostile public opinion to issue several rulings that emasculated the defense in the retrial. Weisberg limited evidence about alleged abuse of the brothers by their parents, testimony he had allowed in the first trial. In addition, the second time around, he refused to instruct the jury on the theory of imperfect self-defense, which would have enabled the jury to return a verdict of manslaughter. The Menendez brothers were convicted of first-degree murder.

But the second trial, unlike the first, was not televised. And Abramson does not allow for the possibility that a camera trained on Weisberg during the proceeding might have made him think twice about gutting the defense. Public trials are aimed at curbing the very autocratic excesses Abramson decries. A television camera would have made the trial a much more public event than the sparsely-covered proceeding it became. Out of the glare of the camera, Weisberg had free reign to rule at will. His rulings limiting the defense "seemed incredible" to Associated Press Special Correspondent Linda Deutsch, who covered both trials. She describes Lyle Menendez's televised testimony in the first trial as "heart-wrenching. And in the second trial," she notes, "it was all kept at a clean distance. Nobody had to deal with it. The prosecutor portrayed them [the defendants] as monsters, and the public—the jury of the public—never saw them in that trial."

Likewise, Defense Attorney Johnnie Cochran believes his former client, O. J. Simpson, was victimized by unfavorable rulings in his civil wrongful death trial because Judge Hiroshi Fujisaki was not under a camera's gaze. He cites, particularly, Fujisaki's allowance of questions about a lie detector test administered to Simpson. "If there'd been TV cameras," says Cochran, "I don't think he would've done it, quite frankly. I really don't."[51]

Mike Tyson's appellate lawyer, Alan Dershowitz, is convinced the boxer suffered because his rape trial was not televised. In his book, *Reasonable Doubts: The Criminal Justice System and the O. J. Simpson Case,* Dershowitz claims the world learned about the case through reporters biased against Tyson. He alleges that the trial judge, Patricia Gifford, allowed herself to be "hand picked by the prosecution." Dershowitz also asserts, she "made numerous rulings that she never would have gotten away with had the case been nationally televised." He cites the judge's exclusion of the testimony of three crucial eyewitnesses who would have claimed that the alleged victim lied about having no sexual interest in Tyson.

Dershowitz maintains the prosecutors made claims in closing arguments they would never have made in front of a national audience. They argued, for instance, that if the victim really had wanted to have sex with Tyson, she would have worn her black see-through panties (which had been freshly laundered and were drying when Tyson called) instead of her polka-dotted ones, and falsely implied the victim was a virgin. Had these arguments been televised, there would undoubtedly have been complaints from feminist viewers.

But Dershowitz probably speaks for many defense attorneys in offering his bottom line: "In every individual case, the answer will be different. Some defendants will benefit and others will lose from their trials being televised."[52]

Public Confidence and Accountability

Supreme Court Justice Felix Frankfurter "longed for the day when the news media would cover the Supreme Court as thoroughly as it did the World Series," because "the public confidence in the judiciary hinges on the public's perception of it, and that perception necessarily hinges on the media's portrayal of the legal system."[53] The institutions of government are created to serve the people, so they must be accountable to the people. Only then will the public have confidence that its government is being fairly administered. American courtrooms house judges and juries who make life and death decisions on a daily basis. The people must know these decisions are just. When television provides the public a window into the courtroom, the judicial system becomes accountable to the public.

Judicial proceedings conducted in secret not only jeopardize fairness; the people cannot be sure justice has been done. As Chief Justice Warren Burger wrote in *Richmond Newspapers,* 'The crucial prophylactic aspects of the administration of justice cannot function in the dark.... A result considered untoward may undermine public confidence, and where the trial has been concealed from public view an unexpected outcome can cause a reaction that the system at best has failed and at worst has been corrupted."[54] Hearings conducted behind closed doors are called, paradoxically, *in camera* proceedings.

In principle, anyway, television offers the most effective means for large numbers of citizens to ensure that justice is being meted out in their courtrooms. Millions watched O. J. Simpson appear to struggle to put on the crime scene gloves in his murder case. To his lead lawyer, Cochran, it was those viewers who saw that Simpson was not "acting"[55] and thus could understand the power of Cochran's argument to jurors: "If the gloves don't fit, you must acquit."

David Danielson, the supervising criminal judge in the San Diego Superior Court, told a group of students: "Nothing is more powerful than the visible wilting of a witness."[56] When people are unable to attend the proceedings in person, television is the only way they can see a witness wilt and grasp how that may affect a trial's outcome.

Court TV

William Kennedy Smith standing trial in *Florida v. Smith*.

Court TV likes to cite its coverage of *Tennessee v. Tate and Blades* as another window on justice in the making. The case involved two black men in Memphis accused of stabbing a prominent white socialite more than 50 times. There were clear racial overtones to the case. Prosecutors claimed that the son of the murder victim had become a drug addict and came to know the defendants, who in turn robbed and killed his mother. As she followed the case daily for Court TV, Rikki Klieman became convinced that "the evidence was clearly not there" for a conviction. In fact, the jury acquitted the black defendants. "And I thought," says Klieman, "this is a great example of the camera being able to show the world that Memphis, Tennessee, doesn't come back with a racist verdict. They got a very fair trial."

When William Kennedy Smith was tried and acquitted for rape in West Palm Beach in 1991, his trial was televised gavel-to-gavel on Court TV. Because the public had witnessed the proceedings first-hand—via the camera—there was an understanding after the trial that he had been acquitted because the prosecution had failed to prove its case, not because he was a Kennedy, insulated from justice by his wealth and name. His lawyer, Roy Black, changed his mind about cameras in the courtroom after the Smith trial: "I like the idea of cameras in the courtroom.... Prior to the Smith case I was adamantly against it. But coverage can change people's minds about the judicial system."[57]

Presenting millions of people with a window in the courtroom where

William Kennedy Smith was tried gave many confidence that justice had been done there. Yet from the televised Smith trial came an angry backlash against cameras in the courtroom. Former camera proponent, Senate Codes Chairman Dale Volker, altered his position after watching the Smith "debacle," as he called it. "I think a lot of us feel that every person in that trial was affected by the cameras—the prosecution, the judge, the defendant," he observed.[58] Indeed, after the Smith trial, rape victims were deterred from reporting rapes to police, according to rape crisis counselors.[59] Television made the Smith court accountable, but at the expense of future victims of rape.

O. J. Simpson's acquittal was not widely accepted despite the assurance of Court TV counsel Ron Olson that gavel-to-gavel television coverage would contribute to "the public's understanding and acceptance of whatever comes from this."[60] But in large measure, acceptance or non-acceptance was a factor of experience, of a verdict viewed through two very different racial prisms. To most blacks, the verdict followed quite logically from evidence they had seen in telecasts of the trial—evidence of police misconduct and racism. While watching the same telecasts, whites focused on the powerful DNA evidence linking Simpson to the murders, and could not understand the "not guilty" verdicts. Both groups saw a somewhat different trial from the jurors who rendered the verdicts, which also affected their acceptance of the outcome.

Likewise, televising the first Rodney King (state) trial did not engender confidence in the verdict acquitting four officers of wrongdoing in the beating incident. The acquittals prompted the most devastating urban insurrection in the history of this country. Television viewers were shocked by the powerful videotaped images of the King beating, aired dozens of times before and during the trial, and could not understand why jurors did not share their outrage. Although the trial was televised, gavel-to-gavel, the public was not forced to sit through all the technical and often tedious mitigating evidence offered by the defense—evidence that apparently impressed the jurors, who were a captive audience. For example, a defense expert witness dissected the videotape of the beating, frame by frame, justifying each blow so that the enormity of the beating escaped the jury. The prosecution failed to drive home evidence suggesting racial overtones to the beating. That evidence, in turn, was lost or discarded by a jury without a single black member. The jury had been drawn, in part, from a conservative community inhabited by many Los Angeles police officers. Here, as in Simpson's murder case, jurors viewed the evidence through their own racial prisms. But many who had watched the entire videotaped segment over and over on the news felt the officers should have been convicted.

Although the camera is often cited as the lens to public acceptance, the verdict in Simpson's untelevised civil trial, that he was responsible for two deaths, was much more widely accepted than the acquittal in his televised criminal trial. But again, attitudes tended to fall along racial lines. And there were clear differences in the civil trial: a lighter burden of proof, Simpson's own faltering testimony, newly uncovered photos of the defendant in the same rare type of Italian shoes that tracked blood from the murder scene, and the racial makeup of the jury—mostly white, in contrast to the largely black jury in the criminal trial. Some civil jurors admitted during jury selection that they thought Simpson was "probably guilty," but insisted they could put those opinions aside—opinions formed largely from watching telecasts of the criminal trial.

Eighty percent of respondents to a Gallup Poll conducted at the beginning of the Timothy McVeigh bombing trial agreed with Judge Matsch's decision to ban public television cameras from the courtroom.[61] Even though the trial wasn't publicly broadcast, people had no problem accepting the jury's verdict convicting McVeigh and sentencing him to death. But in the absence of a courtroom camera, the public had been served with plenty of video clips of the federal building exploding, grieving victims and file shots of a shackled, stone-faced McVeigh being hustled into law enforcement vehicles.

When Elisabeth "Betty" Broderick was tried in San Diego for the murder of her former husband and his new wife, her first trial, which ended in a hung jury, wasn't televised. Prosecutor Kerry Wells feels many people were sympathetic to Broderick's claims of emotional abuse at the hands of her ex-husband until they saw the second, televised, trial. Public opinion changed, in Wells' view, after viewers saw Broderick testify and heard tapes of vulgar messages she had left on her husband's answering machine. Wells observed: "When they actually got an opportunity to see the evidence, their perspectives of the case changed, to my advantage, I thought."[62] The defendant was convicted of two counts of second-degree murder following her second trial. Broderick, however, attributes the difference between the two results not to the camera in the second trial, but to the judge's decision to exclude the testimony of a crucial defense expert on the battered woman's syndrome. She feels: "Trial number two was like trial number one put through a shredding machine." Menendez defense attorney Abramson made a similar claim about the two Menendez trials. Camera or no camera, it is not uncommon for a judge to streamline the defense in a retrial, in response to a prosecutor now fully aware of how to attack the defense.

Televising trials makes the criminal justice system accountable to the public in some respects. But a criminal trial involves a complex process and every trial is unique. It is difficult to isolate the camera as *the* force for promoting public confidence in the judicial branch of government, with so many factors coming into play.

Information for Meaningful Self-Government

Courtroom camera advocates believe televised trials flow logically from mainstream American principles dating back to the Founding Fathers. In a democracy, said the founders, the people must control their governing institutions. The only way to ensure that is through full public access to information about those institutions. In 1822, James Madison wrote, "A popular Government without popular information or the means of acquiring it, is but a Prologue to a Farce or a Tragedy; or perhaps both. Knowledge will forever govern ignorance. And a people who mean to be their own Governors must arm themselves with the power which knowledge gives."[63]

A contemporary, Thomas Jefferson, used even stronger language: "The way to prevent [errors of] the people, is to give them full information of their affairs through the channel of the public papers, and to contrive that those papers should penetrate the whole mass of the people."[64] A well-informed people, said Jefferson, had the right to revolt if their government failed them.

More than 150 years later, the same sentiments echo through landmark legal opinions. In 1974, Justice William O. Douglas wrote that the true sovereign in our constitutional scheme is the people, which has the right to govern in an informed manner.[65]

The same year, Justice Lewis Powell, Jr., declared that the press is instrumental in providing the public with tools of information it needs to govern itself effectively. "In seeking out the news the press ... acts as an agent of the public at large," wrote Justice Powell in *Saxbe v. Washington Post Co.* "It is the means by which the people receive that free flow of information and ideas essential to intelligent self-government. By enabling the public to assert meaningful control over the political process, the press performs a crucial function in effecting the societal purpose of the First Amendment."[66]

One of the major purposes of the First Amendment is the protection of free discussion of the affairs of government. The right of access to criminal trials safeguarded by the Amendment ensures "that this constitutionally protected 'discussion of governmental affairs' is an informed one," according to the Supreme Court in *Globe Newspaper Co. v. Superior Court.* [67]

None of the authors cited above specifies that an informed public need be a public with access to televised trials, which obviously was not an option in the age of Madison and Jefferson. But today's public is a population that, by and large, chooses television as its primary source of information.[68] Indeed, television is the *only* source of news for more than half of all Americans.[69] And by a more than two to one margin, in at least one poll, Americans consider television a more credible source of information than the print media.[70] Can television then be excluded from the workings of the judicial branch of government if the populace is "to govern in an informed manner"?

That is the question posed by advocates of cameras in the courtroom. They note that the Supreme Court has already acknowledged, in its *Richmond Newspapers* decision, that most people acquire information about trials not by firsthand observation but from the news media, who serve as their *de facto* surrogates.[71] Thus, how can you bar the tools of the medium they trust and rely on most?

In fact, Sager and Frederiksen argue, it is the medium that provides the most reliable picture of government at work: "Visually oriented information that is critical to a complete and accurate portrayal of the proceedings, including the atmosphere of the courtroom and demeanor, gestures, and emotions of the trial participants, is readily available to all."[72]

So far, the argument that televised court proceedings are essential to enlightened public governance has not made its way into case law. But it is one of the principles that has helped force open some unlikely doors. The California Supreme Court has allowed camera coverage of oral arguments on at least six of the hottest issues to come before the justices in recent years, including term limits for state officeholders, anti-abortion picketing at health clinics and parental consent to abortion.[73] Not surprisingly, in the state that invented the freeway, the largest audience turned out for arguments on Proposition 103, the voter initiative that lowered auto insurance rates for Californians.

All of the televised arguments during that period involved civil cases. Even though both the prosecution and defense agreed to television coverage of a major "three strikes" case, a majority of the Court refused to admit the camera. The Court ruled in that case that a trial judge has the discretion to set aside a "strike"—a criminal conviction—in cases where the prescribed punishment of 25 years to life would be unduly harsh.[74] That prohibition on camera coverage raised the eyebrows of, among others, Justice Richard Huffman of California's Fourth District Court of Appeal, who chaired the task force that recommended revisions to the state's rules on televised trials (see Chapter 8). Huffman can not conceive of an appellate case where it would be inappropriate to allow camera access if the press were not otherwise excluded.

At the trial level, televised broadcast of some cases may lead to an increased awareness of social problems that require attention. One evening in 1997, three friends aged 20 and 21 had some fun pulling up road signs in Tampa, Florida. Shortly thereafter, three people were killed in a collision at a nearby street corner where a stop sign had been pulled out of the ground. The three friends were all convicted of three counts of manslaughter and sentenced to 15 years in state prison. Although vandalism and theft of road signs is a nationwide problem, Court TV's broadcast of this Hillsborough County case caused public officials across the country to mount national education campaigns about the issue.[75]

Educating the Public

California Supreme Court Chief Justice Ronald George decries the "widespread lack of public understanding" of the judicial branch of government, its role and how it works.[76]

When George was just a year out of law school, another jurist, U.S. Supreme Court Justice John Harlan, suggested that television could help solve that problem. Though siding with the majority in the *Estes* case, which overturned a televised conviction, he wrote that "television is capable of performing an educational function by acquainting the public with the judicial process in action."[77]

Just how well television has lived up to that potential draws opinions ranging from the skeptical to the enthusiastic. California's Justice Huffman lines up solidly with the skeptics when it comes to courtroom television as a force for education. "That's bull!" he exclaims, asserting that the profit motive of commercial broadcasting will always steer coverage to what's newsworthy, though not necessarily educational. "With all due respect," says Huffman, "to cloak [the profit motive] and to wrap the American flag and the First Amendment around it—that is absolute intellectual dishonesty."

Legal scholar Gerald Uelmen argues "the tabloidization of the media and the reduction of news coverage to 10-second sound bites have rendered efforts to educate the public about judicial issues largely ineffectual." He suggested that superficial coverage of complex cases may even have contributed to a national trend to unseat judges who hand down politically unpopular rulings.[78]

A study measuring public understanding of the judicial system both before and one year after cameras were allowed in New York courtrooms, concluded that television coverage of trials had no impact on public understanding of the judiciary.[79]

However, the New York study was conducted before the advent of Court TV and its extended trial coverage, which in the view of many observers has elevated public knowledge about the judicial system, although it is limited to viewers who subscribe to cable television.[80] And advocates and critics of courtroom cameras believe there are specific instances where television coverage provides education that cannot readily be measured in public opinion polls.

Defense Attorney Johnnie Cochran, for example, is grateful there was a television camera in O. J. Simpson's criminal trial for its education about the real world of police work. "Now," he says, "the public, around this country and around the world, knows about the improper handling of the evidence ... they found out this is a national problem...."[81] In the 1960s, said Cochran, accusing a police officer of lying could expose one to the risk of a contempt charge. In the Simpson case, police perjury was conclusively exposed—to a television audience of millions. Whether they agreed with the verdict or not, people who watched the Simpson trial on television saw and heard Detective Mark Fuhrman lie under oath and criminalists Colin Yamauchi and Dennis Fung admit mishandling evidence.

The Simpson trial telecasts also helped expose the nation's "racial divide," says Cochran—that people of different races "live different lives ... have different perceptions. In one community we see the police as oppressors. In another community we see the police as protectors."[82] Hence, the different reactions of whites and blacks to the verdict. Likewise, another high profile case may have opened the eyes of white Americans to the realities of police abuse. San Diego attorney Michael Marrinan, who frequently files misconduct litigation against police, told a group of students that before the wide-scale televising of the videotaped beating of Rodney King, prospective jurors generally denied any direct knowledge of police abuse. Now, he says, questions on the subject during jury selection often elicit references to the King case.[83] The shift is no doubt due, in part, to the repetitive use of the amateur video clip during the televised trial of four officers involved in the beating.

As defense attorneys in the Simpson case challenged the evidence gathered at the murder scene and at Simpson's gated estate, television viewers were treated to primers in the basics of the Fourth Amendment and, as the trial progressed, in other staples of judicial life—due process, burdens of proof, circumstantial and direct evidence, relevance, and that hearty perennial, the leading question. Wrote syndicated columnist William Raspberry: "We learned a good deal about the strengths of our legal system (for instance, the safeguards built in to protect the accused) as well as its weaknesses (including the fact that you have to have money to avail yourself of all those safeguards)."[84]

And even legal scholars with a jaundiced view of television's public educational value rave about its effectiveness in educating future lawyers. Professor Uelmen quickly incorporated taped segments of the Simpson trial into the syllabi of his law school courses, as did UCLA's Peter Arenella, who decries the televising of high profile trials while admitting it educates far more people than televising ordinary cases.[85] In fact, the O. J. Simpson case is a law professor's dream. With transcripts and tapes of the trial now well-established teaching tools in courses such as criminal procedure and evidence, the courtroom has become a classroom.

In terms of educating the public, televising actual court proceedings can correct inaccuracies and distortions portrayed in the fictional events of television entertainment programs. Prime-time fare casts a disproportionate number of crime victims as white.[86] In fact, 43 percent of homicide victims are African-American.[87] Police in popular crime and adventure shows frequently violate the Constitution with impunity by committing illegal searches and seizures or interrogating suspects without giving them their *Miranda* warning that anything they say can and will be used against them. "Far from producing a viewership more knowledgeable and appreciative of the legal and procedural safeguards within the system," wrote a student scholar, "crime-television tends to diminish respect for those protections and devalue their significance to society."[88] That concern was shared by a man who helped fortify the protections. Chief Justice Earl Warren thought the very popular "Perry Mason" was a terrible show because it misinformed the public about the realities of a trial.[89]

But even as aberrant an example as the Simpson murder trial can correct false impressions about the legal system. "Most people in the population had never seen a trial [before Simpson]," says Professor Erwin Chemerinsky. "Now most people in the population have seen at least part of a trial. They know what a courtroom looks like. And they also realize that, unlike 'Matlock' or 'Perry Mason,' it doesn't all get resolved neatly within an hour. So I think the public education aspect of it [was] just terrific."

While potentially valuable, television remains an imperfect force for educating the American public about its legal system. Coverage inevitably is skewed toward atypical, high profile cases. Most commercial television stations offer 90-second to two-minute "wrap-ups" embracing the day's highlights from a major trial, with little time for legal nuance. That may not be much different from the product offered by most daily newspapers. But apart from the biggest cases, TV stations rarely cover trials with the consistency of local newspapers. Television is at its educational best with the kind of extended coverage offered by Court TV and, occasionally, other outlets. It could be even more educational if it were augmented by a legal C-SPAN that provided gavel-to-gavel coverage of ordinary, and not simply high visibility, cases with just enough commentary to help a lay audience grasp legal complexities. The question is whether a large audience would watch such programming. In the final analysis, an informed public depends on citizens proactively seeking information about their justice system from all available sources, including television.

Entertainment and Titillation

"But this is not theater; this is a trial." U.S. District Judge Richard P. Matsch apparently felt a reminder was necessary, as he opened the trial of Timothy J. McVeigh on charges of bombing the Alfred P. Murrah Federal Building in Oklahoma City.[90] The proceedings in a Denver courtroom were being transmitted by closed-circuit television to a theater-like setting in Oklahoma City, where survivors of the blast, their families and relatives of the 168 who died could follow the action.

It was the first use of television in a federal criminal trial, but was available to no more than 330 persons each day—the capacity of the auditorium in the Federal Aviation Administration building. In fact many, including television analyst Andrew Tyndall, felt the absence of a public telecast was an important factor keeping the trial from bursting into the national drama that the Simpson case became. As the *New York Times* reported, "… people never got to scrutinize the witnesses' demeanor, study the prosecutor's hair style and wardrobe, hear the judge's voice, watch the lawyers bicker, see the defendant react—all those things that, as Mr. Tyndall put it, turned the Simpson case from a trial into a drama."[91]

As most Americans know, many such publicly televised "dramas" have played to huge audiences. In the parlance of the television industry, they have been "ratings getters." Telecasts of the murder-robbery trial of Ronny Zamora surpassed the ratings of the popular late-night *Johnny Carson Show*.[92] Viewers sat transfixed as defense lawyers plied their theory of "voluntary subliminal television intoxication"—crimes committed in a state of insanity induced by saturation viewing of television violence.

The ratings for the O. J. Simpson trial in this country and abroad were unprecedented.[93] Sixty-two percent of the country watched at least part of Lorena Bobbitt's trial on charges stemming from the amputation of her husband's penis. For the first Menendez brothers trial, it was 53 percent. And 81 percent of all Americans watched segments of the first trial of the officers who beat Rodney King.[94]

Were they drawn by a desire to be informed? Or entertained? In all likelihood, it was a mix of both. O. J. Simpson's criminal case evolved as an international drama, a modern-day morality play replete with salacious themes of sex, violence, race and Keystone Kops. Viewers were glued to their TV sets as witnesses described the volatile, passionate and tragic relationship between a gorgeous white woman and a larger-than-life black sports icon. Details were elicited about every knife wound and neck slash suffered by the victims. Kato Kaelin, Simpson's whimsical house guest, joked amiably with his questioners as he recounted his conversations with Simpson while driving to McDonald's for hamburgers in the defendant's Bentley a few hours before the murders of Simpson's ex-wife and a friend. The events became America's obsessive soap opera. Yet, as noted, they provided lively case examples for countless law school and civics classes—a random blend of education and entertainment.

Education and entertainment values would clash, quite by coincidence, in the Simpson civil trial. The jury reached a verdict just before President Clinton was scheduled to deliver his State of the Union address. A national crisis ensued as the networks wrestled with which event to cover. MSNBC's anchor John Gibson called the impending collision a "coast-to-coast media train wreck."[95] Noted author Neal Gabler wrote: "To the media, the State of the Union was, finally, a nuisance, a responsibility to fulfill before they could turn to the good stuff. Simpson was their story because it had glamour, drama, suspense. The State of the Union was just a way to kill time."[96] When it became clear that the revelation of the verdict might overlap with the President's speech, a Los Angeles anchorwoman promised to "bring you coverage of what the president has to say after the verdict." President Clinton was "very gratified" the networks did not cut from his speech to the verdict,[97] though at least one resolved its dilemma by splitting the screen and offering coverage of both events simultaneously.

Gabler charges that this "only underscores that entertainment is the primary force of our society, Simpson merely another show and the news another entertainment medium."[98] Simpson's civil trial wasn't even televised. Yet the media was having heartburn about whether to preempt the President with televised coverage of the verdict. And meanwhile they provided their own

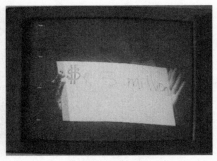

KTLA TV

When verdicts were returned in O. J. Simpson's untelevised civil trial, producers in a listening room across from the courthouse used flashcards to relay the verdicts to reporters. *Left:* Card showing "Y" (yes) as answer to question 5, "Do you find by a preponderance of the evidence that O. J. Simpson committed a battery against Nicole Brown Simpson?" *Right:* Card showing amount of compensatory damages awarded the plaintiffs.

sideshow to a case often labeled a "circus," as producers in a listening room, across from the courthouse, used flashcards to relay the verdict to reporters waiting to go "live" with the results.

Claus von Bulow's 1982 trial in Providence, Rhode Island, for the attempted murder of his heiress wife, was a predecessor to the theater of O. J. Simpson. Nearly every local newspaper and evening television program carried a story on the case, CNN provided live coverage, and even Thames Television in London covered the trial. Neither attorney objected to the presence of the single television camera in the courtroom. Yet the case, like the Simpson criminal trial, took on all the trappings of an international soap opera. R. W. Power describes the powerful drama caught in the eye of the camera:

> Few cases will afford the high drama and popular allure of the von Bulow case: a personable aristocrat who fell from grace. The camera, while now unobtrusive in the courtroom in the wake of improved technology, permitted viewers to see von Bulow's every blink and wrinkle. The camera waits and watches breathlessly, capturing the eternity of suspense the defendant must be enduring.... As the axe falls, the audience scrutinizes the face and hands for reaction—a momentary tightening of the fingers, no perceptible change in facial expression, narrated for those viewers who were momentarily distracted at the vital instant or who want their own impressions verified or corrected. Such television reporting may be a substantiation of the premise that Americans are sufficiently committed to voyeurism to prevent a too robust growth of the right to privacy.[99]

Where does education end and entertainment begin? Professor Chemerinsky feels many cases are inescapably a blend of both. He draws an analogy with a teacher in a classroom who "is both conveying information and is also to some extent entertaining." Teaching, after all, is a performance art. Chemerinsky is "not troubled by the fact that people might watch a trial and also find it to be entertaining in the sense that there's drama, there's mystery, there's theater inherent in the trial."

The question is: should cameras be barred from cases that promise to be entertaining? Leslie Abramson, a noted defense attorney with a notable bias against courtroom cameras, thinks the answer is yes: "We are talking about the right to titillate, we are talking about the right to exaggerate, we are talking about the right to make money."[100] She likens the televised trial to the broadcast of sporting events—"the merchandizing of spectacles." Trial action, Abramson points out, like sports, happens at a predetermined time and place and according to predetermined rules, making it relatively cheap and easy to broadcast. "The problem," she says, "is that the loser of the NCAA basketball final goes home to think about next year; if my client loses his capital-murder trial, he goes to the gas chamber."[101]

But not everyone thinks it's a bad thing that the public becomes emotionally involved in its justice system by dint of an entertaining trial. At a debate on cameras in the courtroom, Professor Fred H. Cate, Annenberg Senior Fellow at Indiana School of Law–Bloomington, argued: "The idea that you could have a community become impassioned or excited about a trial, about any small segment of the governing structure around us, it strikes me as a terrific thing."[102]

Stuart Fischoff, Professor of Media Psychology at California State University, Los Angeles, told a reporter from the *New York Times* that Americans now expect to be entertained by judicial proceedings. He said, "I think America has very quickly adapted to a sense of judicial activities as entertainment." Today, he observes, Americans "expect to see their trials on television" so they can become "hooked."[103]

Big trials have always been viewed as a source of entertainment. In old England and early America, public attendance at court was a way of "passing the time."[104] As noted earlier in this chapter, crowds flocked to the Aaron Burr treason trial in pre-television Virginia in search of high drama. Television has created a contemporary mass amphitheater in the courtroom where millions can watch courtroom drama and keep tabs on their judicial system— or at least part of it. And that may be the real issue. Since most televised trials are murder cases, the public may be inclined to view them as typical of the criminal justice system. Largely missing, except for occasional glimpses on Court TV, are the myriad cases involving petty crimes—thefts, assaults and small drug cases—that provide the bread and butter of criminal court calendars. Missing, too, are the cases resolved by plea bargains, which comprise the overwhelming majority of criminal court items.

The big televised cases, with their entertainment value, have also engendered some of the trappings of sport: commentators who analyze each step, each day, in terms of who "won" or "lost." It's a development decried by, among others, Marcia Clark, lead prosecutor in the Simpson criminal trial. "A criminal case is not won or lost by the motion or by the day," she wrote. "Its outcome is determined by weeks and months of cumulative testimony."[105]

The process of accumulating the evidence may also be entertaining, but at heart it is still a legal process, a search for justice. And it's important that commentators—and their viewers—remember that.

Catharsis for the Masses

When people are emotionally involved in the outcome of a trial, television coverage offers an opportunity for a collective national catharsis, a sense of relief or emotional "cleansing." Of course, broadcasts themselves may create that emotional involvement. Nevertheless, community retribution is a well-established justification for public trials. The theory is that when people see with their own eyes that the culprit has been brought to justice, it has a therapeutic effect, preventing vigilantism. The Supreme Court described this phenomenon in *Richmond Newspapers:*

> When a shocking crime occurs, a community reaction of outrage and public protest often follows.... Thereafter the open processes of justice serve an important prophylactic purpose, providing an outlet for community concern, hostility and emotion. Without an awareness that society's responses to criminal conduct are underway, natural human reactions of outrage and protest are frustrated and may manifest themselves in some form of vengeful "self-help," as indeed they did regularly in the activities of vigilante "committees" on our frontiers.[106]

Kelli Sager, pleading with Judge Ito to keep the television camera in Simpson's criminal trial, cited the public benefit of the "cathartic effect believing that justice is being done." The camera remained and the trial was watched by millions of people. Indeed, many black people experienced that catharsis—a sense that one of their own finally received justice from the system. For most whites, however, that catharsis never came from the televised trial. They felt O. J. Simpson got away with murder.

The Search for Justice

Although 48 states now permit some degree of courtroom camera coverage, none has yet embraced in law the principle that a public trial is necessarily a televised trial. Television remains discretionary in all the states that allow it. And the proposition that "public means televised" is unlikely to win favor with the United States Supreme Court until the high court allows broadcast coverage of its own proceedings. Still, the fact that other courtroom doors are opened to cameras every day implies that many judges and attorneys see merit in the principle. They believe television coverage *is* added insurance that a trial will be truly public in this modern, urban age. Many think it does foster public confidence in the judiciary, provide a check on judicial excesses and contribute to an informed, better-educated citizenry.

Where resistance remains to that concept, it stems largely from concerns that television interferes with the primary purpose of the courts—the search for justice—by somehow changing the process. Rather than providing an accurate mirror of the proceedings, television may transform them into theater, with the attorneys, judges and witnesses as performers. Or at the very least, it drops another, unnecessary variable into the equation for justice. We'll explore that argument in the next chapter.

Chapter Five

Do Cameras Change
the Process?

You can study this until you exhaust yourself... —Justice
Richard Huffman, California Fourth District Court of
Appeal[1]

Justice Richard Huffman has cause for exhaustion. As chairman of a task force
that reviewed California's policy on televised trials in the wake of the O. J. Simpson criminal trial, Huffman may have logged as many hours in study and discussion of the cameras-in-the-courtroom issue as any sitting judge in America. Central to his group's deliberations was an enduring and difficult question:
does courtroom camera coverage impair the dignity, solemnity and fairness of
the legal process? In other words, does it change the process for the worse?

Nearly everyone, including Justice Huffman, thinks cameras have the
potential to change a proceeding, if only subtly. "Do judges act differently in
front of television? Absolutely," says the former trial and now-appellate court
judge. "Of course. They're people and people do..." But the larger half of the
question—do cameras change a proceeding *for the worse?*—is the part that
"exhausts" scholars and analysts.

Despite believing that cameras can alter behavior, Huffman ultimately
endorsed revisions to California's Rule 980 that still allow cameras into courtrooms at the discretion of judges, while equipping jurists with elaborate guidelines to aid their decision-making. "The position we took is, essentially, judicial discretion is a means of achieving fairness and equity," Huffman told the
authors. "It is not an end in itself. And the difficulty one faces in this area, is
that there are no studies available, whatsoever, none, that address the prejudice to the rights of the parties."

In fact, there have been many studies. But critics contend most of them
are flawed by reliance on self-reporting by interested parties, or the use of
simulated, rather than real, courtroom proceedings.

Some studies have been follow-ups to the experiments that have cracked
open courtroom doors to cameras in many states. Among the most quoted and

highly regarded is the evaluation of the California experiment by the consulting firm of Ernest H. Short and Associates.[2] It surveyed participants in 200 legal proceedings ranging from criminal arraignments to trials. Three-quarters of those surveyed said they were either unaware, or only a little aware of the televised coverage, and four-fifths insisted they were either not at all distracted or were distracted only at first by the presence of cameras. In fact, most of the reported distractions arose not from television cameras, but from the repeated clicking of still cameras. Fully 90 percent of the judges and attorneys who were polled reported that the television cameras interfered only slightly or not at all with courtroom dignity and decorum. Three-fourths of jurors said the cameras had no negative effect on the courtroom environment. The 25 percent who said camera coverage did negatively affect the courtroom environment would seem to be a significant minority. However, only two percent reported that the camera's presence affected their behavior, just half the number that reported being affected by the presence of the general media. And the researchers reported that jurors exhibit "slightly greater attentiveness" when cameras are present.

Similar results were obtained by the Federal Judicial Center in its evaluation of a pilot program involving electronic coverage in six U.S. district courts and two courts of appeals. And the Courtroom Television Network, Court TV, is fond of quoting its favorable survey of the 96 judges who presided over the 100 cases covered by the network during its first year of operation. All of the 70 judges responding agreed that television cameras were essentially unobtrusive and had not impeded the judicial process in their courtrooms.

But as Huffman notes, with undisguised sarcasm, all of the respondents in those studies had a stake in successful outcomes. "They're all studies on, 'Well, Judge Foghorn, did you think you did a good job when you ran that case?' 'Oh, yes, I did a wonderful job because I do good work.'" In other words, how many attorneys and judges would admit they played to the camera or allowed it to distract them from their best efforts?

Whatever their self-reporting flaws, it should be noted all the studies arrived at the same conclusion: that camera coverage generally did not affect the proceedings negatively. Those included the California study, which augmented the responses of trial participants with the impressions of courtroom observers.

Some studies of the effect of television on witnesses and jurors in simulated courtroom situations were designed to eliminate self-reporting bias. A study at the University of Wisconsin's Madison campus in the late 1970s cast 36 student volunteers as "witnesses" in a mock trial proceeding. All watched a film depicting an incident. There was virtually no difference in the abilities of two groups to recall elements of the film—one that knew its "testimony" was being taped by a hidden camera, and another whose testimony was not taped. However, a third group of subjects, who faced an obvious camera, provided answers that were more correct, lengthier and more detailed than members of the other two groups. Researchers concluded they were, in effect, better witnesses.[3]

A 1990 University of Minnesota study employed 178 undergraduate students as either witnesses or jurors in three mock trial scenarios: (1) trial with a video camera present, (2) trial with a print journalist present, and (3) trial with no coverage. The witnesses all viewed a five-minute taped reenactment of an armed robbery. Those who testified in front of the camera reported greater nervousness and media awareness than did members of the other two groups. However, researchers found it did not affect performance. Those who testified before a camera recalled just as much correct information and committed no more errors than witnesses who testified with only a print journalist present or no coverage at all.

In addition, wrote the researchers, "perceived witness nervousness was not found to adversely affect juror perceptions of the quality of witness testimony.... [Video-taped] witness testimony was seen as being as clear as [other] witness testimony."

This study also sought to find out if participants who testified before a camera would hold negative attitudes since they generally experienced more nervousness. In fact, that group felt more positively about camera coverage than the other groups, indicating that actual experience with cameras promotes a more favorable attitude.

The University of Minnesota researchers clearly noted the limitations of their study. Their laboratory courtrooms were not the same as actual courtrooms. And their study was confined to a single incident involving armed robbery, which could limit its applicability to other types of criminal or civil cases.[4]

If Not Studies, What?

In the absence of conclusive studies, judges and attorneys have relied on their own reasoning, experience and, in some cases, bias in forming attitudes about cameras in the courtroom. In its 1965 *Estes* decision, the Supreme Court essentially shut out cameras for more than a decade, without any empirical studies to support the view of four justices on the widely arrayed Court that television *per se* was prejudicial, a violation of the Fourteenth Amendment to the U.S. Constitution. Justice Tom Clark wrote for the majority: "The impact upon a witness of the knowledge that he is being viewed by a vast audience is simply incalculable."[5] Chief Justice Earl Warren didn't need any studies to formulate his concurring opinion. "Whether they do so consciously or subconsciously," he wrote, "all trial participants act differently in the presence of television cameras." Warren wrote that even if they make a "conscientious and studied effort to be unaffected" by the cameras, that effort prevents the participants from "giving their full attention to their proper functions at trial."[6] The basis for that assessment isn't clear, since Warren as prosecutor, jurist and California attorney general never participated in a televised proceeding. But televised trials appeared to offend his sense of courtroom decorum. He told his law clerk: "We are asked again to make the determination of guilt or innocence a public spectacle and a source of entertainment for the idle and curious."[7] Warren might have been surprised that "the idle and curious" comprised 51 million viewers in American homes and tens of millions more in workplaces during the "public spectacle" of the Simpson murder verdict, 21 years after the death of the chief justice.

Before the Simpson case, cameras had achieved steadily increasing acceptance in American courtrooms. Even after Simpson's acquittal, a 48th state was added to the courtroom-camera list, as Indiana approved television and still photographic coverage of its Supreme Court on an experimental basis. Implicit in the expanding acceptance of cameras was a growing feeling by judges and other decision-makers that cameras do not necessarily poison the process by changing it in ways that interfere with justice. In part, it may be the "maturation process" that Texas District Judge Mike Westergren talks about—a combination of better, less intrusive equipment and more experience with it. Says the veteran jurist: "There will come a time, I believe, when cameras will be so commonplace that they will not constitute a problem, either in the high profile or non–high profile cases." Yet cameras clearly remained an issue with Judge Westergren a few months earlier when he banned them from the trial of Yolanda Saldivar, convicted of killing Tejano singing star Selena. Westergren says the decision was driven, in large measure, by concerns that television coverage would extend the trial and raise costs, which had already been increased by a change of venue from Corpus Christi to Houston.

Whether cameras actually prolong trials remains a hotly debated issue. The Simpson criminal case, more than eight months from opening statements to verdict, added a major and, many say, aberrant element to the debate. Critics contend the trial was extended by the posturing and proselytizing of lawyers for a television audience containing a potential second jury for a retrial, should the hung jury many expected occur. Even Prosecutor Marcia Clark joins the chorus contending that cameras in the Simpson courtroom "encouraged lawyers to preen for the lens and prolong the life of every goddamned motion to increase their time on the air...."[8] An adversary, defense attorney Gerald Uelmen, agrees. He feels the trial would have been over sooner if it had not been televised, because there would have been no interruptions to deal with issues related to camera coverage.[9] But California history is laced with untelevised trials that exceeded the Simpson case in length, although most had more charges and defendants. They include the Manson family trial (10 months, including jury selection), the Zebra murder trials (more than 12 months) and the Hillside Strangler case (23 months). And despite judicial rulings that

Court TV

Prosecutor Marcia Clark making an argument in the O. J. Simpson criminal trial.

sharply curtailed the defense and its witness list, the untelevised Menendez brothers retrial matched its televised forerunner in length.

One veteran jurist thinks an analysis strictly in terms of the camera's impact on trials is too narrow. "I don't think it's the presence of the camera," says Oakland County, Michigan, Judge Jessica Cooper. "I think it's the presence of the *media*." Cooper, who has tried "dozens" of cases before cameras in more than two decades on the bench, presided over Dr. Jack Kevorkian's highly publicized second trial for violation of Michigan's law against assisted suicide. "I think that in my case," she told the authors, "we had hot-tempered attorneys who were even hotter-tempered because of the presence of the media, not the camera itself. The camera is simply a part of technology.... It's not the technology [that prompted lawyers to preen]. It's the press, and in the Kevorkian case there was a lot of press." Kevorkian was ultimately acquitted.

Cameras—New Players in a Theatrical Mix

No one disputes that courtroom theatrics predate cameras in courtrooms. Lawyers have always "performed" for juries and news reporters. And judges have been charged with controlling excesses. The question is whether cameras

have complicated that relationship and somehow tainted it, as Gerald Uelmen suggests. "Once we convert the courtroom to a 'set,'" he writes, "we transform lawyers, witnesses and judges into performers."[10]

The authors asked dozens of judges, lawyers, witnesses and jurors who
had participated in televised proceedings a central question: did the camera
make a difference? Admittedly, the responses were subject to the same self-
reporting bias as some of the studies cited earlier. But many who did admit a
difference had a common response: they felt the camera's impact initially and
soon forgot about it. Even a seasoned, "professional" witness, Beverly Hills
police detective Leslie Zoeller, admitted feeling "nervous" when he took the
stand to testify in California's notorious Billionaire Boys Club murder case in
1987, his first encounter with a courtroom camera. "Once I started testifying,"
he recalls, "my attention was drawn to the attorneys asking the questions or
the judge. I really didn't notice the camera."

A non-professional witness, Elisabeth "Betty" Broderick, had a similar
reaction. She claims she successfully ignored the camera when she testified in
her own behalf at her second, televised San Diego trial on murder charges.
She found the prosecutor's interruptions during cross-examination a far greater
distraction than the camera.

U.S. postal carrier Bob Rakestraw was a juror in the first trial of Erik
Menendez, which was covered by a remotely operated camera mounted in the
ceiling in a back corner of the courtroom. "I would say within the first week
I had forgotten about it," says Rakestraw, "and I never even thought about it
any more until the end of the trial. So it was just an afterthought with me,
after the first week or so." The trial lasted several months. Rakestraw thinks
his impressions would have been drastically different had court rules allowed
pictures of jurors. In fact, he might have begged off jury duty altogether. "You'd
be, I felt, subject to questioning and subject to ridicule if perhaps someone
disagreed with your verdict." As it turned out, Rakestraw and his fellow jurors
offered almost everyone something with which to disagree—they hung, divid-
ing their votes between murder and manslaughter.

Before presiding over the O. J. Simpson preliminary hearing, Los Angeles Municipal Court Judge Kathleen Kennedy-Powell had allowed cameras in
her courtroom a number of times, usually for brief non-trial events such as
arraignments. Her view is familiar: "My general experience has been that after
a couple of minutes, everybody forgets the camera's there." The exception? No
surprise, the Simpson case. "I don't know if there will ever be another case like
that," she says.

Judge Kennedy-Powell admits to altering her own behavior during the
televised Simpson hearing, in what she considers a positive way. She spent 23
minutes explaining a key decision rejecting a defense motion to throw out
much of the evidence gathered at Simpson's home. Normally, she says, she
would have dismissed the motion with a few words. But normally her rulings

are not subject to second-guessing by millions of her fellow Americans. "I was aware that there were people out there that were unfamiliar with a motion to suppress—in fact, most everybody—and I wanted to make a clear explanation," the judge explains. "I really wanted the public to be able to understand why I reached my decision—agree or disagree, you know, that's fine—but I think everyone is better off knowing what the reasoning was."

Some attorneys also admit cameras change courtroom behavior. Douglas Larson represented the family of Jack Ruby, a man who killed on camera,[11] in a Texas probate case. "The first day the jurors all showed up dressed casually and comfortably," Larson recalls. "As soon as they realized there were TV cameras there, they showed up the next day in their Sunday best." He also states: "Everyone involved was playing to the camera, including me." How? "I was always being really careful so I would look good on camera. I think that's just human nature." The instinct to "look good," in the traditional sense anyway, was not the change wrought by television coverage of the Simpson trial, according to Prosecutor Christopher Darden. "Cameras caused all the lawyers to change our approach and our style," he wrote. "Everyone became long-winded and abrasive"[12]

Perhaps the most ringing affirmation that a camera, placed discreetly, need *not* alter courtroom behavior in a high profile trial comes, ironically, from a strong opponent of courtroom cameras. Defense attorney Jill Lansing represented Lyle Menendez in his first trial. "Everyone involved in that case was someone I knew before," says Lansing, "and everyone behaved the same." That applies to the judge and attorneys for both sides.

Cameras and the Witness List

Lansing's concern is about alterations of a much more fundamental nature—to the witness list, and hence to the very evidence in a trial. In the Menendez case, she says, "there were people who had information whom we wanted to have testify who would not testify because of the visibility of the trial." She cites, in particular, a woman who would describe "the physical aggressiveness" of murder victim Kitty Menendez, which became important in assessing the motivation of Lansing's client in killing his mother. The would-be witness was worried her appearance in the high profile case would ruin her husband's business. Was she afraid of the camera or publicity in general? Lansing isn't sure. But she feels confident camera coverage lures some witnesses to the stand who should not be there—"volunteers" who will "exaggerate or minimize information" for fifteen minutes of television exposure.

Conversely, television coverage may elicit testimony from volunteers with valuable information to share. The Menendez prosecutors reaped the benefits of two such witnesses. One of them, in the assessment of juror Bob Rakestraw, "gave us the most honest testimony that we heard in that whole trial." He refers to Grant Walker, a swimming pool service man who told of hearing the defendants "cursing out" their parents a few days before killing them.

Leslie Zoeller, the lead police investigator in the Menendez case, shares defense attorney Lansing's concern about reluctant witnesses. He relates: "I had quite a few witnesses in the first trial approach me and say, 'How can we get the cameras out of the courtroom? I do not want to testify in front of the camera. I do not want to see my face on television.'" In the end, however, the prosecution did not lose any witnesses. "They always seemed to testify," says Zoeller. However, he thinks some may have been less effective, less elaborative, than they would have been were the lens not trained on them.

Doron Weinberg, a prominent San Francisco criminal defense attorney, is convinced witnesses tailor their testimony to look good on camera. During cross-examination, Weinberg tries to develop an easy rapport with witnesses, a feeling of familiarity. But if the witness knows he's on camera, says Weinberg, he's more guarded, controlled and self-conscious and less likely to be shaken by his questioner.

San Diego attorney Charles Sevilla blames television for scuttling a clemency hearing for client Robert Alton Harris, who in 1992 became the first person executed in California in a quarter-century. "We had guards who had written some letters for Harris," recalls Sevilla, "and were willing to actually go forward at a clemency hearing in front of the governor and say he was a decent, peaceful, stabilizing force on Death Row. But when they heard that it was going to be televised, no way. We lost our witnesses." Harris eventually withdrew his request for clemency, but renewed it later. This time, the governor held an untelevised hearing and denied clemency.

John Keker, a San Francisco attorney who has represented Court TV in several camera access hearings, acknowledges cameras may make intimidated witnesses even less inclined to testify. But he insists there are other factors, as well—for instance, the notoriety of even some run-of-the-mill trials involving gang figures or organized crime. In such cases, says Keker, "the print press and the scuttlebutt in the witness' neighborhood can be just as devastating as the fact that their testimony is shown on television."

Television coverage may affect prosecution and defense witnesses differently. Maine is among the few states to study the effects of courtroom cameras on lay and professional witnesses. One finding: "The negative effect of coverage on a lay witness testifying in a criminal trial is much greater than the effect on a professional witness."[13] The most common professional witnesses are police officers, medical examiners and forensics experts, who usually testify for the prosecution. In that respect, television may offer an edge to prosecutors. And the presence of a camera may affect a defendant's decision whether to take the witness stand in his own behalf. He may fear that any nervousness will be interpreted by the television audience as lying.

There are judicial remedies for camera-shy witnesses—those, for instance, who may fear reprisals for making an in-court identification before a large television audience. The simplest remedy, says media representative Kelli Sager, is excluding cameras during their testimony. But that, she quickly adds, does not justify "throwing cameras out of the trial entirely." She worries about abuse of such exclusions, "because the same argument could be made that people don't want to testify if there are reporters in there, or if members of the public are allowed to sit in there and they have to look their neighbor in the eye. But that doesn't justify closing down the courtroom."

There are also alternatives, short of barring cameras during the testimony of a reluctant witness. The witness' identity can be electronically blurred; his voice, electronically altered. And in some cases, the broadcast of a trial or testimony of objecting witnesses has been delayed until after the trial is over. We'll examine these alternatives in more detail in a subsequent chapter.

Changes—For the Better?

Camera advocates acknowledge the lens' potential to change the process in one respect—to *improve* it, they say. "I think to the extent it has any impact at all," says Sager, "it tends to make people behave better, for the same reason that any time you are being watched, you may be on your best behavior."

Echoing Sager, retired Superior Court Judge Norbert Ehrenfreund, a former San Diego defense attorney and prosecutor, calls television "a great advantage in obtaining the truth." "In my experience," he says, "the witnesses, knowing other people outside the courtroom may be watching, are all the more careful about telling the truth because there may be somebody out there who can see if they're lying"—someone who *knows* the truth, he says.[14]

Then there's one of the most frequently cited benefits of camera coverage: as a check on the excesses of despotic judges. "For the same reason that some judges may not want to have cameras in their courtroom," says Sager, "I think it is in the public's interest to have them there, because they are less likely to act in a tyrannical or illegal fashion if they know they are being watched."

But Charles Sevilla, a staunch camera critic, insists that is cosmetic insurance against misbehavior. "While it may be the outwardly tyrannical judge will pull in his horns if the camera is there" says Sevilla, "inwardly, you will still get the same rulings from the tyrant. They'll just be sugar-coated cyanide tablets as opposed to cyanide without the sugar."

Noted Miami trial lawyer Roy Black, who successfully defended William Kennedy Smith against rape charges, thinks cameras can work both ways on judges—sharpen their performance or corrupt it. Under the eye of a television camera, Judge Mary Lupo made what Black considered well-researched, well-reasoned though sometimes unpopular rulings in the Smith trial. But the same television scrutiny, says Black, can produce rulings that "may be more popular than correct."[15]

In a ruling both popular and correct, according to public opinions polls, Judge Hiller Zobel reduced the 1997 conviction of British *au pair* Louise Woodward from second-degree murder to involuntary manslaughter. However, the relative rarity of such rulings caused many to wonder if Zobel had been influenced by public pressure generated by widely-watched telecasts in the U.S. and the teen-aged defendant's home country. In an apparent effort to blunt such speculation, the judge prefaced his ruling by quoting an earlier Massachusetts barrister, John Adams, that the law is "deaf as an adder to the clamours of the populace." Zobel added, "In this country, we do not administer justice by plebiscite."[16]

California's two Menendez brothers trials engendered a running debate over the conduct of trial judge Stanley Weisberg and the influence that television may, or may not, have had on his rulings. In the untelevised and less-scrutinized retrial, Weisberg issued a series of rulings that sharply limited a defense theory that produced hung juries in the original combined trials. The judge ruled the Menendez lawyers had not laid the groundwork for "imperfect self defense"—the theory that the brothers had acted in the "honest but unreasonable belief" that they needed to defend themselves against imminent death or great bodily injury.[17] That line of defense clearly impressed some of the jurors who delivered split verdicts in the earlier proceeding. But by barring it in the retrial, Judge Weisberg eliminated the option of convicting the brothers of the lesser offense of voluntary manslaughter. Leslie Abramson, Erik Menendez' vocal attorney, accused Weisberg of gutting the defense in an effort to ensure the eventual first-degree murder convictions. And some of her sympathetic colleagues in the legal community wondered if Weisberg would have been as tough on the defense under the same television surveillance as the original trial. An alternate juror who followed the second trial as a spectator had the same question. Judy Zamos thought Weisberg's behavior "was quite different" in the retrial. "He was the main prosecutor upon the bench, in his black robe," she says. "He didn't dare do that when the world was watching him."[18]

There is another factor in the debate over the extent and manner in which television insinuates change into a legal proceeding—the dimensions of the proceeding itself. Does television exert a more powerful influence over participants in a big case, a mega-trial, than in less-publicized proceedings? George Gerbner, dean emeritus of the Annenberg School for Communication at the University of Pennsylvania, contends the answer is yes. "When you change the audience, you change the performance," says Gerbner, a consistent critic of televised trials. "When you enlarge the audience to millions of people, including the communities, families, bosses and voters who determine the fate beyond the courtroom of most of its participants ... you all of a sudden

Court TV

Top: Pamela Bozanich, prosecutor in the first televised trial of the Menendez brothers. *Bottom:* Defendant Lyle Menendez, on trial for the fatal shooting of his parents.

change the stakes from examining the guilt or evidence pertaining to that particular case to reflecting on how the rest of your life is going to shape up. The election of judges depends on how they appear on camera to millions of voters; the possible promotion of a prosecutor into higher office, if he or she wins the case; the careers and the reception of witnesses back in their communities."

Adds Gerbner: "The presence of the cameras [in big cases] may or may not affect the way in which participants in a trial think they feel, but it inevitably affects the way in which they consider their future being influenced by what they do."

In that regard, New York attorney Jack Litman, another courtroom camera critic, cites the bail hearing for Joseph Hazelwood, captain of the tanker *Exxon Valdez* when it ran aground in Alaska on March 24, 1989, creating the worst oil spill disaster in U.S. history. Hazelwood stood charged with three misdemeanors, for relatively minor acts, albeit with vast consequences. The prosecutor asked for $50,000 bail; but Judge Kenneth Rohl, with TV newscasts beaming his actions to a world-wide audience, set bail at $1 million. "This will send a ripple around the world," he declared. A review board eventually overturned his bail order as "constitutionally excessive." Without TV coverage, would the bail have been so high? Litman thinks not.[19]

Scornful of state experiments and studies—"Ninety-five per cent of those so-called experiments do not qualify to be called experiments"—George Gerbner returns time and again to the aforementioned axiom of communications theory: "If you change the audience, you change the performance." Though he has not specifically tested the theory in courtroom settings, "there's no reason to assume that judges are the exception," he says.

In the course of serving as a radio and television commentator during the Simpson criminal case, Peter Arenella was converted, in some measure, to Gerbner's point of view. The University of California–Los Angeles law professor still finds "considerable merit" in the assertion that television inside a courtroom provides an accurate counterweight to sensationalistic excesses outside court—that if you don't televise trials, you increase the public's dependence on tabloid-style coverage. But that view has limits, says Arenella. "It ignores how much televising a high profile trial feeds the media frenzy outside the courtroom. There is a chicken and egg problem here. Courtroom cameras are not responsible for the irresponsible media coverage that takes place outside the courtroom, but their absence from the courtroom tends to diminish the national media's interest in the case."[20]

Conversely, he asks, when big cases are televised, does the outside notoriety feed back into the courtroom and "provide incentives for all of the trial participants to view their own roles somewhat differently, with consequent changes in their behavior and decision-making?" The Simpson criminal case, he says, provides "a telling example" that the answer can be yes, that "televising a high profile case alters the behavior and experiences of all the trial's participants."[21]

JUDGE MATSCH EXPLAINS HOW THE MCVEIGH TRIAL PROCEEDED SO QUICKLY AND RATIONALLY...

David Kellet, San Diego Union-Tribune

In the wake of the second (civil) Simpson trial and again after the Denver federal trial leading to the conviction of Timothy McVeigh for the deadly bombing of the Oklahoma City federal building, Arenella's position won many disciples. There was no courtroom camera coverage of either proceeding. Comparisons between the long, explosive Simpson saga and the two other trimmer, less-volatile proceedings were unavoidable. The quick consensus: the camera, or lack thereof, made a crucial, transforming difference.

But it's important to note some other major differences between the McVeigh case and the Simpson criminal trial that undoubtedly contributed to their different tenors. First and foremost were the sharply contrasting defendants: a glamorous sports and entertainment hero on one hand, an obscure, alienated ex-soldier, on the other. Americans felt they knew O. J. Simpson. He'd been in their dens and living rooms, thrilling them, charming them with a dazzling smile for decades. Except for a single, endlessly repeated shot of a heavily guarded McVeigh in shackles and jail jumpsuit (pictures of the well-groomed, well-dressed defendant weren't available from the courtroom), many Americans had trouble even identifying him. The crime of which he was convicted was so vast as to be incomprehensible, beyond human grasp. Simpson was accused of a mix of murder and passion that was the stuff of prime television fare devoured nightly by millions of viewers. His trial was in Los Angeles, the communications capital; not Denver, built on livestock and energy.

The casts were strikingly different, too. There were no glamorous, flamboyant "dream teams" in the McVeigh trial; just diligent, no-nonsense prosecutors and a government-subsidized defense team—all gagged, by court order. And, almost as important as the contrasting defendants, was a difference in judging: Lance Ito, the patient, permissive Simpson judge, versus Richard Matsch, openly determined to avoid the "Simpson experience" with a tight rein over his case.

Did courtroom cameras make a difference? Undoubtedly. But the two trials would likely have been drastically different even if cameras had been excluded from both courtrooms. "O. J. is about as unique a case as you can get," says defense attorney Charles Sevilla, a view widely echoed by camera critics and advocates alike. "It's not even the typical high profile case. It was in a league unto itself."

Even Professor Arenella concedes the Simpson criminal trial may be an exceptional case that should not rule out cameras from every high-interest, high profile trial. Citing an educational value in airing ordinary civil and criminal cases, Arenella adds: "Televising high profile cases educates a far greater audience but at a far higher price. There are some high-profile cases [Rodney King] whose social and political significance justifies the risks involved."[22] The parenthetical reference is to California's explosive police beating case which evolved into a sweeping examination of police conduct and community racial attitudes.

Do cameras change the process? It may seem that the reader is left to "exhaust" himself with the evidence, pro and con, as Justice Huffman and his colleagues did in reviewing California's courtroom camera rules. Given the growing acceptance of camera coverage even after the Simpson case (see "States' Rights," Chapter 7), it appears that in many cases the changes wrought by a discreetly placed pool television camera using available courtroom light are insignificant. It is not the "99 per cent of all cases" suggested by David Harris, the University of Toledo law school professor who's written exhaustively on the subject. And certainly grandstanding lawyers, reluctant witnesses and a defendant cast in a prejudicial light are, individually or collectively, the by-products of some televised trials. But judges have the discretion to weed out poor candidates for camera coverage, with a mind toward protecting the fairness of the proceedings. And just as they search lawbooks and data banks for precedents to resolve legal disputes, they have a growing body of law to guide them in decisions about admitting cameras. Given the unique ingredients of each item on a criminal or civil docket and the exceptional cases—the Simpson criminal trial, the Susan Smith and John Salvi cases cited in other chapters—it almost inevitably will remain a case-by-case decision. Hopefully, with experience, it will also become an easier, less exhausting one.

Chapter Six

Two Trials: Trial by Jury and the Court of Public Opinion

The only people who heard all the evidence were the people sitting in the jury box, in both cases.—President Bill Clinton, after verdict in Simpson civil case[1]

Even the President of the United States, a politically astute lawyer himself, was mindful of the chasm between the verdict in O. J. Simpson's criminal case and the feelings of many Americans. A vast number of people formed opinions from watching the trial on television. But the trial on television was not the trial seen by the jury.

There have always been "two trials" in highly publicized cases: the trial the jury sees and hears, and the one perceived by the public through its exposure to news coverage. Sometimes there are drastic differences between the two. The advent of cameras in the courtroom has highlighted this contrast in a unique way. In the words of UCLA law professor Peter Arenella: "The picture trumps the words."[2] Convictions have been reversed where the case available to the public overwhelmed the one presented to the jury, infecting deliberations with publicity never offered as evidence.

The case responsible for keeping cameras out of courtrooms for many years was overturned because of prejudicial publicity. A split Supreme Court ruled that Billie Sol Estes' swindling conviction in Texas was infected by television and photographic coverage of both pretrial and trial proceedings.

Pervasive media coverage at the pretrial stage may taint the pool from which the jury will ultimately be drawn. Publicity during trial raises different concerns. Cameras now enable large numbers of people to enter the courtroom, so more people feel they are entitled to judge the case than was so before the advent of cameras in the courtroom.

Prejudicial Publicity in Pretrial Proceedings

Introduction

During pretrial hearings, judges often screen out inadmissible evidence that will be excluded from jury consideration. The first reversal of a criminal conviction by the Supreme Court for prejudicial pretrial publicity came in 1959 in *Marshall v. United States.*[3] Howard Marshall was charged with unlawfully dispensing drugs. The trial judge refused to allow the prosecutor to introduce evidence of the defendant's prior convictions for similar offenses, because it might tempt the jury to convict him based on his prior record.

But many of the jurors had read about the defendant's record in news accounts. The Supreme Court said, "We have here the exposure of jurors to information of a character which the trial judge ruled was so prejudicial it could not be directly offered as evidence." Marshall had raised the defense of entrapment: that he was not predisposed to commit the crime but was induced to do so by the government. The Court felt, "The prejudice to the defendant is almost certain to be as great when that evidence reaches the jury through news accounts as when it is a part of the prosecution's evidence."

Seven years later, the high Court reversed Dr. Sam Sheppard's conviction for the murder of his wife because prejudicial publicity deprived him of a fair trial.[4] The media had reported countless inflammatory tidbits of evidence never heard by the jury in court. Also, news accounts emphasized Sheppard's failure to cooperate with the authorities, even though he had been fully cooperative before his family refused to allow him to be questioned without his attorney present. One headline screamed: "Testify Now in Death, Bay Doctor Is Ordered." The newspapers also harped on his refusal to submit to a lie detector test: "Doctor Balks at Lie Test; Retells Story." They reported that other possible suspects had been "cleared" by lie detector tests.

Although the trial itself was not televised, television and newsreel cameras took motion pictures of witnesses, counsel, the judge, jurors and the defendant outside the courtroom.

The Supreme Court characterized the media blitz as "editorial artillery," which included a front-page charge that somebody is "getting away with murder." A coroner's inquest, where Sheppard was publicly searched and questioned without an opportunity for his counsel to defend him, was broadcast on the radio. Newspapers highlighted incriminating evidence, pointing out discrepancies between Sheppard's statements to the authorities.

According to the Court, "The newspapers portrayed Sheppard as a Lothario, fully explored his relationship with Susan Hayes, and named a number of other women who were allegedly involved with him." Walter Winchell reported in a radio broadcast that Carole Beasley, under arrest for robbery, had stated she was Sheppard's mistress and had borne him a child. "The testimony at trial" said the Court, "never showed that Sheppard had any illicit relationships besides the one with Susan Hayes."[5]

Nevertheless, the high Court concluded, "The jurors themselves were constantly exposed to the news media. Every juror, except one, testified at voir dire [jury selection] to reading about the case in the Cleveland papers or to having heard broadcasts about it. Seven of the 12 jurors who rendered the verdict had one or more Cleveland papers delivered [to] their home[s]; the remaining jurors were not interrogated on the point. Nor were there questions as to radios or television sets in the jurors' homes, but we must assume that most of them owned such conveniences."[6]

Ultimately, the *Sheppard* Court articulated guidelines for judges to shield jurors from prejudicial publicity. These include the use of gag orders, change of venue, sequestration, continuances and, as a last resort, a new trial to be ordered when fairness has been threatened by publicity. Justice Tom Clark, writing for the majority, concluded: "Due process requires that the accused receive a trial by an impartial jury free from outside influences."[7]

Pretrial Publicity Heightened by the Television Camera

The power of pretrial media coverage has increased with the entry of television into the courtroom. When pretrial hearings are televised, future jurors may be watching. Judges typically decide important issues concerning the admissibility of evidence before the jury panel is formed. If the proceedings are televised, prospective jurors may be exposed to evidence excluded from the trial.

During *voir dire*, potential jurors are questioned about their exposure to pretrial publicity about the case. Even though many may know a great deal about the matter before they ever enter the courtroom, they can be selected for the jury if they swear they can still be fair and impartial. Trial jurors, however, may be unable to shed the image of a witness identifying the defendant as the perpetrator at a televised preliminary hearing. This could prove particularly prejudicial if the pretrial identification were ruled inadmissible at trial, due to constitutional or other infirmities.

Psychology professors Gary Moran and Brian Cutler, who have written several publications on the workings of juries, conducted studies of the prejudicial impact of pretrial publicity. They concluded that even modest pretrial publicity may prejudice potential jurors against a defendant. The professors also warned of possible self-reporting bias by jurors who insist they can be impartial. Such claims, they wrote, should not be taken at face value.[8] It is also difficult to put aside biases formed by watching shocking scenes of a federal building exploding or a shackled defendant walking down a hall in jail clothes, which are played over and over again on television before the trial ever begins.

Even though William Kennedy Smith's lawyer, Roy Black, reversed his anti-camera position after his client's acquittal on rape charges, he maintains that television coverage of *pretrial* proceedings remains potentially damaging because it "can infect the pool of potential jurors."⁹ Before jury selection in the Smith trial, Black made a motion to bar television cameras, arguing they would "intimidate" jurors who were about to become "central characters in an internationally known, sensational drama." He predicted the camera would make prospective jurors less candid when asked to answer difficult questions.¹⁰

Black's motion was denied but his prediction came true. During jury selection, a prospective juror was being questioned about the Kennedy family. His vague responses led Black to believe the man had more to say but was reluctant. When the camera was turned off, the potential juror "breathed a sigh of relief and blurted out, 'I can't stand Ted Kennedy,'" according to Black. He feels strongly that cameras should be excluded during *voir dire* because they affect a juror's candor.¹¹ In fact, cameras are barred from jury selection in many states.

Pretrial televising doesn't always harm the defense. Several motions were argued out of the camera's presence before the first Menendez brothers murder trial began. The court permitted broadcast of other motions, however. One such motion involved the defense effort to present testimony by "intergenerational" abuse experts to show that the childhood history of the parents could incline them toward abusive behavior. The public heard this evidence but jurors did not. Although Lyle Menendez's defense attorney, Jill Lansing, does not remember pondering at the time whether jurors might inadvertently watch the experts on television, she admits, "if they were going to see anything improperly, that would have been something that would have been helpful to us rather than hurtful."

Lansing also feels jurors in retrials are contaminated by exposure to television coverage of the first trial.¹² The judge in the two Menendez trials, Stanley Weisberg, had the same concern. In excluding cameras from the second trial, he observed: "The visual images from television coverage of the first trial remained in the minds of many potential jurors long after memories of details faded."¹³

Perhaps the most flagrant disregard for the potential impact of televised pretrial proceedings came in the case of Oliver North, the former White House national security aide indicted on 12 criminal counts for his role in the Iran-Contra affair. North testified before congressional committees for six days. Major television and radio networks carried his testimony live. News shows replayed portions of the testimony and analyzed it.

North's later conviction was reversed because the appellate court could not rule out the possibility that many grand jury and trial witnesses had been affected by North's televised congressional testimony.¹⁴ John Keker, who prosecuted North, begged Congress not to go forward with North's immunized testimony. "We knew it was going to screw things up horribly," Keker told the

authors. "Congress insisted," he says, "because their version of the public interest was that North had to be heard from and [Admiral John] Poindexter [Pres-
ident Reagan's national security advisor] had to be heard from, and they had
to be heard from early and they had to be heard from in the context of a hearing as opposed to a criminal trial. And they weren't going to wait for the independent counsel."

O. J. Simpson's "Dream Team" also worried about the potential for bias
arising out of pretrial television coverage, while favoring broadcast coverage
of the criminal trial itself. Robert Shapiro argued to Judge Ito that the public has a right to know, through the vehicle of the camera, what the jury sees
and hears. But on technical legal issues, said Shapiro, "on evidentiary hearings that may or may not result in matters coming before the jury, we clearly
agree ... that those matters should be excluded from the camera and from the
courtroom, from the public viewing of the courtroom proceedings." Johnnie
Cochran echoed Shapiro's sentiments: "We think that the public, in their right
to know, should see what our jury sees, not the machinations of the pretrial
hearings."[15]

The judge who conducted Simpson's preliminary hearing thinks the
benefits of televising it outweighed any potential detriments. The pool of
prospective jurors for the case had already been deluged with "rumors and
innuendo," notes Kathleen Kennedy-Powell. The televised coverage of the
hearing "put some of those rumors to rest. People were seeing what was actually going on in court, so the information was more accurate than it had been
up to that point. It wasn't 'some unnamed source says this'; 'a source close to
the investigation says that...' There was something concrete and everybody
could hear it and everybody could see it. And I think that was a *good* thing."

Televising a preliminary hearing may help ensure that a defendant is not
railroaded into formal charges. The broadcasting of O. J. Simpson's preliminary hearing ultimately worked to his advantage. Prosecutors exposed the out-
line of their case against him and the defense thereby gained at least one key
witness. Former real estate agent Kathleen Bell watched Detective Mark
Fuhrman's smooth, televised performance on the witness stand and came forward to deliver her own devastating trial testimony for the defense about
Fuhrman's racist remarks during a chance meeting with her.

Still, the possible prejudicial impact of televised pretrial proceedings
clearly concerned the California task force chaired by Justice Richard Huffman.
The advisory panel stopped short of endorsing Governor Pete Wilson's appeal
for an all-out ban on courtroom cameras. But it did recommend broadcast coverage be restricted to events actually seen by sitting jurors—that it be prohibited in arraignments, bail hearings, preliminary hearings, jury selection[16]
and pretrial motions in criminal cases. The state Judicial Council rejected the
proposal, except for the ban on coverage of jury selection.

The Jury Trial and the Public Trial

The court of public opinion is closed and the real court is
open. —U.S. District Court Judge Richard P. Matsch

Though almost all pretrial events in the Oklahoma City bombing case
had been smothered in publicity—an alleged "confession" was even publicized—Judge Matsch tried to apply some damage control. Once the prelim-
inaries were out of the way, he was determined there would be just one trial,
the one taking place in his Denver courtroom. To guard against another one,
staged for public consumption, Matsch imposed a gag order on attorneys to
prevent their "spinning" of a second, self-serving version of events on the courthouse steps. He wanted the public to hear what jurors were hearing, as delivered by news reporters (though not television cameras, which were barred).
The judge may also have been concerned about tidbits from a second, spin-
doctored trial getting back to jurors.[17]

The same, lofty ideal—that the public be exposed to identical information
as jurors—was expressed by Floyd Abrams, arguing on behalf of Court TV to
retain television coverage of the Simpson criminal trial. "If Mr. Simpson is convicted," he told Judge Lance Ito, "it is important that the public have seen for
itself what the evidence is…. If Mr. Simpson is acquitted, it is important that

the public know that the evidence was lacking and that he should have been acquitted.... The best way that that can happen is to allow the public to see for itself and judge for itself and come to its own conclusions about the sobriety and the seriousness and the sense of responsibility that exists in this courtroom, and there is no other way, Your Honor, I would argue to you than having the camera here."[18]

Also pleading with Judge Ito to retain the camera in Simpson's trial was media attorney Royal Oakes, who argued, the camera "is a perfectly accurate reflection of reality," to which Ito replied: "But it does editorialize in the sense that it has a tilt and pan and close focus and it can emphasize what it wants to emphasize."[19] Nevertheless, Judge Ito allowed the camera to remain and after the trial he defended his decision, stating: "If you take the cameras out of the courtroom, then you hide, I think, a certain measure of truth from the public."[20]

But the public saw a different trial from that witnessed by the jury. "In fact, people who stayed glued to every hour of live TV coverage literally did not see the same trial as the jurors legally responsible for judging the case."[21] Simpson attorney Gerald Uelmen, trying to account for the disparity between the criminal verdict and the public's perception of Simpson's guilt, felt if people had simply confined their judgments to what the jury heard in the courtroom, there would have been no problem with public acceptance of the verdict. That may be a bit simplistic, given the complex social and racial dynamics that shaped public attitudes toward the verdict. But without doubt, conscientious trial watchers did see, in the televised version, a great deal of evidence never presented to jurors.

Millions of viewers watched Detective Fuhrman assert his Fifth Amendment right not to incriminate himself after he committed perjury. But Judge Ito refused to allow the jury to see it. The public learned about many alleged incidents of domestic violence not heard by the criminal jury, including a frightened call to a battered women's shelter by a woman fitting Nicole Brown Simpson's description shortly before her death.

Television viewers saw a proceeding, out of the jury's presence, in which Rosa López, housekeeper for a Simpson neighbor, testified she saw Simpson's Ford Bronco parked in front of his home about the same time the murders occurred. Her testimony was riddled with inconsistencies. Focus groups that viewed the videotaped testimony gave it a thumbs-down. The defense decided not to present it to the jury.[22]

Public exposure to events unseen by jurors may cut both ways. Among many viewers, Rosa López's waffling account may have cast doubt upon Simpson's alibi and thus his innocence. On the other hand, Fuhrman's disastrous boasts to a screen writer of brutality, evidence tampering and racism may have made television viewers more receptive to a defense theory of frame-up.

Noted journalist Theo Wilson, who covered major trials over four decades

for the *New York Daily News,* was supremely conscious of the two-trial phenomenon. In a book published shortly before her death in 1997, she wrote,
"*News* readers learned every detail of the big trials, knew exactly what the jury
had heard as opposed to what had transpired outside the courtroom, and
understood why jurors returned the verdicts they did." Wilson cited as an example President Nixon's declaration of Charlie Manson's guilt during Manson's
trial. It was not incorporated into the trial story save a brief reference, but was
used separately in the *News.*

After the Simpson trial, however, Wilson wrote, "I could tell from the
questions the public asked that the viewers couldn't figure out what testimony
had or had not been heard by the jury, and what was plain junk from outside
the courtroom."[23] That view is shared by Professor Peter Arenella, who maintains, "only the hard core viewers who watched the entire [Simpson] trial could
know for sure what 'evidence' was not presented at the trial. Even some of
these viewers might confuse memories of domestic violence evidence they saw
on one of the tabloid shows with the evidence presented at the trial."[24]

Then there is what viewers did not see in the Simpson criminal trial: the
grisly autopsy and crime scene photos of the victims, withheld from broadcast by Judge Ito. "The television jurors didn't see the real jurors horrified by
the pictures," Professor Arenella told a conference on ethics and the media.
"Everyone in the courtroom understood that, but not the [television] viewers."[25] Arenella watched the trial from both sides: the television studio and
the courtroom itself. "The trial I watched and analyzed on television was
remarkably different from the one I attended," he observed.[26]

Associated Press special correspondent Linda Deutsch sat in Judge Ito's
courtroom every day during the O. J. Simpson trial. She, too, is convinced the
public and the jury see different trials: "I don't think what the public sees on
television is what you see in the courtroom…. The public sees a witness closer
than you see them in person. Head shot close-ups are so close that even you
and I do not talk at that kind of a distance. It would be uncomfortable for
anyone to be in that proximity with another person."

Los Angeles Superior Court Public Information Officer Jerrianne
Hayslett ran interference between the court and the press in the Simpson trial.
In her first five and one-half years on the job, Hayslett was exposed to 200 to
300 cases where the courtroom camera was at issue. She echoes Deutsch's
characterization of the contrast between the eye of the spectator in court and
the eye of the camera piped to the viewing public: "The spectator in a courtroom can not zoom-in to sit right on top of the witness who's testifying, can
not turn around and sit in the laps of grieving family members sitting in the
front row or the second row of a courtroom."

Hayslett continues, "So the eyeball can turn from one side to another,
but the eyeball can not zoom out and get that dramatic close-up of a judge
who's frustrated because of lawyers who are acting out. They can't go in for a

close-up of the defendant's hands. The [still photography] camera in the back of the courtroom is a far more realistic view of what the spectator gets."

Though generally favorable to televised coverage, Deutsch feels the television camera may miss the big picture: "You don't get the entire panoply of what's going on in the court. You don't see the spectators, and the reporters taking notes, and feel the tension in a courtroom. All that you see is who's testifying at that moment. And that, in a way, is artificial. But others might argue that's the best we can get."

Jack Litman, who represents criminal defendants in New York, feels the television media actually creates the big picture, but a false one. "Typically," he maintains, "crying spectators are juxtaposed (by television editors) with the defendant's haggard face." Thus, he says, "the public sees the defendant as guilty. That message is not deduced from the televised trial content. It stems from the very nature of television: The message and the medium are one and the same."[27]

The television cameraman in the Simpson trial was connected to a media center that was choreographed by news organizations and news directors across the country. Recalls Hayslett: "They would call in with requests for shots that they wanted—a close up of the defendant now, get a shot of his hands now, the witness on the stand now." That, in turn, "gave a great deal more drama—a feeling of drama, whether it was soft drama or real drama at the time—it changed the perception of the viewer, what the viewer was seeing, because the viewer was then being subjected to the creativity of the news director, as opposed to the activity in the courtroom."

In response to such concerns, the California Judicial Council imposed restrictions on the range of courtroom camera coverage after Simpson's murder trial. Although close up photography of jurors was already prohibited, the rule now also forbids any photographing, recording or broadcasting of jurors or spectators. This includes the reactions of victims or family members.

O. J. Simpson probably welcomes the change. In a panel on "Rivera Live" in August of 1995, Simpson complained, "What the TV camera did is every time something emotional happened on the witness stand, they'd cut to Kim Goldman [sister of stabbing victim Ronald Goldman], or a member of the— of the Browns [family of Simpson's ex-wife], and sometimes members of my family. And they'd make it a little more emotional than it should've been. And I thought that was a disservice to me."

Yale Law Professor Paul Gewirtz characterizes the two different trials in Simpson's murder case, in his article, "Victims and Voyeurs at the Criminal Trial": "At every point there was a trial before the broader public at least as intense as the trial before the jury, and this broader public trial, magnified and distended by the media, profoundly affected what went on in the courtroom. Even intermittently attentive and poorly informed segments of the public felt justified in judging Simpson's guilt or innocence.... The public audience shaped the trial's enduring meaning far more than the jury could. In short, the second trial—the one before the public—largely displaced the first."[28]

Simpson lawyer Alan Dershowitz feels there were not just two trials conducted in Simpson's criminal case, one before the jury and one before the public; there was a *third*—the one portrayed in the predominantly black press which was largely favorable to Simpson. Dershowitz says the defense team, mindful of a possible gulf between the jury verdict and white public perception, was concerned about prejudice to Simpson in the event of a hung jury and ensuing retrial. The defense would face a daunting challenge to find a jury pool that could still apply the presumption of innocence. Appellate courts reviewing claimed mistakes in the trial after a guilty verdict would have a predisposition to find those errors "harmless" because of what courts often deem the "defendant's obvious guilt." For that reason, according to Dershowitz, the defense made conscious efforts to be vocal during the trial. "We defended our client both in the court of law and in the court of public opinion."[29] Gerald Uelmen says both sides, with a view toward a possible retrial, did some things "more for the consumption of the television viewers than the jury."

And much of what they did occurred outside the courtroom, beyond the range of the courtroom camera, in news conferences and "spin" sessions before hungry batteries of cameras outside the courthouse itself. Simpson co-counsel Robert Shapiro wrote an article on how to conduct such events.[30]

Members of the news media who are exposed to evidence from both trials may be inclined to reach their own conclusions as the case proceeds. This creates a "subtext bias," according to Professor Arenella. "In the Simpson case there was little doubt that most of the mainstream media, reflecting the attitudes of their consumers, believed Simpson was guilty of the two murders. This type of 'subtext bias' is inevitable because the media, like the rest of us, comes to conclusions about the defendant's guilt or innocence long before the case goes to the jury."[31] But the jury is instructed to wait until all the evidence has been presented before rendering a verdict after due deliberation.

Commentators—The Medium Becomes the Message

Adding to the distinction between the jury trial and the public trial is the emerging cottage industry of expert commentators and pundits who appear on broadcast coverage of major trials. Although jurors may not be directly exposed to commentators, many of them influence not only the coverage of trials but the proceedings themselves. Paraphrasing the much-quoted words of communications theorist Marshall McLuhan, the medium can become the message.[32] "Most of the regular commentators and pundits [during the Simpson criminal trial] had an obvious bias," contends defense attorney Uelmen. "They had decided which way the case should turn out, and the 'spin' they placed on the day's events invariably led to the result they favored."[33]

Law professors Erwin Chemerinsky and Laurie Levenson, both veteran legal commentators, raised similar concerns in their article, "The Ethics of Being a Commentator II"[34]: "It is not unheard of for judges to follow legal commentary and tailor their rulings accordingly. Trial participants sometimes use commentary to guide what arguments or strategies they will present in court." Indeed, Simpson prosecutor George "Woody" Clarke admitted to the Society of Professional Journalists that commentators influenced his trial strategy. Discussing benefits of broadcasting the criminal trial, he recalled driving home and hearing coverage of the cross-examination of witnesses he had just conducted. "I learned to have a pen and piece of paper nearby even in the car, because I would hear from commentators, 'Well, obviously Mr. Clarke is going to ask such and such during his redirect examination.' I'd think, 'that's a great idea; I never thought of that.' So I'd write that down."[35]

Peter Arenella was a television commentator when photographs were shown to the jury but withheld from the TV audience. His producer told him: "You've got 15 seconds to explain those pictures [to the viewing public]." Arenella "got out two descriptive sentences"—a poor substitute for viewers seeing the real thing.[36]

"The TV juror might miss revealing non-verbal behavior of the witnesses or the defendant that the [courtroom] jurors can see from the jury box. Some witnesses appear more credible on TV than in the courtroom, while others fare better in person than on the tube," wrote Professor Arenella in an article.[37] For example, he cites Detective Mark Fuhrman, who appeared to Arenella "far more credible on television than he did in person…. The subtle and occasional cracks in his demeanor were more apparent inside the courtroom."[38] Professor Arenella's evaluation of Fuhrman's courtroom credibility reflected both his own interpretation of the detective's body language and the reactions of some black jurors to parts of Fuhrman's testimony. "The television audience," says Arenella, "could not see the jurors' reactions because Judge Ito barred camera coverage of the jury."[39]

Lawyers Shift from Jury Audience to Public Audience

A simple human factor may add to the differences between the two trials, the one seen by the jury and that experienced by the public. The participants themselves may act differently when the jury is outside the courtroom and the public is their only audience.

Oakland County, Michigan Judge Jessica Cooper is convinced that "the [attorneys'] arguments got hotter, the sarcasm got deeper" when the jury was absent during the second trial of Dr. Jack Kevorkian for assisted suicide. "They would do things … to posture and preen. And I think that was pretty much for the camera…. They were playing to the camera when the jury went out, and they were playing to the jury when the jury was in."

Likewise, in the Simpson criminal trial, defense attorneys and prosecutors alike behaved differently when jurors sat cooling their heels outside Judge Ito's court. They often screamed at each other, hurled insults and stretched the principles of civility to the limit, forcing even the patient Judge Ito to hold some in contempt of court. But in front of the jury, the hot-blooded environment cooled considerably.

Still, their angry antics, *sans* jury, may have had a purpose, says Professor Paul Gewirtz. Because lawyers in high profile cases know public opinion has a way of "seeping into the courtroom," he writes, they consciously influence the court of public opinion in hopes of reaching jurors—current or future, in event of a retrial. The bottom line: "One audience will become the other."[40]

The Public Plays by Different Rules

The right of the public to pass judgment derives from itself, according to Gewirtz: "I feel, therefore I may judge." He is disturbed by "the public's increasing sense that it is either on a par with or superior to the jury."[41] A jury must follow a discrete set of complex rules in the courtroom. These do not bind the public audience, however, which is free to turn on and tune in or turn off and tune out the proceedings.

"The jury decides, but the public separately decides on different evidence and in accordance with different criteria," writes Gewirtz. He distinguishes the jury, which must be a "constant" audience, from the viewer, who may be an "intermittent" audience. Jurors, he observes, cannot come to the trial one day and be gone the next, but must hear and consider everything admitted into evidence before them. They must wait until they have heard all the evidence to deliberate and judge. And they must follow the court's instructions. The public, on the other hand, is not so limited. It may be biased, it may be exposed to inadmissible evidence and it need not watch every minute of the trial. It is also not bound by the instructions of the judge.[42]

Jurors are repeatedly admonished by the judge not to consider anything that is not presented to them in court. Attorney John Keker maintains, "The jury doesn't see things that the public sees. But if the public followed the same rules that the jury followed, which of course, they don't ... if they followed jury instructions, then they'd have to ignore the stuff that was outside the evidence of the case."

The Public Audience as Thirteenth Juror

Inevitably, however, the viewing public becomes the "thirteenth juror," in the view of UCLA's Arenella. "But it is privy to information that the jury has not considered and is not bound by the legal instructions that the jury tries to follow in good faith." The jury's role and vantage point are unique.

"Watching the trial on television is not an adequate substitute for being in the courtroom every day [as a juror]."[43] Since the community doesn't see the same trial as the jurors, it should defer to the decision of the jury.[44]

Judge William Howard, who presided over the Susan Smith case, warns of the danger of distortion when viewers see only part of the picture: "People often form judgments based upon incomplete or inaccurate information. If viewers see only a selected part of a proceeding, such as a particularly entertaining portion of a witness' testimony or a lawyer's final argument, and if it is transformed into importance by repeated emphasis, the reality is distorted. When it is visualized, rather than verbally summarized, it becomes an unalterable vision of truth."[45]

Of course, even in non-televised trials, the public may form judgments based on sporadic attention to reports on a case. And advocates of televised trials prefer the camera's "unadulterated" eye to the journalistic "filters" who summarize the testimony for the public. But trying to be a "thirteenth juror" remains "a tricky business," warns Arenella. "Only the most conscientious viewer could distinguish the trial evidence from the information she was exposed to in the media."[46] The television jurors form opinions from watching a different trial than the one seen by the jury. Armchair jurors should remember that when they are tempted to second-guess the decision of a jury sworn to render a verdict based on the courtroom evidence alone.

No matter what safeguards are imposed—even if cameras are excluded altogether—the public may have a different view of the case than jurors. People generally tend to follow the proceedings intermittently; they are usually seeing, either on television or in print, selected segments of the trial offered by reporters as their sense of the most important representations of a long proceeding. It is a good faith approximation of—but not the same as—the view from the jury box.

Chapter Seven

States' Rights

A Matter of Self-Determination

The American states that permit courtroom cameras comprise "48 social, or judicial laboratories." That's the view of Ronald George, chief justice of the state that hosted the Simpson "Trial of the Century" and then underwent a complex process to revise its cameras-in-the-courtroom rule. George's view mirrors one of the major principles of the *Chandler* case that revolutionized the law of television in state courts. In holding that courtroom cameras do not necessarily violate due process, Chief Justice Warren Burger quoted a Louis Brandeis opinion from 1932: "It is one of the happy incidents of the federal system that a single courageous State may, if its citizens choose, serve as a *laboratory*; and try novel social and economic experiments without risk to the rest of the country."[1]

Not surprisingly, today's rules authorizing the use of cameras in the nation's courts vary, from state to state, among the 48 that permit judges to open their courts to television. Each has undergone its own unique political process in pushing open the doors to at least some of its courts. In every state, the course has been shaped by three key cases frequently cited in this book: *Estes v. Texas*,[2] *Chandler v. Florida*,[3] and *California v. Simpson*. This chapter examines the three states that spawned those cases and the evolution of courtroom coverage in each.

Texas is analyzed first because of the enormous influence of the *Estes* case in drawing the parameters for televised trials. The *Chandler* case added a dimension of states' rights—states are free to allow cameras in court as long as they do not run afoul of the U.S. Constitution. And the *Simpson* case stirred a backlash that for a time threatened to slam shut many courtroom doors to cameras.

Some judges have run for cover, away from the camera's glare. But the backlash largely disintegrated as it hit America's state houses. As of this writing, only two states, South Dakota and Mississippi, and the District of Columbia do not permit cameras in their courtrooms. In 1996, *Simpson* notwithstanding, Indiana joined ranks with the other 47 states that allow television cameras in court.

The chapter concludes with an analysis of the effect of the "Simpson factor" on courtroom camera laws. And it provides an overview of some of the more common features of the various state camera statutes.

Texas

While Texas was the first state to permit the live telecast of a trial,[4] it also contributed to the demise of cameras in the courtroom for 16 years, following the *Estes* decision.

The Lone Star state steered its own course after the American Bar Association enacted Canon 35, in reaction to the Lindbergh kidnapping trial. Unlike most states, Texas refused to adopt Canon 35, which prohibited photographing and broadcasting court proceedings.[5]

Thus for almost 30 years, when most of the other states were grappling with whether and to what extent to impose Canon 35 on their courtroom etiquette, Texans listened to trials or saw courtroom photographs in their local newspapers when individual judges permitted it.[6] At first blush, it seems ironic that the case which became the benchmark for banning cameras from the nation's courts arose in Texas. But it was almost inevitable that a Texas case would put the lens cap on courtroom cameras because there were fewer restrictions on televised trials in Texas than in most other states. In its 1965 *Estes* case, the Supreme Court ruled that the Texas practice of allowing televised trials violated federal due process. This was an exercise of federal supremacy under Article VI of the U.S. Constitution.

But the *Estes* Court didn't shut the door completely on cameras in the courtroom. It noted, "the ever-advancing techniques of public communication and the adjustment of the public to its presence may bring about a change in the effect of telecasting upon the fairness of criminal trials. But we are not dealing here with future developments in the field of electronics. Our judgment cannot be rested on the hypothesis of tomorrow but must take the facts as they are presented today."[7]

For ten years after the *Estes* ruling, most states were reluctant to jump into the camera fray. But in the late 1970s, several states began opening their courts to cameras. Many conducted experiments of varying length and scope. Each state adopted its own approach, while imposing substantially similar conditions on the media.[8]

Just as the *Estes* majority had predicted, better technology enhanced the process. It became possible to obtain airable video and film images using existing light, obviating the need for intrusive artificial lighting with its cables and cords. The smaller television cameras were less conspicuous and quieter, substantially reducing any disturbance to court proceedings.[9]

In 1972 the ABA replaced Canon 35 with Canon 3A(7), which created a narrow exception to the prohibition of broadcasting, televising or photographing trials. The exception allowed camera coverage under restrictive guidelines "for instructional purposes in educational institutions."[10]

And finally, in 1981, the Supreme Court handed down its *Chandler* ruling, using the Florida case to open courtrooms to cameras.

By 1990 Texas was ready to give cameras in court another try. The state supreme court adopted a rule permitting cameras into Texas trial courts and courts of appeal. The rule contained guidelines requiring consent from parties and witnesses before camera coverage was allowed.[11]

The first televised civil trial in Texas after the post–1965 hiatus was the 1990 probate case of the estate of Jack Ruby. A few calls from the media, including Court TV, to Probate Court Judge Robert Price got cameras back into the trial court. The judge saw no problems with camera coverage of the trial. "We had a commodious courtroom," he noted. "At the very beginning, before jury selection, I told the crew I didn't want [them] to run a bunch of lines.… We were concerned with the safety factor. I didn't want to do anything to distract the attorneys, the principals or the jury." All of the parties, the judge, the lawyers, the clients and the jury "were on their best behavior." "I don't know what I was expecting," says Judge Price, "but I was pleasantly surprised by the decorum and conduct of the press."[12]

Still, Price emerged from that trial with a cautious attitude toward cameras, willing to permit cameras into his courtroom only sparingly. Price says he would bar them from cases involving salacious issues or if he thought they would create any distraction whatsoever. If none of the parties objected, he would then make an independent determination. Alluding to the legal standard used by appellate courts to review the decisions of trial courts—"abuse of discretion"—Price concludes, "you can't abuse your discretion if you say no."

In retrospect, Douglas Larson, attorney for the Ruby family, would have asked for an arrangement now commonplace in hundreds of courtrooms: a camera pool to reduce the number of cameras in the courtroom.[13] He recalls three or four cameras in court at various times, including that of Court TV, which taped the entire trial for later airing. That cable channel was just getting started; *Ruby* was one of its early cases.

Larson reports that Judge Price called the attorneys into his chambers and asked if anyone objected to the presence of cameras; Larson said "no." He won the trial, so it would be hard to say camera coverage damaged his presentation. With hindsight, however, Larson says he would have objected to television coverage, because he felt a certain amount of tension when on camera. "I don't like being on camera," he says.

The following year, Judge Joe Drago III of the State District Court of

Fort Worth, permitted television coverage of a criminal case from opening arguments through the jury's verdict. Patricia Griffin was accused of contributing to the alcohol-poisoning death of her five-year-old son, Raymond "Tinky" Griffin. Judge Drago permitted Court TV to place two stationary cameras at the back of the courtroom. The network provided the tape to local television stations on a shared, or pool, basis.[14] The pooling arrangement addressed concerns expressed by Douglas Larson in the *Ruby* case.

Viewers in thousands of Texas households saw Patricia Griffin collapse in relief after her acquittal. Judge Drago was convinced that camera coverage caused no disruptions and may have actually eased media attention.[15] "If anything, because of the pool situation with all of the television people in a back room, there were less disruptions in and out of the courtroom," Drago said. "You didn't see cameras crowding the jurors every time they came in and out of the court." Attorneys for both sides agreed the cameras caused few distractions.[16]

Despite warm reviews for television coverage of the Griffin case, broadcasters have often found their cameras shut out of the big cases of ensuing years.

In 1994, Texas Senator Kay Bailey Hutchison went on trial for ethics charges that she used state employees and equipment for personal and political uses while serving as Texas treasurer. Judge John F. Onion, Jr., decided to bar cameras in his courtroom after Hutchison's attorneys expressed a concern peculiar to the case. Lead defense attorney Dick DeGuerin argued that the senator's political opponents might extract clips from televised testimony and use them against her in the upcoming election campaign against six little-known opponents.[17]

Said DeGuerin: "There is a likelihood that an opponent would isolate some taped snippet of testimony and put it in a televised political advertisement and repeat it out of context, thus further endangering her right to a fair trial."[18] He was concerned about dirty campaign tactics as well as fair trial issues.

Yolanda Saldivar's murder trial, a year later, seemed tailor-made for television. The victim, Selena Quintanilla Perez, was a *Tejano* singing star, young, sexy, talented and beloved by millions of Latinos. When Saldivar gunned down "Selena," as she was known, outside a Corpus Christi hotel, it aroused the passions of fans throughout the Americas.

Harris County, where Saldivar was tried, received requests from 80 news organizations for credentials to cover the trial. "I can't recall any trial attracting this much attention here," Jack Thompson, the Harris County courts administrator, told reporters. The trial had been moved to Houston because of heavy pretrial publicity about the case.[19]

The media were victims of bad timing. Yolanda Saldivar went to trial as the O. J. Simpson murder case concluded. Without directly alluding to the controversial, televised California trial, State District Judge Mike Westergren made an unequivocal decision to bar cameras. Texas court rules enable a judge to permit the televising of criminal trials if both the parties and witnesses agree.[20] In the Selena case, both District Attorney Carlos Valdez and defense attorney Doug Tinker opposed camera coverage.[21]

Despite the ban on courtroom cameras, Jack Thompson found himself consulting Los Angeles officials, now armed with experience from the Simpson case, about how to deal with a "media horde" outside the courthouse.[22] "I have never been exposed to such a media event, and I hope I never am again," Judge Westergren told a citizens' group after the trial.[23]

When Judge Price said after the Jack Ruby case that he would be hesitant in the future to allow cameras where salacious facts were likely to attract public attention, he might have been talking about the drug possession case of Michael Irvin, star wide receiver of professional football's Dallas Cowboys. Police caught Irvin in a hotel room with two "models" (exotic dancers), two ounces of cocaine, about three ounces of marijuana, drug paraphernalia and sex toys. The story featured a sports star in a seamy sex situation replete with drugs—the very stuff of tabloids. Criminal District Judge Manny Alvarez barred cameras and recording equipment from his courtroom, declaring, "I don't want these cases to get out of hand."[24]

Even before a grand jury indicted Irvin on felony cocaine and misdemeanor marijuana charges, the case attracted enormous publicity. In preventing camera coverage, Judge Alvarez hoped to ensure fairness: "I want to make sure both sides, the state and the defense, are treated the same as anyone else who comes before this court."[25]

Although he banned cameras from his courtroom, Judge Alvarez made one concession to the media: He permitted a single camera to tape court proceedings through a glass window in the courtroom doors. News organizations had to organize a pooling arrangement.[26]

Judge Alvarez had hoped to avoid a spectacle by keeping cameras out of court, but as happened in the Selena case, it simply contributed to the crowd of news people outside the courthouse. Thanks in part to gag orders on the lawyers and a resolution of the case before trial, the case did not turn into the runaway media "circus" many feared.

Irvin pleaded no contest to second-degree felony drug possession and received probation and a fine. His plea avoided both a possible 20-year prison sentence and testimony of prosecution witness Rachelle Smith, one of the women found with Irvin the night of his arrest. She would have testified about other sex parties with Irvin for which he provided drugs.[27] As the story unfolded, Smith's boyfriend, police officer Johnnie Hernandez, was charged for taking out a contract on Irvin's life because he could not abide Irvin's threats to his girl.[28]

In depriving Texans of televised coverage of the Irvin show, Judge Alvarez helped bring courtroom camera coverage in his state full circle—from a permissive attitude, to the *Estes* shut down, to rules permitting cameras if the parties consent, back to a post–*Simpson* trend against cameras in high profile cases.

Florida

While *Estes* was the prevailing word on cameras in state courtrooms, Florida managed to develop rules that have become the most liberal in the nation.[29]

The post–*Estes* era not only saw significant technological advancements that minimized the disruptive influence of courtroom cameras, but also spawned a major shift in the role of television news. Once operated largely as a public service, local TV news became a for-profit commodity with massive growth potential in an increasingly competitive environment. Television replaced newspapers as the main source of news for most of the public. Advanced electronic news gathering became the key to success: the station with the best live, on-the-spot broadcasts of major news got the ratings.[30] In this technological and communications context the Florida courts conducted experiments with televised trials.

In 1975, the Post-Newsweek stations in Florida petitioned the state supreme court to lift the ban on televised courtroom coverage. The court adopted an experimental program to televise one civil and one criminal trial, subject to court-imposed guidelines. These included a requirement that parties, jurors and witnesses consent to coverage of the proceedings.[31] But more than a year passed with no televised trials; consensus between the parties proved impossible.[32]

The Florida Supreme Court amended its earlier guidelines and authorized a second one-year pilot program. It permitted television cameras in all state courts, even without the consent of participants. Media organizations were required to conform to explicit standards of conduct and technology, and reasonable orders and direction of the presiding judge.[33]

A case arose during this experimental period that attracted international attention. It was the murder trial of 17-year-old Ronny Zamora, discussed in earlier chapters. Trial Judge Paul Baker allowed television coverage of the case. He estimated that at times, "several million viewers"[34] were glued to their sets mesmerized by the unique defense—"voluntary subliminal television intoxication,"[35] an overdose of violent TV crime dramas that blurred right and wrong.

Zamora was convicted. And Judge Baker emerged convinced that television coverage of the trial had been a positive experience. In a report to the Florida Supreme Court, he said the *Estes* Court's fears about the influence of the television camera on judges were unfounded, asserting, "a judge's conduct should be subject to public scrutiny." Baker concluded that the public's right to know how a judge comported himself or herself could be accomplished by either sitting in the courtroom or watching television.[36]

Favorable reviews of the Zamora broadcasts paved the way for television coverage of another major Florida case with national interest, the murder trial of serial killer Theodore Robert Bundy. In 1978, two students at Florida State University in Tallahassee were bludgeoned to death in the Chi Omega sorority house, and two other residents were viciously attacked.[37] Six blocks away, another young woman was sexually assaulted and brutally beaten. The university town was traumatized, not knowing if and when the killer would strike again. The answer came in Lake City, 100 miles east of Tallahassee. Twelve-year-old Kimberly Diane Leach was abducted. Her body was found almost two months later. Bundy, with "clean-cut good looks and articulate charm,"[38] became the prime suspect.

Bundy had already been convicted and sentenced to death for the sorority house murders when he went on trial for the death of Kimberly Leach. Presiding Judge Wallace Jopling was faced with a barrage of media interest in the trial. At the outset, he granted a motion to ban press coverage of pre-trial depositions. He recognized that media attendance at these depositions could generate prejudicial pretrial publicity.[39]

Once the Bundy trial began, however, Jopling sequestered the jury and allowed one still and one television camera in the courtroom. But the judge transferred the trial to Orlando because the small town of Live Oak[40] could not withstand the media onslaught. Empaneling an impartial jury had become nearly impossible.[41]

Although Orlando had been exposed to the Bundy case to the same extent as Live Oak, the judge felt the urban environment provided a vastly greater jury pool, more likely to be impartial, if not less informed. Only two out of 175 prospective jurors had not heard of Bundy. Jury selection became a laborious task. The judge individually questioned each person to avoid tainting potential jurors with information others had heard. Media coverage of the Tallahassee murder trials was so widespread that the judge also found it necessary to permit each side in the Leach case 20 peremptory challenges, double the number usually allowed in Florida capital cases.[42]

With a camera trained on him eight hours a day, Bundy felt the strain and protested. Responding to pressure from Judge Jopling, the media agreed to limit their camera coverage of Bundy to no more than 15 minutes per hour. Bundy complained about still photographic coverage as well. He berated the media for publishing photographs that portrayed him in the least appealing light. He commented: "You see this photograph in the front of the [*Miami*] *Herald*. It's kind of a grotesque picture, and I was quite furious when I saw it because ... I'm sure they took lots of photographs yesterday but they loved this one. They could have printed any number of others, but they loved this one because it made me look like an idiot."[43]

The presence of television cameras in the Bundy case took its toll on the defendant. But the media and court managed to work out their differences in a way that was "cordial and mutually respectful" in a highly charged trial where the stated media goal was "a minimum of accompanying confusion or discord."[44]

And despite what problems there were in the Bundy case, the state supreme court declared the year-long experiment with cameras in Florida's courts a success by amending Canon 3(A)(7) of the Florida Code of Judicial Conduct to permit televised coverage in Florida's courtrooms.[45] It left authorization for cameras entirely up to the presiding judge, whose job it would be to control court proceedings, prevent distractions, maintain decorum and assure fairness.[46]

Florida's permanent rule, adopted by the Florida Supreme Court in *Petition of Post-Newsweek* in 1979, states:

> The presiding judge may exclude electronic media coverage of a particular participant only upon a finding that such coverage will have a substantial effect upon the particular individual which would be qualitatively different from the effect on members of the public in general and such effect will be qualitatively different from coverage by other types of media.[47]

This rule requires judges in Florida to "seek out specific information addressed to the issue of the impact camera coverage might have on the participant compared to the effects it might have on other individuals." Although a judge may allow cameras without consent of the accused, the judge must entertain the defendant's objection. An objecting party must show: 1) that camera coverage would have a significantly different effect on participants than on other members of the public; and 2) that the effect of camera coverage would be significantly different from the effect of other types of media coverage. The final decision, however, is up to the judge.[48]

Judges in Florida have allowed televised coverage, over objection, in response to petitions by a widow of a murder victim, a prisoner who feared retaliation and a 16-year-old rape victim. These judges found telecasts would not have a qualitatively different effect from newspaper reports of these proceedings.[49]

Florida's liberal rule, permitting cameras into courts subject only to the judge's approval, soon came under attack in *Chandler v. Florida*. The United States Supreme Court had the opportunity to assess a landscape changed by advances in technology.

In his *Estes* opinion, Justice Clark had suggested the Supreme Court might find itself revisiting the camera issue in "another [future] case."[50] *Chandler* was the case.

Two Miami Beach policemen were charged with burglary, conspiracy, grand larceny and the possession of burglary tools. In what is destined one day to become perfect fodder for a television "dumb cops" series, this case was a drawing card for public interest. Co-defendants Noel Chandler and Robert Granger had underestimated the power of technology one night as they used walkie-talkies during the course of a crime they had plotted together. By chance, amateur radio operator John Sion happened to be scanning the dial when he picked up the incriminating two-way talk between Chandler and Granger.[51] He recorded the conversation and went to the police.

Chandler and Granger tried to have Florida's Canon 3(A)(7) declared unconstitutional,[52] but failed. During trial one television camera recorded a whole afternoon of the state's evidence. It recorded no defense testimony. Ultimately, broadcasters aired two minutes and 55 seconds of the proceedings.[53] After the guilty verdict, the defendants moved for a new trial. They cited television's role in denying them a fair and impartial trial, but provided no evidence of specific prejudice. The Florida District Court of Appeal affirmed the convictions, finding no indication that the limited televised coverage had any negative impact on the defense case.[54]

The United States Supreme Court agreed. Chief Justice Warren Burger, delivering the opinion of the Court, referred to the door left open by *Estes*. He concluded that *Estes* did not prescribe "a constitutional rule barring still photographic, radio, and television coverage in all cases and under all circumstances." Acknowledging that coverage of any high profile trial might compromise fair trial rights, the Chief Justice said the inherent risks did not justify an absolute ban on broadcast coverage of trials.[55] The high court noted that no empirical evidence showed the *Chandler* trial was tainted or trials in general were harmed by televising them. Unless the record showed that television coverage impaired the decision-making ability of jurors, or adversely affected the behavior of the participants, there would be no reversal.[56]

In the absence of a constitutional violation, the Supreme Court concluded, Florida was free to permit televised trials on its own terms. But the *Chandler* Court refused to find an absolute First Amendment right for broadcast media to televise court proceedings. It did, however, permit states to determine when television would be allowed in the courtroom as long as it did not impinge on the right to a fair and impartial trial. Chief Justice Burger wrote: "We are not empowered by the Constitution to oversee or harness state procedural experimentation; only when the state action infringes fundamental guarantees are we authorized to intervene. We must assume state courts will be alert to any factors that impair the fundamental rights of the accused."[57]

By striking a blow for states' rights, the *Chandler* decision reflected the Burger Court's conservative trend of taking power from what was perceived as a liberal federal government and giving it to the states to interpret matters of criminal procedure.[58] Henceforth, individual states would be free to enact camera rules of their own choosing, provided they passed constitutional muster.

With the enactment of Florida's permanent rule enabling cameras to be in courtrooms and *Chandler* authorizing limited televised trials, other states eagerly jumped on the bandwagon. By the time *Chandler* was decided, 19 states already permitted cameras in the courtroom at both trial and appellate levels, while three more permitted televised coverage of trial courts only. Six limited coverage to appellate courts and 12 more were seriously considering opening at least some courtroom doors.[59]

Now, with permission from the United States Supreme Court, Florida television stations routinely broadcast "dozens of trials—both criminal and civil ... each year."[60] Miami lawyer Norman Davis, interviewed prior to the advent of nationwide Court TV, noted that in Florida, "TV cameras help the public believe the judicial system is fair."[61] He cited the positive sociological spin-off of cameras in the courtroom. In 1989, Miami Police Officer William Lozano stood trial for shooting to death an unarmed black motorcyclist and his passenger, triggering a three-day riot. "The local population had the chance to see the entire process," said Davis. "It helped diffuse tensions in the community."[62] Community leaders asked a local public television station to provide nightly, gavel-to-gavel coverage of the trial. The community hoped to avoid a recurrence of the racial violence that had erupted during two earlier trials in cases of white Miami policemen accused of killing black civilians.[63]

The Los Angeles riots sparked by the acquittal of four Los Angeles policemen accused of beating motorist Rodney King exemplify the type of community hostility Miami wanted to avoid. The King trial was also televised. Home video clips of the beating were repeatedly shown to jurors and aired to television viewers. Could telecasts of the King trial have actually helped incite the riots? It is difficult to assess whether television coverage defuses or exacerbates tensions when there is a controversial verdict in a highly charged case.

In 1991, another big Florida case hit the air waves, stirring debate about whether televised trials enhance or diminish public confidence in the justice system. It was the rape trial of William Kennedy Smith, nephew of the late President John F. Kennedy. Smith, a medical school resident, came home to the family's seaside Palm Beach compound one night with a woman he met partying at a local bar. She alleged he raped her. He denied the allegations. Prosecutors filed charges. He pleaded not guilty. Dirty laundry—the woman's grass-stained underwear—was aired. The victim was named, contrary to existing media policy. Smith was acquitted.

The trial was lasciviously fleshed out by the media, which turned out in droves: "WEST PALM BEACH, Fla.—William Kennedy Smith pleaded not guilty to rape Friday in a court hearing that ended in mayhem as reporters and camera crews crushed bystanders and deputies in their quest to interview the defendant," wrote David Zeman, in an article published in the *Houston Chronicle*.[64]

Smith's attorneys filed motions with Circuit Judge Mary E. Lupo to ban television cameras from the courtroom. They argued, "Television would turn

Jury selection in *Florida v. Smith*. Florida is one of the few states that allow camera coverage of jury selection.

the proceedings into 'a sensationalized Hollywood-style mockery of the justice system.'"[65] Judge Lupo did not ban cameras, but she placed restrictions on coverage of jurors. She permitted Court TV to broadcast its first major trial, gavel-to-gavel.

On the opening day of trial, the judge cautioned jurors: "This is not a television show....,"[66] and went on to ensure that journalists did not cast jurors as characters in one. After 78-year-old prospective juror Florence Orbach made the comment: "Who cares who diddled who?" she was besieged by press from all over the country for interviews.[67] As a result, Judge Lupo threatened to strip press credentials from journalists who contacted potential jurors. Although not ordered to stay away from jurors, she warned journalists that if they contacted Ms. Orbach or any other juror, they might face charges for obstruction of justice.[68]

Despite their sensational content, telecasts of the trial exposed a chronic ailment in one appendage of the justice system. Wrote Ron Hutcheson of *The Fort Worth Star-Telegram*: "Viewers got a first-hand look at the legal system's response when a woman accuses a man of raping her." He reported, "They saw the accuser reduced to tears as defense attorney Roy Black tore into her story. They saw her bra and pantyhose. They heard her characterized as a woman in search of sex."[69]

The telecast struck many as simply voyeuristic. Even Judge Lupo told jurors at the close of the trial: "This has not been a movie made for TV."[70] President George Bush commented after the trial, "I must tell you I'm worried about it. I'm worried about so much filth and indecent material coming in through the airwaves and through these trials into people's homes."[71]

However, the case changed the view of Smith's defense attorney about televised trials. This shift occurred a comfortable three years after his client's acquittal. Cameras made it "more difficult—but not impossible—for the defendant to get a fair trial," said Roy Black. "Social exposure to the justice system outweighs the cost to the defendant," he concluded.[72] The acquittal of Black's client no doubt helped nurture this new-found affinity for cameras in court.

In the wake of the William Kennedy Smith trial, television has continued to flourish in Florida courtrooms. Court TV televised more than 60 Florida cases in the six years between the Smith trial and June 1997.

California

The Golden State reacted to the O. J. Simpson murder trial by giving judges unfettered power to oust cameras from their courtrooms, with virtually no recourse for appeal. Ironically, the most watched televised courtroom event in history occurred in what was once among the most camera-restrictive environments in the nation. For many years, cameras were barred from California courtrooms. After extensive study, the Judicial Council had concluded that electronic media coverage of courtroom proceedings interfered with a defendant's right to a fair trial. As a result, California adopted Rule of Court 980 in 1965, the same year *Estes* was decided. It prohibited photographing, recording and broadcasting in the courtroom.

The following year, the California Judicial Council authorized a limited number of short-term experiments with courtroom cameras. They required consent of all trial participants and provided that no photographs be used for general broadcast or commercial purposes.[73] The Assembly Interim Committee on Judiciary had concluded that much of the sentiment against broadcasting in courtrooms stemmed from the days when cameras were loud and disruptive, with "exploding flashbulbs, mazes of wire and loudly whirring cameras." A major concern was: "Many judges feel their discretionary powers—which still include the right to make rulings affecting the lives of litigants—have been unduly abridged by Rule 980." The committee thought television coverage of courts could act as a deterrent to crime because potential criminals could see for themselves "the inexorable, inevitable toll justice extracts from law-breakers."[74]

But the committee's "single most important finding" was that no conflict exists between a free press and a fair trial. A fair trial must necessarily be a public trial, said the report, and a public trial in mid–20th-century America meant the media could use whatever device they had, including television, to broadcast to the public.[75] Not everyone agreed with this conclusion. Hugh R. Manes, a prominent litigator of police abuse cases, testified at the 1966 hearing that free press and fair trial rights often *do* conflict. He recommended that defendants have complete veto power over television in the courtroom, declaring: "I must say that the right of fair trial has no peer when there is a conflict between freedom of the press and fair trial...."

Manes did not think a judge should have the absolute and sole discretion to allow camera coverage of court proceedings. He testified: "I submit that as long as we have the concept of presumption of innocence, that where the defendant doesn't want publicity, he or she ought to have the right to say to the press, 'Leave my courtroom; I prefer to try this case before the judge and jury only.'" He asked the committee to consider a rule "that would recognize the principle that a fair trial is the basic whip of liberty. There can't be any dispute about the importance of a defendant's liberty as against the importance of selling newspapers."[76]

Apart from the brief period of experimentation with limited courtroom photography, Rule 980 remained in effect without challenge until 1980. Then, for the first time in California history, cameras gained access to courtrooms statewide. This rule change occurred after a committee appointed by California Chief Justice Rose Bird recommended it. The Judicial Council adopted an experimental rule allowing film and electronic coverage in courtrooms, provided the judge found that cameras would not be distracting. It originally required the consent of the prosecutor and defendant in criminal cases. However, that was deleted after the United States Supreme Court made clear in *Chandler* that camera coverage over the defendant's objection was not an automatic denial of due process.[77]

In the context of a nationwide trend to allow greater electronic access to judicial proceedings, the Judicial Council hired Ernest H. Short and Associates, Inc., to evaluate and monitor the experiment with courtroom cameras.[78] This made California the first state to conduct a concurrent statewide evaluation of such an experiment.[79] Two major questions were studied: first, whether broadcast equipment would result in a significant distraction for trial participants, disrupt proceedings or impair judicial dignity and decorum; and second, whether the behavior of trial participants would change in a way that interferes with the fair and efficient administration of justice.[80]

The Short evaluation relied on interviews with participants in court proceedings, observations of electronically covered proceedings and general attitudinal surveys of participants. Most judges, attorneys, witnesses and jurors perceived no change in their behavior as a result of electronic coverage. However, 21 percent of jurors and 27 percent of attorneys surveyed—a significant number—noticed negative effects from the presence of electronic or photographic media.[81] Criminal defense attorneys displayed the greatest level of

Testimony in the murder trial of Betty Broderick. *Top:* The defendant. *Bottom:* Witness Patricia Monahan.

opposition. The study also found that courts denied nearly all requests for electronic coverage when rules required consent of the parties.[82] Ninety percent of defenders and 79 percent of prosecutors surveyed strongly disagreed with the removal of the consent requirement.[83]

Nonetheless, as a result of the study, the Judicial Council adopted a new Rule 980 in 1984. It permitted film and electronic media coverage of criminal and civil courtroom proceedings at both the trial and appellate levels on a permanent, rather than an experimental basis. It allowed a judge to "refuse, limit or terminate film or electronic media coverage in the interests of justice to protect the rights of the parties and the dignity of the court, or to assure the orderly conduct of the proceedings." The rule prohibited electronic coverage of jury selection, close-ups of jurors and proceedings in chambers or closed to the public. Also barred was sound recording of conferences at the bench, between attorneys and clients or among attorneys.[84] This rule governed cameras in California courtrooms for 12 years until the Simpson revolution.

One of the few appellate court decisions to interpret Rule 980 was *KFMB-TV Channel 8 v. Municipal Court.*[85] Betty Broderick had shot and killed her ex-husband, Daniel Broderick, a prominent San Diego attorney, and his new wife as they slept. Her preliminary hearing generated enormous publicity. In response to local media requests to televise the hearing, Municipal Court Judge Mac Amos allowed coverage pursuant to Rule 980. However, he prohibited witness statements from being broadcast without further court authorization. The media asked an appeals court to overrule the judge and remove the limitation on broadcast coverage. The court complied. Once the proceedings have been recorded, said the appellate court, the judge has no authority to refuse, limit or terminate its later broadcast, because "the rule does not authorize a judge to become the editor of a television station's news broadcasts of a previously recorded judicial proceeding."[86]

Most significantly, however, the *KFMB* ruling made clear that then-existing Rule 980 created a *presumption in favor* of allowing courtroom access to the electronic media. Justice Howard Weiner wrote for the Fourth District Court of Appeal: "Rule 980 recognizes that media access *should be granted* except where to do so will interfere with the rights of the parties, diminish the dignity of the court, or impede the orderly conduct of the proceedings."[87]

Six years later, in 1996, when the Judicial Council revised Rule 980, it specifically eliminated the presumption in favor of electronic media access to California's courts. The rule now reads: "This rule *does not create a presumption for or against* granting permission to photograph, record, or broadcast court proceedings."[88]

Justice Richard D. Huffman, chairman of the task force appointed by the Judicial Council to study changes to Rule 980 in the wake of Simpson, explains that the new rule evidenced a deliberate effort to "overrule," to "cut away the basis for" the *KFMB* case.[89] "If there's one overriding change," he told *Los Angeles*

Times reporter Henry Weinstein, "it's a deliberate, premeditated" effort to increase the discretion of trial judges to decide whether or not to allow live coverage."[90]

Although Betty Broderick's preliminary hearing was televised, her trial was not; it ended in a hung jury. However, Court TV telecast her second trial to a national audience. Out of her assorted courtroom experiences, Broderick has become a booster of televised trials. The authors interviewed Broderick, who is serving a 32-years-to-life prison sentence for her conviction on two counts of second-degree murder.

Broderick claims she killed out of exasperation at her ex-husband's manipulation and sealing of their civil divorce proceedings, in which she lost custody of their children. She adamantly asserts that televised coverage of that proceeding would have changed history. "If I had had cameras in the civil courtroom from day one," she says, "none of this would have happened. He wouldn't be dead and I wouldn't be here."

She also contends that the absence of television in her first criminal trial kept potential jurors for her retrial from being exposed to a crucial, sympathetic witness. "Court TV wasn't invented in Trial One," she says, "and it's a darn shame." Daniel Sonkin, an expert on battered women, testified for the defense in the first trial but did not testify in the second, televised trial.

Between Broderick I and Broderick II, Court TV televised *California v. Powell*, the state prosecution of the four officers who faced charges arising from their beating of Rodney King. Millions watched the videotape of the beating played repeatedly on news telecasts; the acquittal of the officers sparked the worst urban riot in the history of the United States. Their later federal trial, which ended in conviction of two of the four defendants, was not televised because of the federal no-cameras rule.

Judge Stanley Weisberg, who presided over the *Powell* trial, wound up presiding over another high profile case 18 months later. Once again he allowed television coverage, as Erik and Lyle Menendez stood trial, before separate juries sitting in the same courtroom,[91] for the murder of their parents. Both juries hung, unable to decide whether the verdict should be murder or manslaughter. At the retrial in late 1995, Weisberg had a change of heart. He barred cameras from his courtroom. He did not specifically cite the Simpson case in his ruling, but most observers believe the decision was part of the Simpson backlash.

After the Simpson criminal trial concluded, judges seemed reluctant to permit televised trials. Media lawyer Gene Erbin said the Simpson backlash turned the Los Angeles court system into "a hotbed of abolitionists" against courtroom cameras.[92] Judge James Bascue, then supervising judge for Los Angeles Superior Court's criminal division, agreed. He said, "There are some real reservations in this building to cameras in the courtroom.... The judges don't like them, and the jurors are terrified of them.... We're all still undergoing trauma from the Simpson trial."[93]

Not surprisingly, the Simpson backlash was strongest in California. Governor Pete Wilson proposed a ban on cameras in all California courtrooms, declaring: "We have survived the Simpson trial, but there is no reason to be forced to suffer through the theatrics of another 'trial of the century' in this lifetime."[94]

The Judicial Council responded quickly. Chief Justice Malcolm M. Lucas appointed a task force, headed by Justice Huffman, to reevaluate Rule 980. Meanwhile, a Judicial Council survey of more than 600 California judges revealed that a majority, 55 percent, wanted to ban cameras from courtrooms altogether. In Los Angeles, home of the Simpson case, the number climbed to 67 percent.[95] Only 35 percent of those judges with camera experience, however, favored a total blackout.[96]

About the same time, the California Judges Association's executive board, in a non-binding vote, came out 10–8 against a total ban on cameras. It proposed revising Rule 980 to provide trial judges with standards to use in exercising their discretion on whether to admit cameras.[97] This vote reflected a judicial belief that judges should retain discretion to televise trials.[98]

As the Judicial Council's task force considered revisions to Rule 980, the governing board of the State Bar of California took a position that judges should have discretion to allow cameras in their courtrooms. The organization, to which all practicing attorneys in California belong, had opposed camera coverage for 16 years.[99] Journalist Peter Kaye, one of the non-lawyer members of the board, mused that if the board continued to oppose cameras in the courtroom, the media would have a great story: "State bar rushes pell-mell into the 18th century."[100] James Towery, then president of the California State Bar, would have gone even further than the State Bar. He believed cameras should be permitted absent a finding of prejudice by the trial judge. Towery agreed with Court TV founder Steven Brill, who called for a "rebuttable presumption" in favor of cameras.

Many California judges, however, saw the issue differently. They gave Brill a chilly reception when he addressed a meeting of the California Judges Association in the aftermath of the Simpson criminal trial. During his talk Brill argued that television coverage could restore public confidence in the judicial system. A judge in the audience interrupted Brill and asserted that broadcasters are motivated by profit, not public service. Brill replied tartly: "Does profit bother you that much?" Some judges in the audience booed at that remark.[101]

After extensive study, the Judicial Council task force recommended to the Judicial Council that Rule 980 be reenacted with notable differences: Filming, recording and broadcasting of *pretrial proceedings*—including arraignments, bail hearings, preliminary hearings, and motions to suppress or exclude evidence— and *trial proceedings not observed by the jury or trier of fact* would no longer be permitted, even in the discretion of the judge.[102] The task force felt that televising these proceedings might unfairly prejudice the public against defendants, who often appear in chains and dress in prison garb at these hearings.[103]

While serving as Chief Deputy in the San Diego County District Attorney's Office, Justice Huffman, the task force chairman, had prosecuted a case where pretrial camera footage became an issue. In their efforts to save Robert Alton Harris from California's gas chamber, defense attorneys objected to massive prejudicial pretrial publicity, including recurrent use of a video clip showing a heavily guarded Harris in a jail jumpsuit walking down a courtroom hallway in chains. His appellate attorney, Charles Sevilla, recalls: "This was the image the public got of him for the next 14 years [between his trial and execution], as a person who had to be taken to court in chains despite the fact that it's routine for everybody. But that's the image which was portrayed." Harris eventually became the first person executed by California in 25 years.

Old Rule 980 had prohibited close-up photography of jurors. The task force recommended expansion of this prohibition to include any photography of jurors or spectators.[104] Had this rule been in effect during the Simpson trial, television viewers would not have witnessed the families of Ronald Goldman and Nicole Brown Simpson in tears during emotional testimony.

Justice Huffman described the task force's recommendation for a restriction on permitted video as a "compromise." It was intended to both placate the electronic media who feared a total shutout, and appease judges who wished to completely eject cameras after the Simpson trial.[105]

The Judicial Council held public hearings on the proposed changes to Rule 980. They received strongly polarized views. Daniel Kolkey, legal affairs secretary to Governor Wilson, testified that cameras distort the truth-seeking function of a trial and diminish respect for the courts. Retaining the option of televised trials, he said, "will in essence disrobe the judges" and turn trials into a form of entertainment. A defendant, he added, "is entitled to a trial in a court, not in a stadium."[106] Los Angeles Superior Court Judge Mary Ann Murphy echoed Kolkey: "It is time for the judiciary to declare that we are not part of the entertainment industry."[107] She added, "The media invade the courthouse and run roughshod over everyone in it.... The judges describe their courthouses as under siege by the electronic media."[108] But San Diego Superior Court Judge Judith McConnell, chairwoman of the California Judges Association's committee on cameras, disagreed, saying television is "the only key to the courthouse door for many citizens."[109]

Ultimately, California's Judicial Council declined to declare war on the media. But the judges retained and solidified their strategic advantage. Judicial Discretion—Now More Than Ever! is the theme of new Rule 980. And the words of California Chief Justice Ronald George ring true: "Judges traditionally resist any effort to control their discretion in the courtroom."[110]

In addition to eliminating the presumption favoring cameras, the judges wrote Rule 980 to save time during trial. Judges no longer need hold a hearing—

a "mini-trial" within a trial—when the media apply for camera access.[111] "We want to put a stop to the media coverage issue being more dominant than the guilt or innocence, or truth of the underlying litigation," Justice Huffman told the authors. He accuses the media of taking the position: "You [the judge] can't change anything or we are entitled to a hearing and an appeal ... because after all, we've got rights." Says Huffman, "This is to make clear that you [the media] don't have rights, that the trial court can simply pull the plug as the trial court deems necessary to carry out its efforts."

The Judicial Council also sought to insulate judicial rulings on cameras from appellate review. Judges are not required under the new rule to make factual findings when they decide whether to allow cameras. This means there is no record to be examined by an appellate court, which effectively, if not explicitly, eliminates appeals to higher courts. The media can file for a writ—a request for emergency relief—but writs are seldom granted. In the words of Justice Huffman, "What we are trying to do is to make the [trial judges'] discretion as nearly absolute as one can rationally do in the court process."

California judges have also been granted jurisdiction beyond the courtroom; they can now expel cameras from the entire courthouse. The Judicial Council changed "Courtroom" to "Court," which is defined in the rule as "The courtroom at issue, the courthouse, and its entrances and exits." Sanctions for violation of the rule include termination of media coverage, citation for contempt of court, and monetary or other sanctions as provided by law.[112] But the authority to order monetary or other sanctions must await enabling legislation.

New Rule 980 incorporates the task force's proposal to bar any coverage of jurors or spectators.[113] But the council rejected the task force's recommendation for a blanket ban on cameras in pretrial hearings and proceedings out of the presence of the jury.

Now off limits to cameras (as well as sound equipment) are conferences between attorneys and their clients, witness or aides; conferences among attorneys and conferences between the judge and lawyers at the bench. Proceedings held in chambers or closed to the public are still restricted from coverage.

The Judicial Council made a significant addition to the old Rule 980: a list of 19 guidelines to assist judges in weighing whether to allow cameras in their courtrooms.[114] They are:

- (i) Importance of maintaining public trust and confidence in the judicial system;
- (ii) Importance of promoting public access to the judicial system;
- (iii) Parties' support of or opposition to the request;
- (iv) Nature of the case;
- (v) Privacy rights of all participants in the proceeding, including witnesses, jurors, and victims;
- (vi) Effect on any minor who is a party, prospective witness, victim, or other participant in the proceeding;

(vii)   Effect on the parties' ability to select a fair and unbiased jury;

(viii)   Effect on any ongoing law enforcement activity in the case;

(ix)   Effect on any unresolved identification issues;

(x)   Effect on any subsequent proceedings in the case;

(xi)   Effect of coverage on the willingness of witnesses to cooperate, including the risk that coverage will engender threats to the health or safety of any witness;

(xii)   Effect on excluded witnesses who would have access to the televised testimony of prior witnesses;

(xiii)   Scope of the coverage and whether partial coverage might unfairly influence or distract the jury;

(xiv)   Difficulty of jury selection if a mistrial is declared;

(xv)   Security and dignity of the court;

(xvi)   Undue administrative or financial burden to the court or participants;

(xvii)   Interference with neighboring courtrooms;

(xviii)   Maintaining orderly conduct of the proceeding;

(xix)   Any other factor the judge deems relevant.

Of the 19 factors now written into Rule 980 to guide judges, only the first two mitigate in favor of camera coverage: maintaining trust in the judicial system and promoting public access. The remaining 17 allow a judge to easily exclude cameras from his or her courtroom. Of course, California judges' discretion is effectively challenge-proof anyway under the new rule. And that's the way they want it.

Stan Statham, executive director of the California Broadcasters Association, characterized the new Rule 980 as a setback for cameras in courtrooms. As the measure was adopted, Statham told reporters: "What we got today was a small slap on the wrist rather than being put in handcuffs…. It's not a total ban, but what happened today means there will be less coverage of criminal cases."[115] So far, Statham's words appear prophetic.

The States of the Union

In a swift, dramatic reaction to the Simpson trial telecasts, judges in high profile cases, in California and elsewhere, began barring cameras from their courtrooms. South Carolina Judge William Howard prohibited camera coverage of the Susan Smith trial. Cameras were banned twice from the trial of Richard Allen Davis—once by the original trial judge, and again by a new judge after a change of venue. And as previously noted, Judge Westergren excluded cameras from the Texas trial of Yolanda Saldivar.

Even more striking was Judge Hiroshi Fujisaki's decision to bar cameras, tape recorders, and even sketch artists,[116] from O. J. Simpson's civil trial. He read a statement in court asserting that television coverage of Simpson's criminal trial had "significantly diverted and distracted the participants therein, it appearing that the conduct of witnesses and counsel were unduly influenced by the presence of the electronic media." The evidence, he said, included examples of "playing to the camera, gestures, outbursts by counsel and witnesses in the courtroom and thereafter outside the courthouse, presenting a circus atmosphere to the trial." Judge Fujisaki was concerned that "history will repeat itself unless [the court] acts to prevent it."[117]

Legislators in several states threatened to repeal laws allowing cameras in their courts in the wake of Simpson.[118] In New York, which has conducted a series of four experiments with courtroom cameras over a 17-year period, the lines are drawn: Many judges find little or no fault with the presence of cameras in their courtrooms; however, Governor George Pataki, legislators and criminal defense attorneys point to the O. J. Simpson trial as a reason to stymie the enactment of a permanent rule allowing television cameras in New York's courthouses.[119]

But as the dust settled and the months passed, most states retained the status quo. A few actually expanded coverage.[120] Indiana, which had never allowed television in its courtrooms, became the forty-eighth state to open its courthouse doors to cameras. An experiment authorizing coverage of Indiana Supreme Court proceedings was announced in 1996, one month after the retirement of an anti-camera justice.[121] Tennessee, North Dakota, and Missouri made their temporary rules permitting camera coverage permanent.[122] In 1997, Idaho extended its experiment with courtroom cameras another year.[123]

Laws governing the use of television cameras in court are unique to each state. Most have permanent rules authorizing camera coverage; only a handful remain in the experimental stage.

The majority of states give judges discretion to prohibit or allow and control camera coverage of their proceedings. Only a few require consent of the parties to a case. Many statutes specify that discretion shall be exercised to protect fair trial rights and/or ensure the dignity and decorum of the courtroom.

There are also physical limitations on courtroom cameras in several jurisdictions. Unobtrusive cameras with controlled placement and no enhanced lighting are required in many states. Media organizations must often join together in a pooling arrangement. Some states mandate that television cameras be designed or modified so participants being covered are unable to tell when they are being recorded.

States have different rules about what and who may be covered by cameras. Some prohibit recording or broadcast of proceedings otherwise closed to the public, such as grand jury sessions, child custody and adoption cases, and mental health hearings. Most states allow coverage of civil and criminal cases, but exclude *voir dire* (jury selection) and prohibit or restrict coverage of jurors. Some jurisdictions limit coverage in criminal cases to non-testimonial proceedings, such as arraignments and sentencing hearings. All states prohibit coverage of in-court conferences. Most bar coverage of juveniles, victims of sex crimes and matters involving domestic relations or trade secrets. Some states prohibit coverage of witnesses who appear under subpoena, and many do not allow coverage of victims or witnesses who object.[124]

Whatever the individual requirements of a state's camera coverage law, certain assumptions are common to all. Among those 48 states that now permit the televising of their judicial proceedings, there is a commitment to openness, but always mindful of the bottom line—the fair administration of justice.

Chapter Eight

The Federal Case

The day you see a camera come into our courtroom it's
going to roll over my dead body.—Justice David H. Souter,
U.S. Supreme Court[1]

As blunt as it seems, Justice Souter's statement to a House Appropriations
subcommittee did not shock long-time observers of the federal court system.
The only camera that ever focuses on the nine black-robed justices of the
Supreme Court of the United States is the one snapping the court's annual,
official photograph. Throughout the television age, the Supreme Court has
set the tone for policies that have kept cameras out of most courtrooms in the
federal judicial system, even as 48 states have come to allow some degree of
television coverage of their own court proceedings.

The Supreme Court justices have never collectively explained their opposition to camera coverage of their own proceedings. All nine turned down
requests to be interviewed for this book. In his own case, Souter told the subcommittee he had found that cameras "affected my behavior," when he was a
member of the New Hampshire Supreme Court. He'd felt inclined to pull
punches in asking questions, he said, and worried he would see "the excerpts,
the sound bites, totally out of context on the 6 o'clock news." Souter added:
"The whole point of the Supreme Court is that it is not a political institution and it is not part of the entertainment industry of the United States."[2]

While Souter's assessment of politics in Supreme Court workings is
debatable, his tone is typical of many on the federal bench. Senior U.S. District Judge Laughlin E. Waters of Los Angeles has presided under a no-cameras rule since his appointment to the bench by President Gerald Ford in 1976.
"I've lived with that rule and I've been very comfortable with it," Waters told
the authors. "I personally would not want TV cameras in the courtroom."

"A trial is always an emotional, dramatic event," said federal appeals judge
Jon O. Newman of New York. "Television inevitably escalates the emotion."[3]

And perhaps the best-known opponent of cameras in federal courts, the
late Chief Justice Warren Burger, once offered the sardonic appraisal that "the
trial of a case is not show business."[4] If anyone missed Burger's contempt for

television, he affirmed it dramatically in 1981 by pushing and punching at a cameraman who had followed him toward an elevator.[5]

Even without cameras trained on the proceedings, federal courts are no strangers to escalated emotions. The trial of the "Chicago Eight" anti–Vietnam War protestors, following the 1968 Democratic National Convention, produced several raucus confrontations between the defendants and U.S. District Judge Julius Hoffman. At one point, Hoffman became so angry that he ordered defendant Bobby Seale bound and gagged. Even without the incentive of courtroom television coverage, *Hustler* magazine publisher Larry Flynt demonstrated his disdain for a court order in the John DeLorean drug case in 1981, by rolling into a Los Angeles federal court in his wheelchair clad in a diaper fashioned from an American flag. He then attempted to pay a $10,000 fine with wads of one-dollar bills, plucked from a large carrying case. And in a theatrical moment in the 1993 civil rights trial of four officers involved in the Los Angeles beating of Rodney King, defense attorney Harland Braun rested his case without calling a single witness, after ceremoniously introducing his client's boot into evidence. Braun was trying to impress jurors that Officer Theodore Briseno's light-weight footware couldn't possibly have injured King.[6]

The Camera-shy History

Federal criminal court rules (Rule of Criminal Procedure 53) have prohibited electronic coverage of criminal proceedings since 1946.[7] In 1972, an even broader prohibition was adopted by the Judicial Conference of the United States, the policy-setting body for the federal courts always chaired by the Chief Justice of the Supreme Court. Canon 3A(7) of the Code of Conduct for United States Judges applied to both civil and criminal cases. It barred "broadcasting, televising, recording, or taking photographs in the courtroom and areas immediately adjacent thereto...."[8] Individual judicial districts rubber-stamped the Judicial Conference action with their own anti-camera rules.

The rules have been applied rigidly in federal proceedings. The 1984 libel suit of General William C. Westmoreland against the Columbia Broadcasting System is a prime example. Cable News Network (CNN) formally requested permission to televise the trial, involving Westmoreland's assertions that he had been wronged by a CBS News documentary on the Vietnam War. Neither side objected. District Judge Pierre N. Leval acknowledged that the application "should be granted," citing five reasons, including "the experience of many states that live telecasting need not interfere with the fair and orderly administration of justice." However, Leval denied the application because "the rules of the Judicial Conference and of this court are to the contrary," and he believed the rules were not subject to waiver.[9] The judge was in effect telling broadcasters, "I'd like to help you but I can't. My hands are tied." On November 2, 1984, the Second Circuit Court of Appeals issued a ruling upholding Judge Leval.

Six weeks earlier, the Judicial Conference had affirmed its no-cameras rule, by endorsing the unanimous recommendation of an ad hoc committee that no changes be made. The committee had been asked to study the issue after 28 news organizations petitioned the Judicial Conference to open federal courtrooms to broadcasting and camera coverage. The committee said "the alleged public benefits" of more openness were "outweighed by the risks to the administration of justice." Among the perceived risks: jeopardizing "the required sense of solemnity, dignity and the search for the truth."[10]

And in a case cited earlier, the federal prohibition on courtroom cameras, enunciated in Rule 53, was even applied to a defendant who wanted to videotape his own case. U.S. District Judge James E. Doyle of Wisconsin rejected the request of Gillam Kerley, charged with failure to register for the draft, to record in-court proceedings with compact home video equipment. Doyle's ruling was upheld in January 1985 by the Seventh Circuit Court of Appeals, which wrote: "...we find Rule 53's ban on cameras in the courtroom to be a reasonable exercise of the rulemaking power and not in violation of Kerley's first amendment rights. While many of Kerley's arguments, some of which are drawn from experience with cameras in various state courts, support the notion that some broadcasting of trials may be harmless and constructive, such arguments are better directed at those who make the rules."[11]

The Judicial Conference stuck by its rules even as the Supreme Court's 1981 *Chandler* ruling prompted state after state to open its courtrooms to cameras. The *Chandler* decision had assured states that a televised trial did not, *per se*, violate a defendant's right to a fair trial. But in early 1990, another ad hoc committee, this one chaired by U.S. District Judge Robert Peckham of San Francisco, again rejected appeals by the media and urged the Judicial Conference to keep its no-cameras policy in place.

That action, however, fell on a changed political landscape. The committee's recommendation triggered a letter from U.S. Representative Robert Kastenmeier, the powerful Wisconsin Democrat who chaired the House subcommittee which oversees the federal judiciary. He urged the committee to reconsider its position. That, in turn, inspired a letter from Chief Justice William Rehnquist, the chairman of the Judicial Conference, saying he was "by no means averse to the idea" of some kind of experiment with cameras in federal courts.[12] Confronted with the new pressure from leaders of two branches of government, the ad hoc committee met again and reversed its previous stand. On September 12, 1990, with 45 *states* already allowing cameras in their courtrooms, the Judicial Conference approved a tightly-limited, three-year experiment in federal courts.

The Federal Experiment

The pilot program applied only to *civil* proceedings of the Second and Ninth Circuit Courts of Appeals and the courts of six federal judicial districts: the Southern District of Indiana, Eastern District of Michigan, Southern District of New York, Eastern District of Pennsylvania, Western District of Washington and the District of Massachusetts.

During the first two years of the experiment, cameras made courtroom appearances in 147 cases, most frequently civil rights and personal injury proceedings. The Federal Judicial Center, the research and development arm of the U.S. court system, tracked the experiment as it unfolded, polling participants as it began and again at the two-year mark. The responses prompted the Center to recommend that cameras be given access to civil proceedings in *all* of the nation's federal courts of appeals and district courts. Access would be subject to judicial discretion and strict guidelines, including limits of one television camera in trial court proceedings and two in appellate court matters.

The center summarized the reasons for its recommendation in a sentence that has become the favorite ammunition of many courtroom camera advocates: "The converging results from each of our inquiries suggest that members of the electronic media generally complied with program guidelines and that their presence did not disrupt court proceedings, affect participants in the proceedings, or interfere with the the administration of justice."[13]

Among the findings cited in a report by the Judicial Center: Twenty-eight percent of participating lawyers felt more favorable toward electronic coverage than before the pilot program. Just four percent felt less favorable. Two-thirds—72 of 109 attorneys responding to the Center's survey—indicated that they somewhat or greatly favored electronic media coverage of civil proceedings; 13 percent had no opinion; 21 percent were somewhat or greatly opposed. And perhaps most significant, 93 percent thought the presence of cameras had no effect on the fairness of their trials; while just under four percent felt cameras decreased fairness. The remainder thought camera coverage actually *increased* the fairness of the proceedings. Just one attorney cited an instance in which a witness had declined to testify because a camera was present.

The Center also polled 20 of the most active judges in the program. All but one thought the presence of electronic media had no effect on the administration of justice. Seven district judges and all three appellate judges who answered the question favored extending camera coverage to criminal proceedings. Three district judges said they would favor expansion with some reservations; for example, proceeding on a pilot basis.

In summary, the Center reported: "Judges and attorneys who had experience with electronic media coverage under the program generally reported observing small or no effects of camera presence on participants in the proceedings, courtroom decorum, or the administration of justice."[14]

But ten months later, with three months still remaining on the pilot program, the Center would see its main findings and recommendations rejected. The *ABA Journal* reported: "Showing that it is indeed possible to put the genie back in the bottle, the federal judiciary has decided to reinstitute its ban on cameras in the courtroom."[15] A spokesman said the U.S. Judicial Conference debated the issue for 20 minutes behind closed doors before voting by a two to one margin not to extend camera coverage of civil proceedings. The vote to retain the ban on cameras in criminal cases was unanimous. Chief Justice Rehnquist, who had been open to the experiment, did not participate in the vote ending it.[16]

The 26 appellate and district judges who comprise the Judicial Conference were said to be concerned about the potential impact of cameras on witnesses and jurors and what was referred to as "the sound-bite problem"—the tendency of news organizations to distill the day's courtroom events into a few snippets of testimony or argument laced together with footage of courtroom scenes.[17]

In fact there was some grist for the "sound-bite" argument in the Judicial Center's report. The Center solicited air cuts of stories covered under the cameras-in-the-courtroom experiment. Excluding the extended live coverage of entities such as Court TV, researchers found broadcasters used an average of 56 seconds of courtroom footage per story. Most judges said the educational benefit of camera coverage had been realized only to a "moderate extent or not at all under the program."[18] Broadcast journalists countered, with some validity, that shaping a story around a few sound bites is no different than a print reporter's use of selected quotes, which like a television story, give life and presence to the journalist's summary of events.

The Simpson Factor

The Judicial Conference's avowed concerns about the "sound-bite" problem may well have been side issues to another looming development of the time—the gathering storm clouds over the O. J. Simpson phenomenon. By the time Conference members cast their votes against cameras in federal courts, Simpson's arraignment, preliminary hearing and a host of pretrial proceedings had played on daytime television to prime-time-size audiences. To traditionalists, this was not a window into a corner of the American judiciary; it was a floodlight reflecting back to the blinding headlines of supermarket tabloids, illuminating Marcia Clark's hem length, Judge Lance Ito's burgeoning hourglass collection, and Simpson's own courtroom scribbles. This was worrisome. This was to be avoided, at all costs.

As the Simpson case proceeded, USC constitutional law expert Erwin Chemerinsky toured the nation, addressing groups of federal judges, including a Seattle gathering. "One of the first people who spoke," recalls Chemerinsky, "said one of the really good things about the Simpson case is that it means we're never going to have cameras in federal court. I think federal judges would have been reluctant to have cameras in the courtroom even if there was no Simpson case…. They prefer not to have their idiosyncracies and their behavior exposed to the public. But I think cameras would have come to federal court if not for the Simpson case."

As the courtroom images of the Simpson criminal case began receding into history, a federal judge in New York decided it was time to test the waters again. On March 1, 1996, U.S. District Court Judge Robert J. Ward granted a petition by Court TV to televise a pretrial hearing in a lawsuit alleging that the City of New York had mismanaged its foster care program, putting in jeopardy the lives of neglected and abused children. The judge said the suit raised "profound social, political, and legal issues" and the "public interest would be served" by televising the hearing. Ward opined that the Judicial Conference camera ban did not supplant local federal district rules barring cameras "without written permission of a judge of that court." Implicit in the local rules, said Judge Ward, was judicial discretion to *allow* cameras.[19]

Less than two weeks later, the Judicial Conference eased up—slightly. While strongly rejecting a proposal to reopen district courts to cameras, the nation's top judges narrowly approved a measure to permit television, radio and still photography coverage of federal appellate court proceedings. The vote, behind closed doors, was 14 to 12. The Judicial Conference allowed each of the 13 appeals courts to make its own decision on the matter. Significantly, the Second and Ninth Circuits, which had already experienced camera coverage during the 1991–94 pilot program, were the first to open their courts under the new rule.

A Judicial Conference spokesman hastened to assure reporters that the vote to allow televised appeals was not necessarily meant to endorse the general proposition of cameras in the courtroom and would probably be limited to civil cases. And in an apparent slap at New York's Judge Ward, the Conference urged each circuit to adopt rules barring the broadcast of *district court* proceedings.[20]

Cameras: Coming of Age?

While most within the federal judiciary seem content with the status quo, there are notable exceptions apart from Judge Ward. Square-jawed, athletic-looking John Tunheim was appointed to the federal bench in Minneapolis in 1995 at age 42. To an extent his life has been shaped by televised events— political conventions, the assassination of President John F. Kennedy, Martin Luther King, Jr.'s "I Have a Dream" speech, daily coverage of the Vietnam

War and the Watergate hearings, and Tunheim's own appearances before cameras. Prior to his appointment to the bench, he often argued cases for the state attorney general's office before the Minnesota Supreme Court.

While court is in session, Tunheim stays abreast of other matters by electronic "e-mail" messages dispatched to a laptop (or *bench*-top) computer by his secretary. Since mid–1997, he and his federal colleagues in Minneapolis have held court in what is often called "the most technologically advanced courthouse in the United States." It features "real time" online court reporting, courtrooms wired for multi-media evidence presentations by lawyers, and jury boxes fitted for high-resolution video monitors.

In short, Tunheim is a federal judge who has spent much of his life immersed in technology. And he is comfortable with the concept of making federal courts full partners in the electronic age by allowing television coverage at the discretion of judges.

"I think it would have great educational value," Tunheim told the authors. "As a judge who participates in the activities in the courtroom every day, I don't see anything to fear from it." He admits the possibility that camera coverage could deter or affect the testimony of witnesses is "perhaps one of the more valid concerns." But Tunheim believes that concern would be largely relieved if television coverage became routine in federal courts.

"I think a witness, much like a lawyer and judge and the jury, would soon forget about the fact that the camera is there, if it's stationary, if it's small, if there's no noise coming out of it, if there's not a lot of technical equipment in the courtroom"—in short, the norm in most *state* courts allowing television coverage these days.

Is Tunheim alone in his sympathetic view toward camera coverage? No, he says. "My sense is that among younger federal judges, colleagues who are more of my age and experience ... are much more comfortable with the idea than some of the older federal judges."

Why the resistance among Tunheim's older colleagues? Many have never practiced before a television camera, he notes. "I just think it may be a fear of the unknown and being accustomed to the way things have been going and taking the attitude that if it's not broke, let's not fix it."

Indeed, U.S. Judge Laughlin Waters of Los Angeles certainly sees nothing in need of fixing—not the federal policy on courtroom cameras, anyway. In six decades as an attorney and judge, Waters has never participated in a televised proceeding. He was a good friend of former Chief Justice Earl Warren, who once wrote that broadcast coverage was "inconsistent with the Anglo-American conception of 'trial'" and suggested a journalist would have better luck getting cameras on the moon than on the floor of the Supreme Court.[21] Waters did watch television coverage of the O. J. Simpson criminal trial. That cemented his views. "I observed the problems that developed," he says, "the delays that ensued with the use of the camera, and I felt that our rule was a well-justified rule."

But opposition to camera coverage at the federal level is not purely a matter of age. Like David Souter, Justice Anthony Kennedy arrived at the U.S. Supreme Court at a relatively youthful 51. His formative years as a lawyer unfolded in an era when television, more than any other medium, forged public attitudes toward civil rights, the Vietnam War and the Watergate scandal. But in his confirmation hearing, Kennedy clearly leaned against cameras in the courtroom. "The press is part of our environment," he told the Senate Judiciary Committee. "We cannot really excise it from the environment. But in the courtroom, I think that the tradition has been that we not have that outside distraction, and I am inclined to say that I would not want them [cameras] in appellate court chambers."[22]

Kennedy then offered a revealing anecdote, dating from his days as a member of the Ninth Circuit Court of Appeals. It involved a high-profile case in Seattle. "The courtroom was packed," he recalled. "And we were at a critical point in the argument. I was presiding. And a person came in with all kinds of equipment and began setting it up. And he disturbed me. He disturbed the attorneys. He disturbed everybody in the room. And he was setting up an easel to paint our picture, which was permitted. If he had a little Minox camera, we would have held him in contempt."[23]

The Supreme Court nominee appeared to equate that experience, involving a courtroom sketch artist, with the typical experience of scores of state courtrooms where trials are televised every day. It suggests he was ignorant of emerging technology and modern practice, involving cameras that are pre-positioned or remotely-operated and record the proceedings silently. But his incomplete vision of reality had shaped his opposition to courtroom camera coverage.

Eight years later, Kennedy was no longer "inclined" to oppose camera coverage of the Supreme Court, as he'd said at his confirmation hearing; he was now dead set against it. He told a House subcommittee the Court is "different from the other branches" of government and should do its work "without the intrusive commentary that follows the camera" and the "potential for changing the behavior of the judges and lawyers that appear before us."[24]

In general, Supreme Court justices rarely shed light on the reasons for their opposition to television coverage of their own proceedings. One who has is Justice Sandra Day O'Connor. During an alumni forum at Stanford University, her alma mater, Justice O'Connor was asked if there is any argument for televising the activities of the Supreme Court. Her answer: "If our court were to initiate such a drastic change, it would undoubtedly influence all lower courts to follow suit and to think they had to. So it's not a change to be lightly made..."[25]

Her statement blatantly disregards current reality and historical fact. It was, after all, the Supreme Court's own *Chandler* decision in 1981 that encouraged many states to ease their restrictions on courtroom cameras. And her concern

Court TV

Court TV chief anchor Fred Graham.

that a change in the Supreme Court's anti-camera policy might "influence" lower courts to change ignores the horses already released from judicial and legislative barns. In the years since *Chandler,* the ranks of states allowing cameras into at least some of their courts have swollen from 27 to 48.

The Supreme Difference

Many legal scholars think the arguments for barring cameras from courtrooms are weakest when applied to the Supreme Court. There are no witnesses or jurors to intimidate, no sleazy cases to fuel sensationalistic coverage. Court TV founder Steven Brill likes to quip: "You can't say the lawyers will be nervous because the lawyers are always nervous because it's the Supreme Court."

As noted earlier, divining the reasons for the high court's resistance to broadcast coverage has not been easy. In an oft-quoted 1994 article in *TV Guide,* Court TV chief anchor Fred Graham recounted the remarks of justices in unguarded moments and his own interviews with retired justices. He concluded that the Court's ban on television and radio stems from two major instincts: protection of personal privacy and preservation of the Court's mystique.

Graham recalled watching Justice Harry Blackmun during his customary noontime stroll. Blackmun, author of the landmark abortion rights decision, *Roe v. Wade,* stood and looked on, unrecognized, as a group of raucous anti-abortion protestors railed against the rights established by the bystander's most famous opinion. Similarly, noted Graham, other justices take lunchtime walks and conduct their personal lives with near-anonymity. And he recalled the words of Justice Byron White at a conference in his home state of Colorado, shortly before his retirement. White said some future group of justices will open the Court to cameras and wonder, "What was wrong with those old guys?" who resisted the television era. But for now, he said, "I am very pleased to be able to walk around, and very, very seldom am I recognized. It's very selfish, I know."[26]

In other words, by keeping cameras and microphones out of the Supreme Court, the justices have their cake and eat it, too. "It permits them," concluded Graham, "to enjoy being among the most powerful figures in Washington, yet avoid the hassles of being recognized in public."[27]

Likewise, part of the Court's power stems from its aura, its detachment from the average citizen. Chief Justice Rehnquist seemed to underline that when he told a 1992 judges' conference he did not expect the Supreme Court to allow camera coverage any time soon. If the justices failed to acquit themselves well on-camera, he said, "it would lessen to a certain extent some of the mystique and moral authority" of the Court.[28] He may have had in mind the lapses of an aging Justice William O. Douglas, during his last years on the Court, or the sometimes cranky, unfocused behavior of Justice Thurgood Marshall in his latter months.

Retired Justice Lewis F. Powell told Graham he had always voted to keep cameras out, explaining that "the Supreme Court is unique, and one way to keep it special is to maintain its isolation that has existed over the years. Its uniqueness is enhanced because it is not on TV, while most of the other courts are."[29]

Critics contend the Supreme Court is denying taxpayers the same window into the top echelon of the judicial branch of government, and its $164,000-a-year employees, that stands open into the legislative and executive branches. What's lost in the process, say critics, is a remarkable opportunity for education about the least-understood governmental arm. It is not education about abstract concepts, insists James Towery, former president of the California State Bar, "because U.S. Supreme Court arguments have such a direct impact on the public. We can all think back to seminal cases that have been argued before the Supreme Court, where televising those arguments would have had an extraordinary affect on the public. The *United States versus Nixon* leaps readily to mind. Some of the school desegregation cases. I think the Supreme Court has missed some real opportunities by being old-fashioned, by refusing to permit televising its proceedings."

New York Judge Roger J. Miner of the Second Circuit Court of Appeals participated in the Federal Judicial Conference courtroom cameras experiment in 1991–94. He echoes Towery. "The people of the nation," wrote Miner, "should have the opportunity at their leisure and in their homes to see and hear the men and women of the Court and of its bar as they search for answers to the important issues of the day. Only the eye of the camera can provide that opportunity, for in these times it is the principal eye on justice."[30]

Across the country, Miner's colleague on the Ninth U.S. Circuit Court of Appeals, Judge Stephen Reinhardt of Los Angeles, is even more emphatic. "I don't understand why the high court and other Courts of Appeals do not permit TV cameras," he told an interviewer. "It would go a long way toward educating the public and de-mystifying the judicial process. But many judges don't like change. I'm surprised they don't want to wear wigs."[31]

The Supreme Court has been characteristically inscrutable in its response to such arguments. At the same Colorado conference where retired Justice White spoke of the joy of near-anonymity, Justice Sandra Day O'Connor said: "Eventually we will probably have television. But it probably won't be for a good while."[32] As best as can be determined—such matters are rarely settled in public—no more than three justices have ever voted to admit cameras. Justices Brennan, Marshall and Stevens sided with the Mutual Broadcasting System in its 1986 request to broadcast oral arguments in a challenge to the Gramm-Rudman balanced-budget law. Justice Brennan told Court TV's Fred Graham he was the only "yes" vote the last time the Court voted on the subject before his 1990 retirement.[33]

More recently, Justice Ruth Bader Ginsburg hinted at the possibility that she might be open to televising arguments before the Supreme Court. Without addressing the high court specifically, she told an assembly of University of Virginia law students she favors cameras in courtrooms, if they provide gavel-to-gavel coverage. "The problem is the dullness of most court proceedings," she said. "It's often tedious."[34]

Clearly Chief Justice Warren did not think Supreme Court proceedings were "tedious" in 1955 when he inaugurated the practice of audiotaping some of them. The tapes were turned over to the National Archives for the use of scholars. But the Court remains protective of them, as Professor Peter Irons found out in 1993. When the University of California–San Diego political scientist moved to market excerpts of historic Supreme Court arguments, in violation of the Archives lending agreement, the justices threatened unspecified "legal remedies" to prevent it. Irons ignored the threat and hit book and record stores with the ironically-titled *May It Please the Court*, a collection of taped segments, accompanied by a narrative and transcripts. The Court never followed through with its threat.

Meanwhile, the Court's work has been only minimally public. With just 80 seats available for the general audience, visitors have been rationed to as little as three minutes of viewing time before relinquishing their seats to the next persons in line. A full 23 hours before the Court was scheduled to hear arguments in *Webster v. Reproductive Health Services*,[35] a key 1989 round in the running battle over abortion rights, would-be spectators began lining up in front of the Supreme Court building. A sidewalk entrepreneur scalped the eleventh place in line for one-hundred dollars.[36] Apart from a handful of regulars seated in the main section of the court, reporters must squeeze into two rows along one side of the courtroom behind massive stone pillars. Many can not even see all the justices. They keep track of who's speaking via whispered exchanges of information, those with unobstructed views sharing information with the obstructed. Sometimes the court's public information officer helps, too.

Justice Souter's terse statement at the head of this chapter clearly indicates that some justices remain unmoved by pressures to admit cameras to their proceedings. Suggesting the public lacks interest in most of the Court's work, Justice Antonin Scalia once told an audience: "I am about to appeal to the principle that law is a specialized field, fully comprehensible only to the expert." He said the "this-is-too-complicated-for-you-to-understand" argument "has unique validity in the field of judging."[37] Eight years later, Justice Scalia asked that reporters be barred from his speech to 900 people at a packed meeting of Town Hall, the Los Angeles civic organization.[38] Scalia does not appear to be a jurist anxious to extend the reach of the First Amendment.

One day, the Supreme Court could be in the strange and perhaps strained position of enforcing its own ban on cameras while it hears arguments that there is an implied constitutional right to camera coverage. There has already been at least one lower court ruling to that effect. On May 1, 1996, U.S. District Judge Robert Sweet of New York ruled that Court TV could televise arguments on a motion to dismiss *Katzman v. Victoria's Secret Catalogue,*[39] a proposed class-action suit accusing a famous lingerie marketer of discriminating against women in offering discounts. Judge Sweet said the First Amendment requires hearings open to the public, and by extension the news media—including the broadcast media—absent compelling reasons for closure.[40]

Meanwhile, Congress stepped into the fray in response to survivors of the April 19, 1995, bombing of the Alfred P. Murrah Federal Building in Oklahoma City that killed 168 persons. Lawmakers in 1996 attached to the Anti-terrorism and Effective Death Penalty Act a provision mandating closed-circuit telecasts of federal trials when a trial is moved far from where the crime occurred.[41] The Oklahoma City case was moved 625 miles to Denver. U.S. District Judge Richard P. Matsch authorized a courtroom television feed to an auditorium seating 330 people at a Federal Aviation Administration facility in Oklahoma City. The order permitted only survivors and relatives of victims to attend. It excluded journalists. Judge Matsch appointed a "special master" to enforce rules and maintain decorum.

In some high profile cases, judges have authorized closed-circuit, not-for-broadcast audio feeds to a press room to enable overflow crowds of reporters to monitor court proceedings. Dozens of reporters tracked the 1981 drug trial of former automaker John DeLorean that way, as did journalists covering the 1993 Rodney King federal civil rights trial, both in Los Angeles.

Each minor deviation from the norm raises hopes in the news community that it will be a step toward a true break from the no-cameras tradition.

But as we've seen, the hopes have not been justified, except in tightly-limited experiments. Tradition has prevailed, apparently driven by fears that opening federal court proceedings to cameras would somehow cheapen them and their judicial product.

Apart from tradition, there appears to be no fundamental reason why federal courts should not be opened to electronic coverage on the same discretionary basis that's become the norm in most state courts. "I think the concerns are essentially the same," says legal scholar and defense attorney Gerald Uelmen. "I don't see any reason for a flat ban on cameras in federal courtrooms. I think it could in some respects be a healthy presence in terms of how federal cases are conducted."

But that, of course, overlooks another, perhaps critical factor in the reluctance of the federal judiciary, led by the Supreme Court, to open its doors to cameras. Every judge and every justice is appointed to the bench for life, immunized from public pressures. They don't need television exposure to keep their jobs. They can enjoy power with near-anonymity. And if the O. J. Simpson epoch taught them anything, it is that television coverage carries risks. It can grind up the reputation of a respected colleague like Lance Ito simply for appearing too patient, too compliant. So federal judges may ask themselves, why change? Why take chances with an impartial electronic witness that can beam your every slip-up, every excess, to thousands or millions of taxpaying spectators, all in the name of giving them greater access to their own court system? As Justice David Souter might note, it's easier to throw your body, with all its judicial girth, in the way of any camera that tries to roll into your courtroom.

Chapter Nine

Court TV

Court TV's goal is to substitute real law for *L. A. Law*[1]

Steven Brill has told the story so often, it is part of broadcast industry lore. The idea for the Courtroom Television Network, better known as Court TV, was conceived in a "two-minute epiphany" during a 1989 taxi ride in mid-town Manhattan, as Brill listened to radio coverage of a local murder trial.

"As a reporter covering the legal system," Brill told the authors, "I'd always been amazed how jurors, who are actually the only non-lawyers who see the system close up, had a very different impression of the system than other members of the public—that their whole idea of how the legal system worked was changed once they *saw* it, as opposed to the sound bites they get on television, or the tabloid newspaper headlines, or most of all, Hollywood's depiction of legal situations...

"I knew, therefore, it would be good journalism to bring people that same picture of the system.... And I started thinking about cable television and it just sort of all came together."

Brill envisioned Court TV as a "combination of C-SPAN and soap operas"—the former, a reference to the cable cooperative that covers largely the legislative branch of government; the latter, to "the dramatic appeal of people who are going through very difficult situations." The legal process, he says, is "the only form of dramatic, non-violent combat that we have."

Since its first broadcast in a dank basement at New York's 36th Street and 3rd Avenue on July 1, 1991, Cout TV has become a widely recognized, 24-hour-a-day[2] cable television fixture available to 32 million homes. Its 250 employees are spread over six floors of a modern, high-rise building three blocks from its founding quarters and in several other cities. Its profitability remains problematic. Before leaving Court TV in 1997, Brill claimed his creation had passed the break-even point and was turning a small profit. But in an interview at the end of 1997, Erik Sorenson, who had taken over day-to-day leadership of the network, disputed Brill's assertion. "Regardless of whatever hype you or anybody else may have heard or read anywhere else," he said, "Court TV in its six-and-a-half-year history has yet to make a dime of profit."

He estimated Court TV would likely cross into the black in late 1998 at the earliest.

In its first six years, Court TV broadcast all or segments of more than 500 trials. Months after signing on, the network provided live, gavel-to-gavel pool coverage for Florida's William Kennedy Smith trial, one of the most heavily watched courtroom events in history. On a typical day, Court TV's cameras cover at least five legal proceedings, ranging from the O. J. Simpson "trial of the century" to night court in Memphis, Tennessee.

"We are at moments the most boring network ever invented," former executive producer Steve Johnson told an interviewer. "And then at the other extreme, we have moments that are absolutely compelling."[3]

Few would dispute that the latter included the verdict acquitting Simpson, watched by an estimated 150 million people on a variety of broadcast outlets using a feed provided by Court TV. Nielsen Media Research reported an astounding 91 percent of all home television sets that were "on" at that hour were tuned to the Simpson verdict. Overall, the Simpson case provided the highest day-to-day ratings Court TV had ever enjoyed. It was not long after the October 3, 1995, Simpson verdict that Brill claimed Court TV was breaking even financially. But at the time he bristled at suggestions that the Simpson case had "made" Court TV. Brill once called the long-running case "cursed," telling an interviewer: "I would rather this event had never happened."[4] Brill claims that other high profile trials have, at times, topped the average rating of the Simpson trial on Court TV, including a medical malpractice case that aired in the mornings before reporters covering the early weeks of the Simpson case signed on from Los Angeles. Others exceeding the Simpson trial ratings for brief bursts, by his account, included the first trial of four police officers acquitted in Simi Valley, California, in 1992 of charges in the beating of motorist Rodney King and, less than two years later, the final days of the first trial of Erik and Lyle Menendez for the murder of their parents.

In addition to its broadcasts of trials and other legal proceedings, Court TV offers viewers a variety of law-oriented programs, including *Prime Time Justice*, a nightly reprise and analysis of the day's courtroom news; *Trial Story*, history and analysis of significant trials of recent times; and *Cochran & Company*, a discussion of legal issues by former O. J. Simpson defense lawyer Johnnie Cochran, other analysts, guests and telephone callers.

Court TV's Fans and Critics

Court TV has won praise from a surprisingly wide array of sources, including Steven Bochco, the creator of *L. A. Law* and other top-rated television series with legal and law enforcement themes. Court TV, he says, is "the best show on TV."[5] Even an arch-critic of televised trials, George Gerbner, dean emeritus of the Annenberg School for Communication at the University of Pennsylvania, has kind words for Court TV. "I think on the whole Court TV performs a good service," Gerbner told the authors. "First of all, it's cable; therefore it's not foisted on every home, around the clock … it provides a much more well-rounded sampling of court cases. Much of it is civil and not criminal. And it doesn't depend only on sensational trials."

Likewise, Texas District Judge Mike Westergren praises the "education" Court TV offers viewers, despite rejecting the cable network's request to televise the trial of Yolanda Saldivar, convicted in Westergren's courtroom of killing *Tejano* singing star Selena. Like Gerbner, Judge Westergren is "impressed" with the diversity of cases covered by Court TV. "They don't just do high profile cases," he noted.

But despite the variety served up by Court TV, even some of the network's boosters think it presents an incomplete picture of the American justice system and, therefore, a potentially distorted one. "The predominant feature of Court TV's programming has always been the full-dress trial, usually with a jury," noted Professor David Harris of the University of Toledo College of Law in a widely-quoted 1993 article.[6] "This programming structure ignores an important reality about American criminal cases: few of them actually go to trial. In fact, only about six percent of all criminal cases make it to the trial stage. The vast majority of cases are resolved without a trial…. Thus the focus of Court TV on trials may create the impression of a system that serves each and every defendant a generous helping of due process, when in fact that is true in only a few cases. Resolution of most cases does not take days or weeks, as the Court TV viewer might think; rather, most criminal cases are resolved in a few minutes of mumbled questions and incantations in a crowded courtroom, before a judge taking plea after plea."[7]

Could a commerical network such as Court TV sustain an audience with a mirror-image representation of the justice system, containing long sessions of "mumbled questions and incantations"? Harris concedes it most likely could not. "I'm not certain," he says, "that lots and lots of people would tune in day after day to just, in fact, see what's going on downtown in their courtrooms." He praises Court TV for providing at least a sampling of non-trial proceedings, and concludes: "Court TV still offers a far more complete view than anything that has come before. There is real potential for Court TV to help people understand the courts and the law. As such, it is a welcome addition to television coverage of the criminal justice system."

Court TV's Air Fare

The process of selecting cases to be covered by Court TV involves an advisory panel of sorts—a team of "trial trackers" in touch with local "stringers" following hundreds of cases around the country. Each week the trial trackers gather around a conference table with top executives of the cable network. Typically, they sift through 20 to 30 proposed cases and select four or five to be covered in the ensuing two weeks—two to be televised live and three to be taped and played back later in segments or in their entirety. In the words of its own publicity materials, "Court TV weighs several factors when choosing which trials to air, including how important and interesting the issues in the case are, the notoriety and newsworthy nature of both the case and the people involved, the quality of the 'story,' its educational value, and the expected duration of the trial (Other factors being equal, lengthy trials are avoided)."[8]

Brill initially opposed covering the 1994 trial of Lorena Bobbitt, accused of malicious wounding after slicing off the penis of husband John. Said Brill: "When that case was on the radar and it was described to me, I said, 'This is too sleazy. This is like a Jay Leno joke. We shouldn't do it.'" But women employees, moved by the defendant's claims that she acted in a desperate, last ditch response to repeated spousal rape, urged Brill to reconsider. "This case is not a joke," one said. Brill gave in. The trial was placed on Court TV's schedule for taped coverage. Parts were eventually televised live. "And I was really glad that we did it," Brill says, "because in watching her [Lorena Bobbitt] testify, it really brought home the issue of domestic violence and spousal abuse. If you watched an hour of her testimony, you wouldn't be doing Jay Leno jokes."

Court TV—The Advocate

Not surprisingly, Court TV has become a leading force—perhaps *the* leading force—for cameras in the courtroom. Court TV provided not only the pool camera coverage of the O. J. Simpson trial but its most colorful defense, when Judge Ito threatened to eject the camera after an erroneous report by a local television station about leaked DNA results. Evoking the words of the defendant's own plea, Court TV attorney Floyd Abrams told the judge, "…I would like to say the camera pleads absolutely a hundred percent not guilty. It didn't do anything wrong. It hasn't shown anything wrong. It hasn't portrayed anything outside the court rules."[9]

In speech after speech, Court TV founder Brill told audiences: "Trials were not supposed to be merely un-secret; they were intended to be very public. Indeed they were meant to be as public as possible." He evoked the action of the nation's iconic third chief justice, John Marshall, who moved the treason trial of Aaron Burr from a courtroom to the Virginia House of Delegates to accommodate an overflow crowd. Brill suggested that Marshall today would throw open his courtroom to a television camera to accomplish the same end in an age when "the community's interest in many trials … extends far beyond a town or city's borders."[10]

Brill's view of the propriety of cameras is sweeping: they should be allowed in any courtroom where reporters are allowed. That would exclude only family law cases and matters where national security is at stake, plus testimony where the anonymity of the witness is critical—undercover police officers, for instance. From Brill's perspective, the Sixth Amendment "fair trial" issue was settled long ago, in favor of cameras, when the Supreme Court ruled in the 1981 *Chandler* case that courtroom cameras do not, in and of themselves, disrupt a fair trial. He once used a speaking appearance before an American Civil Liberties Union chapter to scold the ACLU for its national policy supporting courtroom cameras only if defendants want them. "Imagine that," he chided his audience, "Richard Nixon deciding on cameras at his trial. Or Rupert Murdoch negotiating with a serial killer for coverage."[11]

Some of Court TV's analysts allow for more exceptions to camera access than Brill. Harvard law professor Arthur Miller thinks, for instance, that Judge William Howard may have made the correct decision in barring cameras from South Carolina's Susan Smith murder case. He cites the privacy issues arising from the small town setting of the trial. "It's a different culture in South Carolina," says Miller. "It's just a different culture from California."

Miller also sympathized with the ruling that barred cameras from the Norfolk County, Massachusetts, courtroom where John Salvi III was tried and convicted in 1996 of killing two abortion clinic workers. The issue was volatile; the defendant, notes Miller, had "great proclivity for disrupting the process and you had some witnesses who were very, very apprehensive." Some feared Salvi would use a televised trial as a soapbox. Miller concludes: "I think most people think the decision [keeping cameras out] was probably right." In fact, the motion to exclude cameras was not strenuously opposed by Court TV, which had offered to block out electronically the faces of reluctant witnesses. Brill concedes "it really was a special case." Salvi was later found dead in his cell at the Cedar Junction prison in Walpole, Massachusetts, in what authorities reported was suicide by asphyxiation. A plastic bag was found tied around his head.

Brill dismisses allegations that cameras insinuate themselves into court proceedings, altering the behavior of participants. "The physical imposition of that simple, lone, silent camera on the wall," Brill told one audience, "is no greater, arguably less so, than a reporter scribbling on a pad. Sure, witnesses might be more nervous in high profile cases. Sure, the lawyers might be more nervous (and probably better prepared). Sure, the judge might act a little differently, and maybe better. Sure, some people might be afraid to come forward, and others might be more eager to come forward. But that has to do with publicity, not cameras. And that argument—about publicity—was decided when the Constitution was written," says Brill, citing a staple of his speeches, the Supreme Court's 1980 *Richmond Newspapers* ruling, declaring a public right to attend trials.[12]

After Brill's departure, Erik Sorenson inherited the role of lead advocate for courtroom cameras. "I recognize there are criticisms of the concept," he told the authors, "and I recognize there are some valid concerns about having cameras in the courtroom. But would I rather live in a country that banned cameras from courtrooms, or would I rather live in a country that under the right circumstances allowed cameras? The latter."

Brill, a Yale-educated New Yorker, had never practiced courtroom law when he founded Court TV. He veered instead from law school into a successful career in legal journalism, with stops along the way as an assistant to New York Mayor John Lindsay and consultant to The Police Foundation. He wrote a best-selling book, *The Teamsters*, and in 1978 founded *The American Lawyer*, a legal affairs magazine which ultimately spawned nine regional publications. After founding and guiding Court TV through its first five years, Brill in early 1997 reluctantly allowed his longtime partner, Time Warner, to buy out his publishing and television interests. The *Los Angeles Daily Journal* suggested he was "a casualty of the type of boardroom intrigue that his publications became famous covering."[13] But his influence lingers on, in much of the programming and personnel.

The Court TV Cast

At Court TV, Brill assembled an on-air staff composed largely of lawyers who, like the founder, had a bent for journalism. Chief anchor and former Fulbright scholar Fred Graham covered the Supreme Court for *The New York Times* and served as law correspondent for CBS News dating back to the Watergate era. Carol Randolph practiced trial law and worked as a talk show host before joining Court TV. Jan Rostal was an assistant federal defender in New York. Rikki Klieman left a lucrative, high profile Boston law practice to become a Court TV anchor and analyst.

Klieman is a walking advertisement for cameras in the courtroom, a defense attorney who thinks camera coverage *helps* defendants. She told the authors: "I had never had an occasion in all of the years that I practiced in Massachusetts to ever have a client of mine object to a camera in the courtroom. And it, frankly, would never have dawned on me to object to a camera in the courtroom because I always saw it as my best ally."

The Court TV analyst insists her views have never changed since cameras entered Massachusetts courtrooms in 1978. "I was prosecuting at the time," she recalls, "and the camera became part of the furniture to me. It was in the back of the courtroom. It was usually at the back of my head. I was so used to it that I just assumed it was there and it was always going to be there."

Klieman firmly believes a court camera provides a check against "arbitrary

Court TV

Rikki Klieman, Court TV anchor and commentator.

and capricious judges." Do cameras affect the courtroom behavior of lawyers? Klieman contends the effect, if any, is to make them sharper and better prepared. The O. J. Simpson criminal trial, she says, was an exception where lawyers "parade[d] like peacocks for the camera. But I think that was Simpson," she says, adding: "I think there was something about the whole atmosphere of Simpson that was theatrical and I think that's bad."

Klieman makes no apologies for her own theatrical aspirations as a new graduate of Northwestern University in 1970. A brief, less than illustrious fling at Broadway convinced her to seek another career. But she admits it was, in part, "the theater bug" that bit and convinced her to accept a job at Court TV, where anchoring is "show business, plus education. An anchor on Court TV doesn't operate like a network anchor, in the sense that we're not there to give sound bites. We're there to explain and to educate the American public about the system of justice at all levels."[14]

Court TV's critics hasten to point out that its power to "educate" is conditioned by its ability to win and hold an audience. Despite downplaying the Simpson trial's contribution to Court TV's bottom line, Brill and his successors have struggled to regain the drawing power of the Simpson telecasts.

They hired defense attorney Johnnie Cochran as a commentator and host. Thanks to the televised Simpson trial, Cochran had become as recognizable as his famous defendant. And they brought Sorenson on board as executive vice president. Sorenson is a hardened veteran of many ratings wars as a local television news director and executive producer of the CBS Evening News. He joined the effort to beef up Court TV's off-hour, non-trial ratings. Cochran was paired with Atlanta prosecutor Nancy Grace in a prime time talk and analysis show called *Cochran & Grace*. The program eventually evolved into *Cochran & Company*, sans Grace, a forum of topical legal subjects ranging from the Oklahoma City bombing case to the "First Amendment rights" of professional basketball's roguish Dennis Rodman. Rodman's appearance, after he was heavily fined for making derogatory remarks about Mormons, was touted in a prominent *New York Times* advertisement, for Court TV, reading: "In 3 Seconds, He Cost Himself $50,000. And to Think, We Have Him for a Whole Hour."[15]

Other post–Brill innovations included a morning show, *Legal Cafe*, featuring discussions of such consumer-friendly issues as prenuptial agreements and getting fired—all in a voguish cafe-bar.[16] But like other non-trial offerings, *Legal Cafe* struggled for an audience. It was shifted to an evening time slot and eventually abandoned, another reminder of Court TV's inherent dilemma. "Court TV is so strongly perceived as a trial network," notes Sorenson, "it has been impossible to recruit people to watch at night, because everybody knows that courts don't meet at night." But to make money, Court TV must draw a larger audience to its after-court offerings. Even Cochran's name recognition hasn't done the trick. While evening ratings have tripled, "it's three times almost nothing," says Sorenson—about 60,000 households, as of the end of 1997. Sorenson estimates it would take at least 100,000 to push the network to the break-even point.

One of courtroom cameras' sharpest critics views Court TV's self-description of "educator" as no more than a cynical ploy. "The people at Court TV," writes defense attorney Leslie Abramson, "insist that their broadcasts also serve an important educational and public-service function. To borrow a phrase

Court TV

Leslie Abramson (*left*), defense attorney for Erik Menendez, speaks with Court TV anchor Terry Moran on *Prime Time Justice*.

from Lee Bailey's final argument in the Sheppard retrial, that's ten pounds of hogwash in a five-pound bag. If Court TV was out to educate people it would look like C-SPAN. In fact, it most closely resembles ESPN [a sports network], right down to the expert 'color commentators' and breezy wrap-up shows."[17] It should be noted that Abramson has herself worked as a paid legal commentator for ABC News.

But prestigious segments of the legal community believe Court TV *can* legitimately take credit as an educational force. A sideline business has placed tapes of Court TV's trial coverage in scores of law schools across the country. After he helped defend Simpson in his criminal case, Professor Gerald Uelmen began integrating Court TV's video coverage into his courses at Santa Clara University School of Law. Uelmen has agonized over the courtroom camera issue, but not over the contributions of Court TV. "Court TV," he says, "had already established a stronghold in legal education long before the Simpson trial."

James Towery, former president of the California Bar, discovered Court TV during the O. J. Simpson preliminary hearing. "I thought at the time," he says, "that that was the first time that tens of millions of Americans had seen what a preliminary hearing is. That was an isolated example of what I thought was the educational power of televising legal proceedings." That proceeding, incidentally, is cited as a judicial model with nearly the same frequency that the Simpson trial is labeled an aberration. Both were nationally televised, gavel-to-gavel.

Court TV also boasts of several "educational products," including *Court TV Online*, a computer service offering information on wills, sales contracts and other legal staples, plus a library of court documents. The network offers a weekly, one-hour classroom series called *Class Action*, commercial-free programs using Court TV's library of courtroom footage to treat contemporary legal and social issues.

The Future of Court TV

As with any commercial broadcasting enterprise, the success of Court TV depends in large measure on its ability to attract new viewers. With that in mind, the network launched new programming in April 1996 aimed at the youth audience. Teen Court TV was a three-hour block of broadcasts airing Saturday mornings, a slot traditionally dominated by cartoons and sportscasts. Among the offerings: *Justice Factory*, a weekly visit behind the scenes of the justice system; *Your Turn*, a teen justice-oriented talk show, and *What's the Verdict?*, a weekly gathering of teenage "juries" that analyzes the taped highlights of youth-oriented trials. For instance, one of the early teen juries dissected *Michigan v. Provenzino*, in which the parents of a wayward teenager were held legally responsible for his string of burglaries. Adding to the program's youthful accent initially was the anchor, a casually-dressed Dan Abrams, looking younger than his then 29 years, and the quirky, MTV-style lens angles, as the camera cut among the participants. The programs won critical reviews, but fought hard for even a meager share of the cartoon and sports-rich Saturday audience.

Before selling his interest in Court TV, the ever-optimistic Steven Brill envisioned a future in other venues, including the Supreme Court of the United States. "I don't think that is a terrible longshot," he said. "I think we will, in some way, be in the Supreme Court on an experimental basis within the next couple of years." The biggest impediment, he observed, is the justices themselves. "Maybe I'm naive, but I think they can be made to see the logic of this. It is not going to be barn-busting television, but I think that it would obviously be good for us and good for everybody if we could televise those [Supreme Court] arguments, and I think sooner or later we will."

Brill's most grandiose dream was to go "global," in the same way that a sometime model, Cable News Network (CNN), has spread its influence around the world. "If we have an audience in the United States," he said, "then I think we'll have an audience elsewhere." As a tentative step in that direction, Court TV broadcast portions of the first Bosnian war crimes trial from the Hague, Netherlands, in 1996. By commercial television standards, the trial of Dusko Tadic, the Bosnian Serb accused of "crimes against

Court TV

Bosnian Serb Dusko Tadic, on trial for "crimes against humanity."

humanity," lacked dramatic appeal. But it won Court TV wide acclaim in the court of broadcast criticism for its educational value.

Brill claimed to have won entrée to the courts of Russia, Italy, the Philippines, South Africa and some South American nations. The list includes nations where an independent judiciary is something of a novelty—a novelty that could attract viewers unaccustomed to judicial openness. But cameras are banned in the courts of Britain and several other European nations that might offer Court TV its first logical overseas extension. "It's an interesting notion, but I think it's quite a ways off," says Sorenson, who inherited Brill's concepts.

Inevitably, Court TV will face the same question overseas it has confronted at home since signing on the airwaves in 1991: Is it right for someone to make money off the misfortune and anguish that underlie most court cases?

Brill has a ready answer: Many professions profit from the misfortunes of others. "You can say that about doctors. You can say that about funeral directors. You can certainly say that about the CBS Evening News. Most of the events covered are not joyous things. If you get high ratings on your coverage of the assassination of Yitzhak Rabin, does that make you a bad person?" In fact, Brill's outspoken defense of courtroom cameras and capitalism once won him boos from a group of judges.[18]

The "bad person" question is, of course, rhetorical. Brill knows it, and also understands that the top-rated programs in many nations are soap operas with fictional representations of the real-life tragi-dramas Court TV regularly beams to a growing audience. He did, after all, conceive of Court TV as part soap opera.

There have been many suggestions for improving or augmenting Court TV. As one means of offering a more representative sampling of the justice system, Professor Harris proposes adding a new service to the cable television menu: Community Court TV, affiliated with Court TV in a manner similar to Public Broadcasting Service's link to local public television stations. "Community Court TV would widen the scope of what the Court TV viewer sees; sensational trials would be rare," writes Harris. "The viewer-citizen could get an objective look at her own court system, the behavior of local judges, whom she may have elected, and the seriousness of proceedings (or lack thereof) in her own community. In addition, the perception that Court TV might nurture, that the criminal justice system is chock-full of serious cases, especially murders, would be countered directly."[19]

Obviously, such a service would not be feasible in the few states where cameras have little or no legal access to courtrooms. And there's a major question as to its commercial viability. Alternate funding, such as the subscription drives employed by local public broadcasting, might be necessary. But in principle, anyway, the idea appealed to Steven Brill, perhaps on a state-by-state basis. "You can't really do a report on how criminal justice works and how the system operates in say, Florida, on a national channel," said Brill. "You can, if you have a separate channel that is your local Florida channel."

All of this presupposes an audience appetite and local entrepreneurs or agencies willing to fulfill it. The continuing struggle for profitability at Court TV, even with the backing of giants such as Time Warner, underlines the difficulties. As Erik Sorenson told an interviewer: "After six years and an investment of over $100 million, you'd like to be in the black."[20] Something for local Steve Brills to ponder.

Chapter Ten

Some Camera (and Trial) Saving Alternatives

> Many blame the pervasive presence of television cameras
> for the current problems of pretrial publicity, but high profile
> trials attracted enormous public attention long before televi-
> sion, and excesses of zealous reporting appear to have been
> the norm, rather than the exception.—Professor Gerald
> Uelmen, Santa Clara University School of Law[1]

Turning around the words of the California legal scholar, television is just one
more ingredient in an old debate: how to stand fast for a fair trial in the face
of a publicity storm. Television cameras weren't even allowed in Indiana courtrooms when Leslie Irvin was convicted of murder in Gibson County Circuit
Court on December 20, 1955—the first conviction overturned by the Supreme
Court solely on the basis of prejudicial publicity. TV news, still in its childhood, contributed relatively little to tainting a jury pool awash in stories of
Irvin's purported confession to six murders and 24 burglaries. The accounts
were based on press releases dispensed by the county prosecutor.

But the emergence of television as the dominant communications tool
of the age, its mushrooming expansion by cable and satellite, and the erup-
tion of tabloid TV have all focused new attention on the need for remedies
to counteract the impact of prejudicial pretrial publicity. The previous chapters have focused largely on the issues arising from coverage of court proceedings by cameras stationed *inside* courtrooms. In this chapter we look
at the broader issue of news coverage in general and the tools available to craft
a fair trial in the midst of a publicity-charged environment. Within this
context we examine in detail some of the alternatives to barring courtroom
cameras.

We have previously cited the 1966 Supreme Court reversal of Ohio Dr.
Sam Sheppard's murder conviction as the shot heard round the judicial world
on the subject of prejudicial publicity. Writes legal scholar Robert Stephen:
"The decision sent a clear warning to trial courts that unless a defendant's fair

trial rights are more carefully safeguarded, reversals will result with increasing frequency in media circus cases."[2]

But the case is equally important for suggesting there *are* safeguards to a fair trial, even in a "circus" atmosphere. They include a change of venue and delay of the trial—in legal parlance, a "continuance"—until the atmosphere has cooled. The trial judge rejected defense motions for both of those remedies.

The Supreme Court also said a sequestered jury was at times a proper and necessary safeguard. As the Sheppard trial approached, three Cleveland newspapers had published the names and addresses of all prospective jurors. Some of the potential jurors were contacted by citizens interested in the trial's outcome. Even during deliberations of the jurors, who were sequestered, photographers posed them in two groups for pictures to appear in a local paper.[3]

In addition, the high court suggested that the creative use of gag orders, imposed on trial participants, could have kept many of the more inflammatory sideline stories to the trial itself out of the media. Among the tales cited: that Sheppard twice refused to take a lie detector test and declined to be injected with truth serum.[4] Finally, the Supreme Court said a new trial should be ordered if publicity threatens the fairness of a proceeding.[5] In short, says Stephen, "the Sheppard Court thrust an affirmative duty on trial courts to take any and all necessary actions to provide a fair trial when a case becomes a media circus."[6]

One jurist who clearly took that message to heart was U.S. District Court Judge Robert Takasugi of Los Angeles, who presided over the 1981 trial of automaker John DeLorean on cocaine charges. His conduct is often cited as a model of sound trial management of a sensationalized case. Amidst a tempest of international pretrial publicity, Takasugi ordered a continuance of the trial, in hopes the storm would abate. During the continuance, the media obtained surveillance tapes which appeared to show DeLorean fully involved in the drug transaction of which he was accused. Takasugi issued a restraining order barring broadcast of the tapes. Airing them, he declared, would have "a devastating effect" on the defendant's right to a fair trial. He said there was absolutely no way "to remove the taint upon the minds of potential jurors" that seeing the tapes would inflict.[7] But the court of appeals said, in effect, that was speculation, that Takasugi's order was overbroad, that there were other ways to protect the defendant's rights, including a strong *voir dire*—the screening of jury candidates.[8] The appellate court overruled Takasugi. Broadcasters aired the tapes.

Dutifully, Takasugi prepared an extensive questionnaire for jury prospects, designed to measure the extent of their exposure to prejudicial publicity. Although federal judges normally conduct most of the questioning of prospective jurors, Takasugi gave attorneys a chance to question jury prospects individually about their exposure to news coverage. The judge liberally excused jurors for cause and gave the opposing lawyers additional peremptory challenges—three for the government, five for the defense. He used a number system for jurors in a not-entirely-successful effort to shield their identities.[9]

To protect themselves against prejudice and guard against improper discussions, the jurors selected a temporary foreman.[10] And Judge Takasugi consulted frequently with a media committee about courtroom decorum. Though he was bound by federal rules barring cameras from the courtroom, the judge allowed an audio feed of the proceedings to be piped to a listening room to accommodate overflow members of the press corps.

Throughout the proceeding, Takasugi remained vigilant for prejudicial pretrial publicity. At one point, he ordered all motions sealed, a move prompted by the headline-making assertion in a motion by Prosecutor James Walsh. Walsh suggested DeLorean's Belfast-based sports car company had ties to the Irish Republican Army, the underground group fighting British rule in Northern Ireland. The Associated Press led a media charge to the Ninth Circuit Court of Appeals, which ruled that Takasugi's sealing order was unconstitutional prior restraint. Walsh's allegation about DeLorean and the IRA proved unfounded.

In the end, DeLorean could not complain that heavy pretrial publicity, including the damning surveillance tapes, had prejudiced the case against him. After a week of deliberations, the jury acquitted the famous industrialist, agreeing with the defense that DeLorean had been "entrapped" by federal agents into committing the crimes.

Each of the tools traditionally used to counter prejudicial publicity—strong *voir dire*, sequestration, continuances, change of venue, gag orders—has its strengths and weaknesses and, in some applications, is subject to legal challenge. A closer analysis of each follows.

Voir Dire

Voir dire is the French term for the examination of prospective jurors in an effort to weed out the biased and incompetent. The U.S. Constitution does not mandate that jurors be ignorant, only impartial. Or, as the authors of one scholarly article put it: "The aim was not necessarily to find jurors who were unaware of the innuendoes and community gossip, but to impanel people who would base their decision on the facts presented at trial."[11]

In fact, in a preamble to jury selection in the second (civil) O. J. Simpson trial, Judge Hiroshi Fujisaki acknowledged that all potential jurors had likely been exposed to some degree to Simpson's criminal trial. As the judge and lawyers screened several hundred prospects, the closest they came to an "unaware" juror was a young student who said she was so busy with her studies and part-time job that she didn't "even know when the [criminal] trial started or ended." That prompted defense attorney Robert Baker to quip, "Shannon Lucid orbited earth for six months and she knows more about this case than you do," a reference to a U.S. astronaut who spent a half-year in the Russian Mir space station.

Many attorneys believe *voir dire* is the most critical factor in the outcome of a case and the key to a fair trial. Increasingly, jury consultants—specialists trained to ferret out the unfavorable or untruthful from a jury pool—fill chairs at counsel tables. Like Judge Takasugi, more and more judges use questionnaires to augment courtroom questioning of prospective jurors about their impartiality. Some prospects complained of writer's cramp after filling out three questionnaires in the Simpson civil case; one, checking the candidate's availability for a long trial; another, probing for biases of a general nature—against law enforcement, various racial and ethnic groups and so forth—and a third posing questions about a candidate's exposure to news coverage and whether it would prevent him or her from being fair and impartial.

But while questionnaires and consultants can enhance the effectiveness of *voir dire,* they can not guarantee a panel of twelve impartial jurors, free of taint from pretrial publicity. "Ultimately," notes Gerald Uelmen, no stranger to questionnaires, "the acceptability of a juror depends upon the credibility and persuasiveness of his claim that his fixed opinions can be disregarded and guilt or innocence judged impartially on the evidence."[12]

Charles Whitebread, a University of Southern California law professor, and co-author Darrell Contreras offer this bottom line: "Unfortunately, a streamlined *voir dire* may inadvertently result in empaneling a juror who has a hidden agenda. However, even the most extensive *voir dire* could not elicit hidden prejudices from potential jurors."[13] Though *voir dire,* literally, means "to speak the truth," people do not easily admit they are biased. And while a vigorous jury selection process remains a first-line remedy for heavy, damaging pretrial publicity, it is inherently vulnerable to human shortcomings.

Sequestration

Courts traditionally view sequestration as "a drastic remedy which cannot be recommended lightly."[14] It entails isolating jurors, during their off-duty hours, in a hotel or other quarters where bailiffs can control their movements and exposure to publicity. Courts usually sequester juries only when saturation news coverage cannot be avoided. It was a controversial part of three explosive California cases: The murder trial of Charles Manson and his "family" in 1970, the second (federal) trial of four police officers on charges stemming from the Rodney King beating in 1993, and the Simpson criminal case two years later. While sequestration shields jurors from media reports during a trial, it does not correct for any prejudice stemming from pretrial publicity.

Besides the cost of sequestration, it inflicts a perverse twist, by forcing "jurors to bear the burden of compensation for the highly publicized acts of the trial participants."[15] Before condemning Manson and his followers to what eventually became life sentences, Manson's jurors served an eight-and-one-half-month "sentence" of their own in a Los Angeles hotel, including much of the Christmas holiday season. One juror attempted suicide. Others complained of going "stir crazy."[16]

In the Simpson murder case, juror Tracy Hampton tearfully asked to be excused, telling Judge Ito, "I can't take it any more."[17] Juror Francine Florio-Bunten likened sequestration to a "mushroom-like thing—like being kept in a dark room."

Sequestration poses other problems, as well. Jurors must remain away from jobs, homes and families for extended periods of time. That not only narrows the pool of available jurors, but also may skew its composition. In addition, the rigors of extended sequestration could lead to a "snap" verdict.

Critics speculate that happened in the Simpson case, when jurors acquitted the defendant after a scant four hours of deliberations. The jurors have disagreed, insisting that nearly nine months of testimony had led them logically and unanimously to reasonable doubts of Simpson's guilt. "While we may really never know what influence this forced separation had on the jury's four-hour verdict," writes legal commentator Roger Cossack, "we do know that several members of the jury were quite angry about the length of time they were locked up and told Judge Ito about their frustration during the famous 'jury revolt.' I have practiced trial law for more than two decades, and neither I nor any of my colleagues had previously heard of or seen a jury revolt."[18] The revolt was sparked by the transfer of several popular bailiffs who had been overseeing the jurors' sequestration.

Defense lawyers rarely favor sequestration because of the widely held theory that it favors the prosecution by fostering a sort of "Stockholm syndrome," in which jurors bond with their captors—the bailiffs who supervise them. "Most jurors love the bailiff," says jury consultant Karen Jo Koonan. "They [the bailiffs] are nice to them; they provide what they need; they try to be helpful, and ... they are law enforcement. They are the establishment and those are the people the jurors can identify with, and some people say that causes them to be more prosecution-oriented." That obviously did not prove true in the Simpson criminal case.

Aware of the problems of extended sequestration, some judges presiding over high profile cases have limited such restrictive measures to jury deliberations. That happened in the case against Damian Williams and Henry Watson, accused of the near-fatal beating of truckdriver Reginald Denny as the 1992 Los Angeles riots broke out. In 1987, a panel of jurors actually requested sequestration in the 21st day of deliberations in the retrial of Sagon Penn on five felony counts stemming from the fatal shooting of San Diego Police Agent Thomas Riggs and wounding of two other persons. The request came after co-workers commented about the case to some jurors during a recess in deliberations. Judge J. Morgan Lester granted the request, over a mild objection by the defense.[19] The jury ultimately acquitted Penn of first degree murder. The panel deadlocked, 11 to 1, for acquittal, on the other charges.

Many states used to require that jurors be sequestered during deliberations. Even as the practice has faded, New York has adhered to it, requiring that deliberating juries be sequestered in all criminal trials in New York. But in an experiment launched in 1995, New York judges limited sequestration to juries weighing verdicts for violent crimes such as murder, rape and armed robbery.

Still, sequestration remains a legitimate, if extreme, option in trials swamped with prejudicial pretrial publicity. Judge Ito may have felt the Simpson trial was in need of drastic measures after several prospective jurors told of involuntary exposure to news accounts of the case, including a man who had overheard a headline on the transistor radio of a fellow passenger while riding to court on a bus. Defense attorney Johnnie Cochran quoted another jury prospect as saying: "It's in the air. It's everywhere. It's when I go to my gym in the morning to work out. It's when I walk into any place. It's everywhere."[20]

Continuances

The continuance, or delay, of a trial may dampen publicity and cause details to recede in the public mind; but it can also conflict with the constitutional right to a speedy trial. A defendant may waive that right, but he or she risks a resurgence of publicity as the new trial date approaches. Consider the case of Theodore Kaczynski. A delay of well over a year and a half between his arrest and his Sacramento trial on charges of carrying out two so-called "Unabomber" attacks helped push his case to the back pages of newspapers and off television newscasts. But it also allowed time for other potentially damaging developments. Details surfaced about the other bombings Kaczynski allegedly carried out. News organizations went to court and won access to some evidence not previously publicized. All of this added grist to the skepticism of some psychologists that time actually erodes the harmful effects of pretrial publicity.[21]

Continuances may also be poor servants of justice. Witnesses' memories may fade as time passes, or witnesses may be lost altogether, thereby jeopardizing the fact-finding process. Delay may also increase the backlog of an already over-crowded court system. Putting all that together with the arguable premise that publicity which recedes will not return, Michigan District Court Judge Peter D. O'Connell concludes, "continuances may be effective on medium publicity cases, but have little effect on the high publicity trials."[22]

Change of Venue

National awareness does not automatically result in national prejudice. That principle, embraced in the *Irvin* ruling[23] cited earlier, has been the driving rationale behind moving several high-visibility criminal cases away from the scene of the crime. A prime example was the change of venue for the trials of Timothy McVeigh and Terry Nichols, the accused co-conspirators in the Oklahoma City federal building bombing that killed 168 persons on April 19, 1995. Although the blast and its aftermath created continuing front-page news in almost every community in America, "the Oklahoma City bombing *changed the lives* of many of the residents of Oklahoma City. This was a situation in which the city was too closely related to the event to ensure a fair proceeding."[24] At least no one in Denver, where the trials were transferred, lived next door to a bombing victim or commuted to work daily past the shredded remains of the federal building. Residents knew about the bombing, without being directly affected by it.

Ideally, a change of venue moves a trial to a location where jurors have had relatively little exposure to pretrial publicity. With modern mass media, however, that is increasingly difficult. Take, for example, the California prosecution of Richard Allen Davis on charges of kidnapping and killing 12-year-old Polly Klaas. On September 18, 1995, Superior Court Judge Lawrence Antolini abandoned a two-month struggle to seat a jury in Sonoma County, where the victim lived and died. The judge complained that "almost everyone" was aware of an alleged confession in the sensational case.[25] Many in the community had participated in a search for the girl before her body was found.

The trial was eventually moved 110 miles south to San Jose, after a survey indicated it would produce a less-tainted pool of jurors.[26] But defense lawyers soon filed a motion for another change of venue. They claimed the jury pool in Santa Clara County was only slightly less biased than the original pool, so pervasive was publicity in the case. Davis was eventually convicted in a trial retained in San Jose.

Critics contend that at least one change of venue may have altered a verdict, without changing the degree of juror immersion in pretrial publicity. The state prosecution of four police officers accused of beating Rodney King was moved less than 30 miles from Los Angeles to Simi Valley, in neighboring Ventura County. Residents there are exposed to Los Angeles television and radio programming. Some of the same newspapers are available. But jurors are drawn from a geographic area generally more conservative and less racially diverse than Los Angeles. And, as noted earlier, Simi Valley is home to many police officers. The Simi Valley jury acquitted the four police defendants. A year and a riot later, in a Los Angeles federal trial, two of them were convicted of civil rights violations.

San Diego attorney Charles Sevilla, the appellate lawyer for executed murderer Robert Alton Harris, thinks his client's trial was an ideal candidate for a change of venue. Harris was accused of killing two boys, including the son of the arresting officer, in a case that stirred a publicity whirlwind in San Diego County, but nowhere else. Recalls Sevilla: "This was a poisonous atmosphere for those months in terms of getting a fair trial for the defendant and the case should have been ... change of venued out." It was not.

Obviously, a change of venue carries a price; Ventura County inherited $223,491 in unsolicited court costs for the King case. The cost of moving the McVeigh and Nichols trials to Denver was much higher than that. When they transfer cases, judges turn aside a traditional value. In the words of legal writer Mark Stabile: "The Supreme Court has recognized that local communities and judicial systems have an interest in settling disputes locally; one locale should not be permitted to unburden its own court system by shifting cases to other locations."[27] The Sixth Amendment to the Constitution mandates the right to a speedy, public trial "by an impartial jury of the state and district wherein the crime shall have been committed." But subsequent interpretations have held that does not bar a change of venue if extensive publicity prejudices the potential jury pool.[28] And even in an age of instantaneous and ubiquitous news coverage of splashy cases, a change of venue is likely to remain a viable, if sparingly used, remedy for a jury pool poisoned by pervasive publicity.

Gag Orders

The simplest, most direct check on prejudicial pretrial publicity would be a directive from the bench, barring the media from reporting anything that might taint a jury pool. But the Supreme Court has taken a dim view of gag orders on the press, calling such prior restraints the "least tolerable infringement" on First Amendment rights.[29] The Court's definitive word came in the 1976 *Nebraska Press Association v. Stuart* decision. The justices unanimously overruled a judge who had barred publication of a confession and other items in the case of Erwin Simants, accused of killing six members of the Henry Kellie family in Sutherland, Nebraska, a town of about 850 residents. To warrant such prior restraints on the press, said the Court, a party must show the publicity generated in the absence of an injunction (or gag order) would be so prejudicial that the defendant could not possibly get a fair trial, that no alternative measures would mitigate the effect of the publicity, and that the injunction would guarantee a fair trial.

As a practical matter, the stringent standards established in the *Nebraska Press* decision prohibit almost all gag orders against the press. But the same ruling suggested that restraints on the speech of *trial participants* might sometimes be appropriate. It quoted from the *Sheppard* decision cited earlier:

> Neither prosecutors, counsel for defense, the accused, witnesses, court staff nor enforcement officers coming under the jurisdiction of the court should be permitted to frustrate its function. Collaboration between counsel and the press as to information affecting the fairness of a criminal trial is not only subject to regulation, but is highly censurable and worthy of disciplinary measures.[30]

The result is a growing use of gag orders covering lawyers, litigants and court officers as a front-line weapon against jury contamination. By mutual agreement, the court gagged lawyers in the first Rodney King beating trial. Judge Hiroshi Fujisaki imposed a sweeping order, covering even "employees and agents" of the attorneys in the Simpson civil case, declaring, "There are no reasonable or workable alternatives..." in a case already immersed in publicity.[31] And a gag order was imposed by Judge Richard Matsch in the trial of Oklahoma City bombing defendant Timothy McVeigh, but not before defense attorney Stephen Jones had unleashed a pretrial media campaign, including television interviews, to soften his client's image, to portray him as "a home-grown American boy."[32]

Occasionally, appellate courts find gag orders overly broad or simply overkill. U.S. District Judge Kevin Duffy of New York stunned participants in the trial of those accused in the 1993 bombing of the World Trade Center with the following directive:

> There will be no more statements [in the press, on TV, in radio, or in any other electronic media] issued by either side or their agents. The next time I pick up a paper and see a quotation from any of you, you had best be prepared to have some money. The first fine will be $200. Thereafter, the fines will be squared.[33]

Courtroom observers quickly calculated that a four-time offender would owe $1.6-billion. But no such fine was ever levied. Twenty-nine days after Judge Duffy imposed it, the Second Circuit Court of Appeals overturned the broad gag order, ruling it was unsupported by findings that alternatives would be inadequate and violated the attorneys' First Amendment rights.[34]

Some states have adopted rules of conduct which restrict extrajudicial statements by attorneys. In the closing months of the O. J. Simpson criminal trial, California's Supreme Court promulgated California Rules of Professional Conduct, Rule 5-120 (1995). It provides, in part:

> A member who is participating or has participated in the investigation or litigation of a matter shall not make an extrajudicial statement that a reasonable person would expect to be disseminated by means of public communication if the member knows or reasonably should know that it will have a substantial likelihood of materially prejudicing an adjudicative proceeding in the matter.

Many defense attorneys worry that such regulations, and gag orders in general, leave prosecutors and police free to "leak" damaging information about their clients anonymously, while leaving them unable to respond publicly. "It is absurd," writes legal scholar Lloyd B. Snyder, "to have a system in which public officials, such as police officers, may make public statements about criminal investigations, while at the same time, [state] bar disciplinary rules prevent the person most capable of speaking effectively on behalf of the defendant [his defense attorney] from doing so." [35]

In an effort to address that concern, California's Rule 5-120 contains a paragraph allowing an attorney to "make a statement that a reasonable member would believe is required to protect a client from the substantial undue prejudicial effect of recent publicity not initiated by the member or the member's client." In other words, it allows tit for tat.

Journalists have traditionally looked askance at gag orders, which cut off sources of information. Media organizations, represented by Kelli Sager, strenuously opposed Judge Fujisaki's gag order in the Simpson civil case. Sager argued that the public's interest in the free flow of information "far outweighs the remote possibility that any further public comment by the attorneys, parties or witnesses about this case could taint the jury pool or prejudicially affect the outcome of the trial in this matter."[36] At the time she filed her motion to vacate the gag order, August 16, 1996, the Simpson publicity train had already chugged along at full speed for more than two years.

Theo Wilson, the late *New York Daily News* trial reporter, also spent much of her distinguished career opposing gag orders. However, the frequent "spin" sessions by attorneys in the Simpson criminal case caused her, reluctantly, to modify her view. "Because of the actions of the lawyers in that case," she wrote, "it seems to me that limited gag orders may become a hard necessity of life.... If limited gag orders will make it possible to bring cameras back into the trial room, and prevent the excesses of the O. J. trial outside the courtroom, so be it."[37]

Options to Banning Cameras

Even in high publicity cases, judges may want to allow courtroom television coverage to ensure that the public receives an unbiased, unfiltered picture of the proceedings, bereft of rumor and courthouse step "spin doctoring." However, it may be inappropriate to televise testimony of reluctant or youthful witnesses, those in the federal witness protection program or victims of sex crimes.

In those cases there are options short of banning cameras altogether. Coverage can be curtailed during the testimony of a particular witness. If a witness balks at being televised, the judge should determine whether the reluctance specifically relates to the camera or to testifying in general. Legal writer Gregory McCall suggests judges explore the basis of a witness' fear of electronic coverage and determine whether it would interfere with his or her testimony to such an extent that it would damage the defendant's fair trial rights. "If the court determines that the witness' objection to cameras is valid," writes McCall, "the Sixth and Fourteenth Amendments require that cameras be excluded."[38]

Electronic alternatives may eliminate the need to turn off the camera during the testimony of specific witnesses. A witness' face can be electronically blurred and her voice altered. Or a "dot" can be electronically placed over a face, as was done with the alleged rape victim during Court TV's telecast of the William Kennedy Smith trial in 1991. In cases where a witness is concerned only about his image, and not his voice, being broadcast, stations have aired the audio portion of the testimony over a graphic displaying a printed, "crawling" transcription of the witness' words.

During the 1991 trial of Elisabeth "Betty" Broderick on charges of murdering her ex-husband, a prominent San Diego attorney, and his new wife, the defendant's daughter felt uncomfortable testifying on camera. "Lee is very shy," Broderick told the authors. "She thought the camera would make her nervous." So Judge Thomas Whelan ordered the camera trained elsewhere in the courtroom during the daughter's testimony. Only her voice was broadcast, with "no ill effects," according to the judge.[39]

Judges may also be tempted to exclude cameras during certain pretrial proceedings in an effort to eliminate another possible source of contamination of potential jurors. Such hearings may involve evidence that will never be presented to the jury. A blanket pretrial exclusion of cameras was proposed and eventually rejected when California's courtroom camera rules were revamped in 1996. Critics of the proposal pointed out that television is only one potential source of prejudicial publicity. Jurors can also be tainted by accounts in newspapers and magazines. And as it demonstrated in its 1986 *Press-Enterprise* ruling, the Supreme Court does not look kindly on efforts to exclude all media from pretrial proceedings.

In most states judges have wide latitude in controlling the operation of courtroom cameras. They may prohibit shots of jurors—some states have blanket prohibitions—and pictures of individual spectators. They can order camera coverage cut during sidebar conferences, so such conversations are not aired before transcripts are released. They have total discretion over placement of the camera, making it as unobtrusive as possible. And in cases where they fear simultaneous broadcast would threaten a fair trial, judges can order a delay in the telecast, even until the end of the trial.

Finally, judges have the ultimate power; they can stop the proceedings and start over. In its *Sheppard* ruling, the Supreme Court clearly stated that where fairness is threatened by publicity, a new trial should be ordered. As Justice Tom Clark wrote in his majority opinion, "the trial courts must take strong measures to ensure that the balance is never weighed against the accused."[40]

Are the Remedies Themselves Threatened?

Used individually, or combined in groups, the Supreme Court has placed faith in the remedies described in this chapter to treat the ill effects of invasive publicity in high profile cases. But some worry that the remedies themselves are under seige. "In a climate in which media saturation coverage cannot be effectively controlled," writes Professor Gerald Uelmen, "the effective use of these traditional tools will carry even more of the burden of ensuring the fairness of trials. Yet the prevailing trend is to limit these devices to save time, reduce expenses and protect the privacy and convenience of jurors."[41]

Uelmen worries about such measures as Proposition 115, the ballot initiative approved by California voters in 1990 in an effort to "streamline" their justice system. One of those streamlining provisions allows judges to conduct all *voir dire* questioning of jurors, without the input of counsel. In practice, some judges exercise their discretion to allow questions by attorneys as well, as occurred in both Simpson trials. The Supreme Court's 1991 *Mu'Min v. Virginia* decision was another blow to the effectiveness of *voir dire* in weeding out jurors tainted by publicity. A five to four majority of the Court declared that a trial judge need not question jurors about the *content* of news reports to which they've been exposed.[42] Although 8 of 12 jurors in the death penalty case admitted exposure to pretrial news coverage, the trial judge accepted their assurances that they could decide the case fairly and impartially without probing further into the nature of their exposure.

Are the remedies adequate to counteract prejudicial pretrial publicity? It's hard to know, says Uelmen, citing a lack of empirical study of the effects of vigorous *voir dire*, sequestration and other tools of trial management. "We are flying blind," he says, "and yet many voices call for us to turn off the radar."[43] But the painstaking *voir dire* in the Oklahoma City bombing case, the change of venue and the exercise of gag order powers by Judge Richard Matsch indicates faith by some in the strength of the traditional remedies to heavy pretrial publicity. Such trials become examples to others, ensuring that the reliance on those remedies will continue and perhaps even grow.

Chapter Eleven

Cameras—Now
and in the Future

The debate over cameras in courtrooms simmered for 60 years and boiled over in one explosive "trial of the century." In post–Simpson America, views have become increasingly polarized. Most people take an all-or-nothing approach that misses the complexities of the competing interests. Many criminal defense attorneys oppose cameras out of hand because of perceived prejudice to the rights of their clients. Journalists, pushed by competitive pressures and an innate drive for access, piously wave the First Amendment. Meanwhile, judges jealously guard absolute discretion over everything that goes on in "their" courtrooms. In May 1996, the Michigan Court of Appeals found state district Judge David Bradfield of Detroit had gone too far when he turned down five requests for still camera access in a six-month period and stated that his policy was to never allow cameras in his court. The appellate court ordered him to consider the merits of each request on a case-by-case basis.

The issue is multi-faceted. There are few easy answers. In the course of preparing this book, the authors have analyzed the consequences and ramifications of saying yes or no to television without benefit of the ultimate laboratory test: a play and replay of the exact same trial, with and without camera coverage. Nevertheless, it is possible to make some observations and recommendations.

Early camera coverage entailed some disruptive elements—added lighting, power cables and the sometimes noisy process of changing film magazines. Today, the presence of a single, small pool video camera placed above the jury box or at the back of the courtroom, sometimes remotely operated, does not generally create physical disruption. Judges must guard, however, that its mere presence does not affect the conduct of lawyers, witnesses, jurors or themselves.

There is no cogent reason for keeping cameras out of the United States Supreme Court. It is in this apex of the third branch of government, arguably the least understood branch, that the law of the land is shaped. No judicial proceeding is more educational than sessions of the Supreme Court. Moreover, a common argument against television coverage—that jurors and witnesses could be influenced simply does not apply. There are no jurors or witnesses. Even the widely quoted critic of televised trials, Professor George Gerbner, dean emeritus of the University of Pennsylvania's Annenberg School for Communication, thinks telecasts of Supreme Court arguments would be a public service. "Certainly whatever qualms or objections there may be to courts of appeal being televised," he says, "do not come near to the validity of the objections to basically high profile criminal trials in real time."

Many newspapers have editorialized for a more open Supreme Court, including the Cleveland *Plain Dealer*. In the words of one opinion piece: "With such a cloak of secrecy guarding the third branch of government, no wonder very few Americans can name even two or three of the justices. No wonder the public has so little understanding of what the high court does."[1]

The same reasoning applies to the lower appellate courts. The trial is over and jurors have gone home. Only legal issues remain to be decided, issues in which the public may have great interest. There is little chance of prejudice to the defendant. Television cameras should be routine fixtures in both state and federal appeals courts.

Cameras in trial courtrooms present a knottier problem. It is here that the public has the greatest interest but justice may be the most vulnerable. Different considerations abound in criminal and civil courts. There is a strong concern for fairness in both. But the Constitution gives the defendant in a criminal case special rights, in an attempt to even the playing field when the powerful machinery of the state gears up to prosecute him. The balance between the public's right to know and the fair trial guarantee is a delicate one. Every case is unique and must be analyzed in light of its own special facts. However, some generalizations can be useful.

Television coverage, as well as print coverage, of pretrial hearings raises issues that may be different from the coverage of actual trials. Prospective jurors watching a preliminary hearing or the debate of a pretrial motion may formulate positions about the guilt or innocence of the accused based on evidence not presented at trial. Jurors may retain these preconceived opinions no matter how often a judge admonishes them to keep open minds. It is a benchmark of our jurisprudence that a case be decided only upon the evidence presented in court. When jurors have had access to other information, fairness may be in jeopardy. Yet, even in pretrial proceedings, those considerations must be balanced with the need for openness to ensure that a defendant is not "railroaded."

A presiding judge must exercise discretion in ruling on each request to televise a proceeding, trial or pretrial, based on its peculiar circumstances. The judge should balance the public's right to access against any indications that television coverage would materially change the proceeding. If confronted with strong evidence that a camera's presence would endanger the integrity of the process, the judge should bar it. But he or she should consult the opposing parties before making the decision. Great weight should be accorded the position of the defendant, who has the most at stake in a criminal case. And judges should remain vigilant for attorneys who, in their enthusiasm to enhance their careers via television, may unduly pressure their clients into consenting to courtroom cameras.

Other considerations to be factored into the judicial equation include the goal of maintaining public confidence in the justice system, the impact televised coverage may have on selecting a fair and impartial jury, the potential for exposing witnesses to the televised testimony of earlier witnesses, privacy considerations, the financial impact of broadcast coverage, the order and dignity of the proceedings and protecting fair trial rights.

There are clearly situations where camera coverage should be barred or modified: when it is imperative to ensure the testimony of an important, reluctant witness; in juvenile proceedings; during the testimony of victims of sex crimes who don't wish to be identified; and when national security or the safety of a witness is at stake.

Conferences between attorneys and their clients should not be recorded, to protect the client-attorney privilege. Nor should conferences among attorneys; between attorneys and witnesses or aides; or between attorneys and the judge at the bench. Likewise, proceedings in a judge's chambers or that are otherwise closed to the public should be off limits to cameras. However, judges should be vigilant that the use of chambers conferences and closed hearings does not become a convenient shield from public accountability.

Neither jury selection nor the faces of jurors should be shown because that could add pressure to the jurors' primary task of focusing on the evidence and reaching a verdict. Judges should also exercise firm discretion in allowing shots of spectators, since emotional displays by families or victims may impassion television viewers against the defendant and undermine public acceptance of the jury's verdict.

That does not necessarily mean barring cameras altogether, as New Jersey Superior Court Judge Andrew J. Smithson chose to do in the 1997 trial of Jesse K. Timmendequas. The defendant was accused of killing seven-year-old Megan Kanka, in a case that generated a rash of "Megan's Laws" around the country— laws requiring officials to notify communities when sex offenders move into their midst. The judge was confronted with an appeal by the victim's parents: "It's going to be hard enough for us to sit in a courtroom," they told him, "let alone have to have cameras on us, seeing all our reactions, or the devastation of what we have to go through."[2] Judge Smithson could have allowed television coverage and placed the audience off limits. Instead he imposed a total ban.

Civil Considerations

In civil cases, the balance should be struck more heavily on the side of the public's right to know, since the life or liberty of the defendant is not at stake. But significant privacy interests must be considered. For instance, parties to an acrimonious divorce proceeding may be averse to airing the intimate details of their private lives, notwithstanding a strong public interest in seeing and hearing those details. On the other hand, plaintiffs in a class action products liability suit may want to publicize their grievances.

Civil litigants who can afford private arbitration as an alternative to a public trial can buy their privacy. That option should be extended to less affluent litigants, as well, to equalize access to more palatable, less stressful forums for dispute resolution.

Open the Federal Courts

The considerations that apply to television cameras in state proceedings apply equally to federal courts. With trial judges exercising final discretion, mindful of fair trial concerns, cameras should be allowed in U.S. district courts to the same extent they are permitted in the courtrooms of nearly all 50 states.

U.S. District Court Judge Laughlin Waters opposes courtroom cameras in general. But he sees no striking distinctions between the two systems, state and federal, that warrant different rules. "Maybe the difference is in the fact the federal judges have lifetime appointments and the state judges stand for re-election," says Waters. "That may color one's approach as to how this particular problem should be addressed." Indeed, judges in the federal system have fewer distractions to keep them from running their courtrooms as they see fit. Since they do not face re-election, they are less accountable to the electorate than their state counterparts. State judges, who must answer to voters periodically, may be acutely sensitive to how they are perceived by television-viewing constituents. Although the independence of the judiciary is a strong ideal in our system, state judges who face confirmation elections must heed political winds to survive on the bench.

But if the independence of the state judiciary is threatened by too much accountability, the opposite is true of federal judges, who face virtually no public review. U.S. District Judge John Tunheim, for one, would like to see more public scrutiny and thinks television is a good way to ensure that. Says Tunheim: "I think the public should see what's going on in the courtrooms. There isn't any routine coverage day in and day out and there's a lot of very interesting issues that are played out every day in these courtrooms.... [P]eople just don't have any idea what's going on." The same factors that guide state judges in deciding whether to allow camera coverage, case-by-case, could be used by federal judges as well.*

---

*As this book went to print, the U.S. House of Representatives had passed the Judicial Reform Act of 1998 (H.R. 1252, Sec. 6), which included a provision granting authority to presiding federal appellate and trial court judges to admit television cameras into federal courtrooms. The corresponding bill introduced in the Senate omitted the section about cameras; however camera lobbyists still hoped to introduce a stand-alone bill in the Senate.

The O. J. Simpson Aberration

The debate over cameras erupted in the mid–1990s largely because of one novel case—the O. J. Simpson murder trial. Cameras were part of a unique confluence of factors that had not been present for any other big case in history. Although we have cited the Simpson case repeatedly, we warn against the tendency to allow it to skew and bias the debate over cameras in the courtroom. In the words of Professor Robert A. Pugsley, of Southwestern University School of Law, "The experiments with televised trial coverage blessed by *Chandler v. Florida* and carried out so successfully in California and many other states should most definitely not be aborted in response to one aberrational event."[3] And indeed, when the initial shock in the aftermath of Simpson wore off, threats to repeal laws permitting courtroom cameras in various states virtually evaporated.

Former U.S. Attorney General Griffin Bell, an advocate of cameras in federal courts, says that, if anything, the Simpson murder trial reminded us that a lens is blind to good and bad. "Courtroom cameras won't always show the people what they want to see," he wrote. "Cameras won't necessarily ensure fairness or satisfactory conclusions. Cameras allow us to witness the commonplace failures, as well as the triumphs, of our legal system. If changes in the administration of justice are needed, cameras are likely to hasten such reforms."[4]

Post-Simpson Reforms

Indeed, telecasts of the Simpson trial led to a public cry for a variety of reforms, some eventually enacted into law, others discarded as ill-conceived when calm returned. Amid fears of a hung jury in the Simpson case, California legislators hurriedly drafted a bill to end the requirement of unanimous jury verdicts in criminal cases.[5] It called for a ten to two vote to convict or acquit. The bill eventually died. Ironically, had such a law been in effect during the Simpson trial, it would only have hastened an already quick verdict. On their first straw vote, the Simpson jurors were split, ten to two, for acquittal.

There were also proposals in California to abolish or reduce the number of peremptory challenges, which would have resulted in the speedier, if less-discriminating, selection of juries. They were opposed by prosecutors and defense attorneys alike and were eventually shelved. Two measures were enacted as a direct result of frustration with the Simpson trial: a gag rule[6] and a new hearsay exception.[7]

Simpson television coverage also helped push into law in California a number of measures to deal more forcefully with domestic violence. At least nine such laws make it easier to jail batterers and increase penalties for violent domestic acts.

The Simpson case also stimulated legislative action beyond the borders of California in at least 14 other states saturated with television coverage of the trial. All have passed or considered domestic violence legislation similar to California's.[8]

Television Commentators

The Simpson saga brought into prominence—and controversy—the emerging cottage industry of legal commentary. Though the civil trial was not televised, local stations and networks still augmented their coverage with analysis by a variety of legal scholars and private attorneys. They were both praised and panned. Lanny Larson, the *Fresno Bee*'s television critic, was among the more acid in evaluating their performance. "Had the Simpson civil trial been televised," he wrote, "people would already have known this wasn't all that complicated. What confused me was explanations by people who benefit financially from keeping things complicated."[9]

The most frequent criticism of commentators arises when they're lured beyond analysis into scorekeeping, where they opine "who won" in the examination of a particular witness or other courtroom event. Two of the more respected legal commentators, Professor Erwin Chemerinsky of the University of Southern California and Dean Laurie Levenson of Loyola of Los Angeles Law School, take the criticism seriously. They have written and spoken exhaustively on the ethics of commentary. "A commentator can greatly help himself or herself by offering only those services that legitimately fall within the role of a legal analyst," they write. "Once one ventures into the realm of soothsayer/gamekeeper by predicting or 'scoring' a proceeding, one will almost by definition be acting without the appropriate competency.[10] 'Legal journalism that borders on sports reporting is bad news for the profession and a disservice to the public.'"[11]

Commentators who stay within the boundaries prescribed by Professors Chemerinsky and Levenson can perform a valuable, educational service for television viewers. When they stray from those parameters, they invite criticism not only upon themselves but of the courtroom telecasts they augment. Viewers appreciate help in understanding a trial proceeding. They don't need help in judging it.

Taking the Camera One Step Further— To the Jury Room?

Today, the laws of seven states and the federal courts prohibit the recording of jury deliberations, and in a majority of states, secrecy of deliberations is a well-settled issue of case law.[12] But if cameras are allowed into the courtroom, should they also be permitted in the jury deliberation room? The very idea rubs against the grain of most jurists. "I would never let that happen," roars Richard Huffman, the California appellate court justice. "They'd [broadcast jury deliberations] over my cold broken body, because you are making celebrities out of the jurors."

W. S. Holdsworth claimed it would have been "almost impious" to probe the workings of the early jury, which were equated with a divine process. He wrote, "when the jury was first introduced the method by which it arrived at its verdict inherited the inscrutability of the judgments of God."[13]

Though television had not been invented in 1933, Supreme Court Justice Benjamin Cardozo worried about any breach of privacy for jury deliberations. "Freedom of debate might be stifled and independence of thought checked," he asserted, "if jurors were made to feel that their arguments and ballots were to be freely published to the world."[14]

And two latter-day scholars, Abraham Abramovsky and Jonathan I. Edelstein, suggest: "Jurors may censor themselves to avoid appearing soft on crime, to avoid perceived alignment with unpopular social or political opinion, or simply because they fear appearing foolish on television."[15]

Whatever the risks of recording jury deliberations, there are some who think it is worth taking, at least on a limited, experimental basis when all the parties and jurors agree. Though millions of Americans serve on juries every year, millions more have never served. For them, the jury process is cloaked in mystery, reinvented to some extent by every group of citizens that walks into a jury room. What riper field for public education?

Accordingly, in 1986, the Public Broadcasting Service (PBS) won permission to tape and air the deliberations of a Wisconsin jury debating the fate of Leroy Reed, charged with the unlawful possession of a firearm. Although no one disputed that Reed was technically guilty, jurors were unanimous in finding him not guilty, because they felt he never should have been brought to trial.[16] They engaged in "jury nullification," by acquitting the defendant despite proof of his guilt beyond a reasonable doubt.[17] In effect, they placed the spirit of fairness over the letter of the law. Law Professors Alan Scheflin of Santa Clara University and Jon Van Dyke of the University of Hawaii characterize juries that nullify as "merciful."[18] But do juries tend to be more merciful when they are being televised?

That question arose 11 years later, when CBS News broadcast portions of jury deliberations in three Arizona cases. Again a viewing audience was treated to an example of jury nullification.[19] Modesta Solano was charged with possession and transportation of drugs for sale, after she and co-defendant Urbano Hernandez were caught with four suitcases full of drugs. Solano admitted in a taped conversation that some of the drugs were hers. But after 12 hours of deliberation, the jury hung, six to two, in favor of conviction, because the holdouts were concerned that Solano's co-defendant, who had turned state's evidence, could get off with probation, while Solano faced up to 12½ years in prison for each charge.[20] They thought the discrepancy was unfair, even though Maricopa County Judge Michael Ryan had forbidden jurors to consider punishment.[21]

Interviewed after declaring a mistrial, Judge Ryan described one especially outspoken holdout as legally wrong but morally right. "He just didn't feel comfortable with what went on here, and so he's interjecting his personal and moral beliefs into it … his conscience," said the judge.[22]

In her second trial, also shown in the CBS News special, Modesta Solano was convicted by a new jury, after a 45-minute deliberation.[23] The prosecution usually has an advantage in a retrial because the weaknesses in the state's case have been exposed in the first trial. In Solano's case, the evidence presented at the first trial—and jury deliberations—were analyzed by the judge, jurors and commentators on videotape, giving the prosecution an even greater advantage the second time around.

The two other cases covered by the CBS News program included a robbery trial that ended in conviction and an aggravated assault case that resulted in a hung jury. A retrial of the latter case, which was not televised, produced an acquittal.[24]

Chief Justice Stanley Feldman of the Arizona Supreme Court says granting permission for cameras to enter the jury room to record and broadcast the four proceedings was "a difficult decision." "We are intruding into the sanctity of the jury room," he told CBS News correspondent Ed Bradley, "and there was a fear that we might, by observing, change the—the process, change the result."[25] That concern, in the judge's thinking, was outweighed by the opportunity to educate. If we believe our legal system is so good, said Feldman, the people ought to have a look at it and judge for themselves.[26]

Jurors later denied that the remotely operated cameras had affected them in any way. One said, "The cameras were so inconspicuous" that "you couldn't even tell they were on … you forgot they were there."[27] Could some jurors have been wanting to affirm their independence of thought? Possibly.

Jury consultants at the National Jury Project had always been curious about whether their research was borne out in the jury room. They answer in the affirmative, after watching the CBS News special. Trial consultant Karen Jo Koonan says the dynamics of the juries whose deliberations were broadcast were similar to what they would expect from their research. "It didn't feel foreign," she reports. "Jurors take their roles seriously."

While hardly high profile, the cases chosen for coverage by the PBS and CBS documentaries were not necessarily a cross-section of the justice system. The dynamics of each case are unique. Excluded from consideration for the CBS News special were murder or child molestation trials or cases where jurors might be subject to retaliation. Since all participants, including jurors, had to consent to the broadcast, the jury pool was no longer a random sample of the community. It was a self-selective sample.

But proponents argue that such programs complete the educational function of informing the public about the workings of the justice system. To them, it seems anomalous that people who are permitted to observe a trial from start to finish, and become intimately familiar with every detail of the case, must then be cut off at the jury room door from information about how and why the outcome of the case is determined. If knowing that their deliberations are being recorded for broadcast makes jurors more careful about doing justice instead of self-conscious about what the community expects, perhaps televising them would serve a useful purpose.

But given the traditional sanctity accorded the process, it's hard to imagine that the televising of jury deliberations could become commonplace, especially if winning the permission of all 12 jurors were a prerequisite. If the goal of televising jurors in action is education, it could be argued that there should be hidden cameras, to minimize the possibility of affecting the proceedings. But using hidden cameras, without informing jurors, raises thorny privacy issues. And there are political opponents such as Representative James Libby, the Maine legislator who introduced a bill making it a crime to record jury deliberations. Given the ratings zeal of commercial television stations, he says, "a danger exists that networks may selectively edit in a way that maximizes sensationalism but compromises authenticity."[28]

For now, anyway, it appears that televised jury deliberations will remain the province of documentaries, shot and produced under tightly circumscribed conditions.

Focus on the Future

The proceedings that occur within courtrooms are a different matter. As public information officer for the Los Angeles Superior Court system, Jerrianne Hayslett has been exposed to several hundred cases in which courtroom cameras were an issue. "Cameras, I think, are here to stay," she says, "and I think they will continue to be a growing factor in imparting information to the public, and not just in this country." She receives frequent queries on the subject from abroad. But Hayslett laments what she sees as a lack of a "long-term strategy" to manage cameras in courtrooms. "Judges often do not want to entertain the idea of cameras in the courtroom because that was not taught them in law school," she says. "It wasn't part of their orientation when they became judges. I think it should be."

Then there are the courtrooms themselves, "the courtrooms of pre-camera days," she notes. "Courtroom construction goes on. Yet nobody is building any modifications or any accommodations into their facilities for cameras.[29]

They don't want cameras hanging out there in the courtroom where they're visible to everyone. Is anybody doing anything like having cameras built into the courtroom itself?"

Hayslett raises an important concern. But who would pay the added costs of equipping new courtrooms for television coverage? The court system is perennially strapped for funds. Cases take months and even years to get to trial because of a shortage of available courtrooms and personnel. Would the taxpaying public agree to the added costs of camera-ready courtrooms in the interest of being better informed? Or should commercial broadcast organizations pick up the tab, since their product is ultimately sold for profit? There is precedent of sorts for that in California, where broadcasters absorbed the costs, on a pro-rated basis, for added press room and electrical facilities for the Rodney King beating trials, the Reginald Denny case, the Simpson murder trial and others. Perhaps the added costs of television-friendly courtrooms could be a shared arrangement between broadcasters and taxpayers, since both ultimately benefit.[30]

The profit motive of commercial broadcasting plays into the equation in another respect as well. It drives programming. Just as Court TV needs occasional "ratings-getters" to survive financially, other networks and local stations will generally choose to cover trials with inherent public interest—the legal events viewers *want* to see. That, in turn, may be different from those they *need* to see to have a well-rounded perspective of their judicial system. Saul Halpert, a respected 40-year veteran of Los Angeles local television ratings wars, puts it in less decorous terms: "In picking and choosing what to cover and how, TV news managers generally opt for the sensational and the spectacular over the merely significant. What I learned was that my employers were less overwhelmed by their zeal to serve the public interest than their need to meet the bottom line R & R—ratings and revenue."[31]

Televising trials gavel-to-gavel on a legal equivalent of C-SPAN, the Cable-Satellite Public Affairs Network, would offer the public a non-commercial option, immune from ratings and profit pressures. Harvard law professor Alan Dershowitz once proposed such an entity, which he dubbed "J-SPAN." It would cover the legal system without the need to select flashy cases to attract large audiences.[32] The fare would include routine cases, unedited and with just enough commentary to help a lay audience through legal thickets. The aim: to provide as broad a sampling of the justice system as possible. It's an idea endorsed by *Washington Post* television critic Tom Shales. He wishes Court TV were like C-SPAN with no commercial breaks. "You know," says Shales, "'Before we go to today's murder trial, here's Art Linkletter with a word on life insurance.' I think it lacks dignity."[33]

Replicating the infrastructure of Court TV, however, would be an expensive venture, without the promise of commercial return. Like Court TV, it would only be available to the fraction of Americans equipped with cable service. Unlike

C-SPAN, most of the proceedings covered by a network dedicated to the judicial branch of government do not occur under one roof. Much of C-SPAN's coverage is provided by fixed cameras in the congressional chambers and hearing rooms of the U.S. Capitol. Offering a representative sampling of the judicial process would require an ever-shifting array of camera installations in hundreds of American cities. Who would fund such an enterprise? A non-profit cooperative of the cable industry, such as C-SPAN, is unlikely. That leaves government—and a hard question posed by Court TV founder Steve Brill: "There's two-million trials going on in the United States every year. Who's going to pick from among those two-million?" Dershowitz, says Brill, "can criticize the choices [Court TV] makes, as can anyone, but the whole point of a free press is that you and I get to make the choices, not the government." Perhaps a citizens'advisory committee might choose J-SPAN's broadcast fare. But who would select the members of the advisory panel? And how could the process be kept free of political and legal bias?

These legitimate questions may be premature. At this point, there seems to be no impetus in Washington for creating such a quasi-governmental broadcast entity. That is not surprising, given a federal court system that continues to bar coverage of its proceedings, except for tightly limited experiments. If truly informing the public is our goal, J-SPAN should be a national priority.

Cameras on the Road to Truth and Justice

In the stormy aftermath of the Simpson affair, there is an almost chronic blurring of pretrial publicity, commentary, courtroom camera coverage and out-of-court reporting. Each poses unique, separate issues. It is important for judges, lawyers and the public to understand that in applying antidotes to potential problems. Pretrial publicity raises its own array of problems that may not be solved by banning television coverage of the actual trial. In fact, trial coverage may actually correct some of the inevitable inaccuracies of pretrial stories based on leaks and spin-doctoring. An informed debate becomes critical.

It is all part of the mix of justice in the television age. A trial remains a "search for the truth." But "truth" is an ephemeral concept. In the words of Professor Gerald Uelmen, "No trial has ever exposed the truth. A trial is simply a struggle for an acceptable level of human certainty."[34] The American justice system is adversarial. It should be a contest of worthy opponents. If attorneys on both sides are competent and well-prepared, with comparable resources, the battle will be justly fought. Unfortunately, few defendants have the wealth and access to the legal defense teams enjoyed by O. J. Simpson.

The process must be protected so that justice will prevail. "I stubbornly cling to the vision of our courts as bastions of thoughtful reflection and dispassionate analysis," says Uelmen. "Television cameras do little to enhance either, and can do much to corrupt both." He thinks, however, it "boils down to a question of degree."[35] Broadcasters and First Amendment champions may frown at that dour assessment, which overlooks the potential of a discreetly placed courtroom camera to be part of the public truth-seeking process. As former Attorney General Bell said: "Cameras allow us to witness the commonplace failures, as well as the triumphs, of our legal system."[36] But it is incumbent upon everyone to be reasonable, thoughtful participants in the process—not knee-jerk advocates—and to recognize that there are times when a courtroom camera must give way to legitimate concerns about justice, just as in others it may be its helpmate.

List of Persons Interviewed

S.L. Alexander, associate professor of communications, Loyola University, New Orleans

Barry Bagnato, correspondent, CBS News

Harland Braun, criminal defense attorney, Los Angeles

Elisabeth "Betty" Broderick, defendant, *California v. Broderick*

Steven Brill, founder, Court TV

Charles "Ted" Bumer, criminal defense attorney, San Diego (deceased)

Erwin Chemerinsky, professor of law, University of Southern California School of Law

George "Woody" Clark, deputy district attorney, San Diego

Jessica Cooper, judge, Oakland County, Michigan

Joyce Daubert, plaintiff, *Daubert v. Merrell Dow Pharmaceuticals*

Linda Deutsch, special correspondent, Associated Press

William Dinwiddie, senior deputy sheriff, Los Angeles County

Francine Florio-Bunten, alternate juror, *California v. Simpson*

Robert Gawthrop, U.S. District Court judge, Eastern District of Pennsylvania

Ronald George, chief justice, California Supreme Court

George Gerbner, dean emeritus, Annenberg School for Communication, University of Pennsylvania

Fred Graham, chief anchor, Court TV

David Harris, professor of law, University of Toledo College of Law

Jerrianne Hayslett, public information officer, Los Angeles Superior Court

Lois Heaney, trial consultant, National Jury Project

William Howard, circuit judge, Charleston, South Carolina

Richard Huffman, justice, California Fourth District Court of Appeal

Samuel Jackson, city attorney, Sacramento, California

John Keker, attorney, San Francisco

Kathleen Kennedy-Powell, judge, Municipal Court, Los Angeles

Rikki Klieman, anchor, Court TV

Karen Jo Koonan, trial consultant, National Jury Project

Jill Lansing, criminal defense attorney, Los Angeles

Douglas Larson, attorney, Mesquite, Texas

Jack Litman, criminal defense attorney, New York
Arthur Miller, professor of law, Harvard Law School
Robert Price, probate court judge, Dallas
Bob Rakestraw, juror, first trial, *California v. Erik Menendez*
Kelli Sager, media attorney, Los Angeles
Ira Salzman, criminal defense attorney, Los Angeles
Charles Sevilla, criminal appellate defense attorney, San Diego
Erik Sorenson, executive vice president, Court TV
James Towery, attorney, San Francisco Bay Area
John Tunheim, U.S. District Court judge, Minneapolis
Gerald Uelmen, professor of law, Santa Clara University School of Law
Jerome Wallingford, criminal appellate defense attorney, San Diego
Robert Wandruff, clerk/administrator, California Supreme Court
Laughlin Waters, U.S. District Court judge, Los Angeles
Doron Weinberg, criminal defense attorney, San Francisco
Mike Westergren, district judge, Corpus Christi, Texas
Judy Zamos, alternate juror, first trial, *California v. Lyle Menendez*
Leslie Zoeller, detective, Beverly Hills Police Department

Chapter Notes

Preface

1. Sanders, "Darden Argues Against Cameras in Courtrooms at First Annual Defense Research Institute Meeting," *Chi. Daily L. Bull.*, Oct. 10, 1996, p. 1.

Chapter One

1. 381 U. S. 532, 595–596.
2. Lindner, "Put Out the Camera's Eye in the Courtroom," *Los Angeles Times*, Feb. 19, 1995, p. M6.
3. Brill, "Point Counter Point," *California Bar Journal*, Dec. 1994, p. 12.
4. Transcript, 980 Hearing, *People v. Orenthal James Simpson*, No. BAO97211 (Cal. Super. Ct., Nov. 7, 1994). The prosecution and representatives of the media argued in favor of continuing televised coverage.
5. Associated Press, "Broadcast Coverage Banned from Susan Smith's Trial," *Los Angeles Daily Journal*, Jul. 3, 1995, p. 4.
6. Dobbin, "Critics Wonder—Do Cameras Capture or Cripple Justice?" *The Sacramento Bee*, Aug. 13, 1995, p. A18.
7. Locke, Associated Press, "Judge Rejects TV Coverage of Richard Allen Davis Kidnap-Murder Trial," September 6, 1995.
8. Harris, "The Appearance of Justice: Court TV, Conventional Television and Public Understanding of the Criminal Justice System," 35 *Ariz. L. Rev.* 819–820 (1993).
9. Brandeis, *Other People's Money,* Nat'l. Home Libr. Found Ed. (1933), p. 62.
10. *Richmond Newspapers, Inc. v. Virginia,* 448 U. S. 555, 571 (1980).
11. Transcript, 980 Hearing, *People v. Simpson, supra* note 4.
12. Mecoy, "Simpson Trial Alters Our View of Justice," *The Sacramento Bee*, Aug. 13, 1995, p. A1.
13. David Halberstam, *The Fifties*, Villard Books (N.Y., 1993), p. 678.
14. *Id.* at 679.
15. Cable-Satellite Public Affairs Network, which provides non-commercial coverage of governmental activities, focusing largely on the legislative branch.
16. On September 8, 1995, Judge Ito ruled jurors would be told that retired detective Fuhrman was "not available for further testimony" and his "unavailability" could

be weighed in assessing his credibility as a witness. A day later, however, a state appellate court barred Ito from issuing his proposed instruction.

17. *Nebraska Press Ass'n v. Stuart,* 427 U. S. 539, 547 (1976).

18. *Bridges v. California,* 314 U. S. 252, 260 (1941).

19. *U. S. v. Dickinson,* 465 F.2d 496, 499 (5th Cir. 1972) *cert. denied,* 414 U. S. 797 (1973). Judge Brown was concerned about the free press-fair trial dichotomy.

20. Oh and Yamamoto, "Cameras in the Courtroom Can Destroy the Process," *Criminal Law News* (State Bar of California, Spring 1995), p. 1.

21. Brill, *supra* note 3, at 12.

22. McCarthy, "California Attorneys See Hung Jury in Simpson Trial," *California Bar Journal,* June 1995, p. 6.

23. *Id.*

Chapter Two

1. Ginger, *Six Days or Forever?* Beacon Press (Boston, 1958), p. 103.

2. *Id.* at 96.

3. Milton, *Loss of Eden,* HarperCollins (New York, 1993), p. 300.

4. Hallam, "Some Object Lessons on Publicity in Criminal Trials," 24 *Minn. L. Rev.* 453, 485–486 (1940).

5. Milton, *supra* note 3, at 323.

6. Kennedy, *The Airman and the Carpenter,* Viking (N.Y., 1985), p. 258.

7. *Id.* at 298.

8. *Id.* at 334.

9. *Id.* at 259.

10. Milton, *supra* note 3, at 297.

11. Reed, "Canon 35: Flemington Revisited," Freedom of Information Center Report, No. 177, Mar. 1967, p. 5.

12. Geis, "A Lively Public Issue: Canon 35 in the Light of Recent Events," 43 *The American Bar Association Journal* 420 (1957).

13. *Waco Times Herald,* Dec. 6, 1955.

14. United Press, Atlanta, Dec. 7, 1955.

15. *Waco Times Herald,* Dec. 7, 1955.

16. Geis, *supra* note 12, at 421.

17. Report of Referee in re. Hearings Concerning Canon 35 of the Canons of Judicial Ethics, 17915 Colorado 8 (1956).

18. *In re:* Hearings Concerning Canon 35, 296 P.2d 465, (Colorado 1956).

19. *Estes vs. Texas,* 381 U.S. 532, 551–554 (1965).

20. *Id.* at 578 (citations omitted).

21. *Id.* at 617.

22. *Id.* at 540.

23. *Chandler v. Florida,*449 U. S. 560 (1981).

24. 422 So. 2d 325 (1982).

25. Tello, "Photojournalism Stands Trial with Ronny Zamora in Florida," *News Photographer,* Nov. 1977, pp. 10–12.

26. *Chandler,* 449 U.S. at 562 (emphasis added).

27. See "Summary of Cameras in the State Courts," National Center for State Courts, Feb. 1, 1997.

28. "Cameras in the Courtroom: Florida's Bundy Case Tests the Fairness of Televising Trials," *Time,* July 27, 1979, p. 76.

Chapter Three

1. California voters in 1990 amended the California Constitution to extend the right of a fair trial to the prosecution. Article I, section 29, now reads: "In a criminal case, the people of the state of California have the right to due process of law and to a speedy and public trial."

2. Levy, *Emergence of a Free Press,* Oxford Univ. Press (N.Y., 1985), p. 227.

3. The federal due process clause is contained in the Fifth Amendment to the United States Constitution: "No person shall ... be deprived of life, liberty, or property, without due process of law." The Fourteenth Amendment applies the protection of due process to proceedings in state courts: "No State shall ... deprive any person of life, liberty, or property without due process of law."

4. 273 U.S. 510 (1927).

5. *Id.* at 532.

6. 381 U.S. 532, 540 (1965).

7. See *United States v. Valenzuela-Bernal,* 458 U.S. 858, 867 (1982).

8. *Chambers v. Florida,* 309 U.S. 227, 236–237 (1940).

9. *Estes v. Texas,* 381 U.S. 532, 538–539 (1965).

10. *In re Oliver,* 333 U.S. 257, 270 (1948).

11. Klieman, "But a Camera in the Courtroom Should Not Take the Blame," *Chicago Tribune,* Oct. 10, 1995, p. 15.

12. Newton, Ford & Weinstein, "Fuhrman Tapes Aired: A Recital of Racism, Wrath," *Los Angeles Times,* Aug. 30, 1995, p. A1.

13. *Estes,* 381 U.S. at 535, 545–554.

14. *Sheppard v. Maxwell,* 384 U.S. 333, 335, 358, 362 (1996).

15. *Chandler v. Florida,* 449 U.S. 560, 574–575 (1981).

16. Earl Warren was Chief Justice of the United States Supreme Court from 1953 to 1969; Warren Burger served as Chief Justice from 1969 to 1986.

17. Litman, "Minority Report of the Committee on Audio-Visual Coverage of Court Proceedings," New York, Dec. 1994, p.44.

18. *Evaluation of California's Experiment with Extended Media Coverage of Courts,* Ernest H. Short and Associates, Inc., Sep. 1981, p. 225.

19. Oh and Yamamoto, "Cameras in the Courtroom Can Destroy the Process," *Criminal Law News* (State Bar of California), Spring 1995, p. 1.

20. Litman, "Show Trials? Cameras in the Courtroom Can Easily Prejudice the Rights of the Accused," *Los Angeles Daily Journal,* Feb. 22, 1996, p. 6.

21. Oh and Yamamoto, *supra* note 19, at 2.

22. State Senate Judiciary Committee Hearing on Jury Reform, Jul. 27, 1995, Los Angeles, California.

23. Thaler, *The Watchful Eye: American Justice in the Age of the Television Trial,* Praeger (Conn., 1994), p. 188.

24. Litman, *supra* note 17, at 37.

25. Memorandum from the Criminal Justice Section to the Members of the House of Delegates, New York State Bar Association, Jul. 1994, p. 5.

26. "The Media and the Trial," ABC News Viewpoint, Ted Koppel, Oct. 5, 1995.

27. Thaler, *supra* note 23, at 128, 129.

28. *Id.* at 128.

29. McCall, "Cameras in the Criminal Courtroom: A Sixth Amendment Analysis," 85 *Colum. L. Rev.* 1546, 1557 (1985).

30. *Estes,* 381 U.S. at 547.

31. *Id.* at 549, 568.

32. *Id.* at 548.
33. *Id.*
34. Twenty-ninth annual Roger J. Traynor California Moot Court Competition, Mar. 16, 1997, University of San Diego School of Law.
35. *Estes,* 381 U.S. at 565.
36. Minow and Cate, "Who Is an Impartial Juror in an Age of Mass Media?" 40 *Am. U.L. Rev.* 631, 637, (1991).
37. *Patterson v. Colorado,* 205 U.S. 454, 462 (1906).
38. See Cooley, Bess & Rubin-Jackson, *Madame Foreman, a Rush to Judgment?* Dove Books (Beverly Hills, 1995), pp. 147–165.
39. Kenworthy and Booth, "Bomb Jurors Profoundly Affected; Sympathy Declared for Oklahomans," *The Washington Post,* Jun. 15, 1997, p. A1
40. Leslie Abramson, interview on *Cochran & Grace,* Court TV, Feb. 18, 1997.
41. *Nebraska Press Association v. Stuart,* 427 U.S. 539, 561 (1976).

Chapter Four

1. 331 U.S. 367, 374 (1947).
2. *Press-Enterprise Co. v. Superior Court (Press-Enterprise II)* 478 U.S. 1, 10 (1986).
3. Mapp, Jr., *Thomas Jefferson: Passionate Pilgrim,* Madison Books (Maryland, 1991), p. 133.
4. Brodie, *Thomas Jefferson: An Intimate History,* Norton (N.Y., 1974), p. 406.
5. Transcript, 980 Hearing, *People v. Orenthal James Simpson,* No. BAO97211 (Cal. Super. Ct., Nov. 7, 1994).
6. Chemerinsky and Levenson, "The Ethics of Being a Commentator II," 37 *Santa Clara L. Rev.* 913 (1997)(emphasis added).
7. *Richmond Newspapers, Inc. v. Virginia,* 448 U.S. 555, 569 (1980).
8. *Gannett Co., Inc. v. DePasquale,* 443 U.S. 368, 419 (1979) (Blackmun, J., concurring).
9. *Richmond Newspapers,* 448 U.S. at 565.
10. *Id.* at 566, quoting T. Smith, *De Republica Anglorum 101* (Alston ed., 1972) (emphasis added).
11. *Gannett,* 443 U.S. at 380.
12. *Id.* at 391.
13. *Richmond Newspapers,* 448 U.S. at 580, n. 17. The Supreme Court noted that although it was not called upon in this case to determine whether the public has a right to attend civil trials, civil as well as criminal trials had historically been presumptively open.
14. *Id.*at 587, fn. 3, quoting Justice Powell's dissent in *Saxbe v. Washington Post Co.,* 417 U.S. 843, 862–863 (1974).
15. *Branzburg v. Hayes,* 408 U.S. 665, 681 (1972).
16. *Richmond Newspapers,* 448 U.S. at 581 and n.18.
17. *Id.* at 573; see *Houchins v. KQED, Inc.,* 438 U.S. 1, 8 (1978).
18. Address of Justice Potter Stewart, Yale Law School, Nov. 2, 1974, reprinted in Stewart, "Or of the Press," 26 *Hastings L.J.* 631, 634 (1975).
19. See *Leathers v. Medlock,* 499 U.S. 439, 447 (1991) (Strict Security test applied).
20. See Zimmerman, "Overcoming Future Shock: Estes Revisited, or a Modest Proposal for the Constitutional Protection of the News-Gathering Process," 1980 *Duke L.J.* 641, 667–668 (1980).

21. *Id.*
22. *Anderson v. Cryovac,* 805 F. 2d 1, 9 (1986).
23. *Globe Newspaper Co. v. Superior Court,* 457 U.S. 596, 606–607 (1982).
24. *Id.* at 607–611 and n. 27.
25. *Press-Enterprise Co. v. Superior Court, (Press-Enterprise I)* 464 U.S. 501, 510 (1984).
26. *Nebraska Press Association v. Stuart,* 427 U.S. 539, 561 (1976).
27. *Press-Enterprise II,* 478 U.S. at 7.
28. *Kerley v. United States,* 753 F. 2d 617, 620–622 (7th Cir. 1985).
29. *Id.* at 620 (citing *Globe Newspaper Co. v. Superior Court,* 457 U.S. 596, 606–607 [1982] [emphasis added]).
30. *United States v. Hastings,* 695 F. 2d 1278, 1280–1284 (11th Dis. 1983), cert. den., 461 U.S. 931 (1983).
31. *Kerley,* 753 F. 2d at 621.
32. *Id.* at 621–622.
33. *Chandler v. Florida,* 449 U.S. 560 (1981).
34. *Westmoreland v. Columbia Broadcasting System, Inc.* 752 F. 2d 16–18, 23–24 (2d Cir. 1984), cert. den., 472 U.S. 1017 (1985).
35. *Hastings,* 695 F. 2d at 1283–1284.
36. *Westmoreland,* 752 F. 2d at 23.
37. 923 F. Supp. 580, 589 (1996); rhg. den., 939 F. Supp. 274 (S.D.N.Y. 1996); jud. aff'd., 113 F. 3d 1229 (2d Cir. 1997).
38. Sager & Frederiksen, "Televising the Judicial Branch: In Furtherance of the Public's First Amendment Rights," 69 *S. Cal. L. Rev.* 1519 , 1520, 1549 (1996).
39. *Id.* at 1541, 1549.
40. Abramson (with Flaste), *The Defense Is Ready: Life in the Trenches of Criminal Law,* Simon & Schuster (N.Y., 1997), p. 280.
41. Margolick, "Simpson Judge Sets Hearing on TV and Radio Coverage," *The New York Times,* Oct. 4, 1994, p. A19.
42. 381 U.S. 532, 540.
43. Boyarsky, "Words Without Images Are Half the Story," The Spin, *L.A. Times,* Nov. 26, 1996, p. A26.
44. 570 F. 2d 1080, 1083 (2d. Cir. 1977).
45. *Cable News Network, Inc. v. American Broadcasting,* 518 F. Supp. 1238, 1245 (N.D. Ga. 1981).
46. 14 Ohio App.3d 376, 382–383 (1984). Trials in Ohio, however, are not routinely televised.
47. *Richmond Newspapers,* 448 U.S. at 572–573 (quoting *State v. Schmit,* 139 N.W. 2d 800, 807 (Minn. 1966)) (emphasis added). Although the Supreme Court was unable to agree on a majority opinion in *Richmond Newspapers,* the members of the divided Court did concur in the importance of public access to the appearance of fairness.
48. See *In re Oliver,* 333 U.S. 257, 270 (1948).
49. Thaler, *The Watchful Eye: American Justice in the Age of the Television Trial,* Praeger (Conn., 1994), p. 14 (interview with Jack Litman).
50. Abramson, *supra* note 40.
51. *Cochran & Grace,* Court TV, February 18, 1997.
52. Dershowitz, *Reasonable Doubt: The Criminal Justice System and the O.J. Simpson Case,* Touchstone (N.Y., 1997), pp. 145–146.
53. Piccus, "Demystifying the Least Understood Branch: Opening the Supreme Court to Broadcast Media," 71 *Tex. L. Rev.* 1053, 1087 & nn. 186–187 (1993) (citations omitted).

54. *Richmond Newspapers,* 448 U.S. at 571.

55. Symposium, "Courts and the Mass Media: The Ethical Issues," 37 *Santa Clara Law Review* 991 (1997).

56. Twenty-ninth annual Roger J. Traynor California Moot Court Competition, Mar. 16, 1997, University of San Diego School of Law.

57. Roman, "O.J.'s Defense Banks on Cameras in Court—High-Profile Trials Ended in Acquittals," *The Washington Times,* Nov. 7, 1994.

58. See Thaler, *supra* note 49, at 79 (quoting Volker in Spencer, "Embattled Cameras-in-Courts Bill May Face Close Vote in Senate," 6/8/92 NYLJ 1, [co. 4]).

59. National Victim Center, *Rape in America* (National Victim Center, April 23, 1992), quoted in Thaler, *id.*

60. Transcript, 980 Hearing, *People v. Orenthal James Simpson,* No. BAO97211 (Cal. Super. Ct., Nov. 7, 1994).

61. "Mass Media," *Communications Daily,* Mar. 31, 1997.

62. Panel discussion, San Diego Chapter, Society of Professional Journalists, S.D., Apr. 11, 1996.

63. Letter to W.T. Barry (Aug. 4, 1822), in 9 *Writings of James Madison* 103 (G. Hunt ed., 1910) quoted in *Polilo v. Deane,* 74 N.J. 562 at 571 (1977).

64. Lasswell, *National Security and Individual Freedom,* McGraw-Hill (N.Y., 1950), p. 63.

65. *Pell v. Procunier,* 417 U.S. 817, 839 (1974) (Douglas, J. dissenting).

66. *Saxbe v. Washington Post Co.,* 417 U.S. 843, 863 (1974)(Powell, J., dissenting).

67. 457 U.S. 596, 604 (1982), citing *Mills v. Alabama,* 384 U.S. 214, 218 (1966).

68. Zoglin, "The News Wars," *Time,* Oct. 21, 1996, p. 61.

69. Piccus, *supra* note 53, at 1083 (citing Roper study).

70. Gibson-Carpenter & Carpenter, "Race, Poverty, and Justice: Looking Where the Streetlight Shines," *Kan. J.L. & Pub. Pol'y,* Spring 1994, 99, 106 (citing Roper study).

71. *Richmond Newspapers, Inc. v. Virginia,* at 572–573 (*supra,* n.7) (quoting *Nebraska Press Assn. v. Stuart, 427 U.S. at 587).*

72. Sager & Frederiksen, *supra* note 38, at 1542.

73. Interview with Robert F. Wandruff, Clerk/Administrator of the California Supreme Court.

74. *People v. Romero,* 13 Cal. 4th 497 (1996).

75. Clary, "For Fallen Stop Sign, Vandals Face Life—Criminal Justice: Act, Consequences Merge After 3 Die at Florida Intersection," *Los Angeles Times,* Jun. 11, 1997, pp. A1, A13; Clary, "Deadly Sign Prank Sends 3 to Prison. Law: Young Friends Each Get 15 Years for Pulling Up Stop Sign and Causing Death of Three Teens Whose Car Collided with a Mack Truck," *Los Angeles Times,* Jan. 21, 1997, p. A16.

76. Symposium, *supra* note 55, at 1021.

77. *Estes v. Texas,* 381 U.S. 532 (1965)(Harlan, J., concurring).

78. Uelmen, "Judges Hear the Crocodiles Snapping," *Los Angeles Times,* Feb. 19, 1997, p. M1.

79. Thaler, *supra* note 49, at 80 (citing Petkanas, "Cameras on Trial: An Assessment of the Educational Effects of News Cameras in Trial Courts" [Ph.D. diss., N.Y.U., 1990], p. 112).

80. See chapter 9, *infra.*

81. Symposium, *supra,* note 55, at 989.

82. *Id.* at 990.

83. National Lawyers Guild, panel on Alternative Forms of Legal Practice, Thomas Jefferson School of Law, San Diego, Apr. 10, 1997.

84. Raspberry, "Why Courtroom TV Is Educational," *San Diego Union-Tribune,* Feb. 7, 1997, pp. B6.

85. Arenella, "O.J. Lessons," 69 *S. Cal. L. Rev.* 1233, 1257 (1996).

86. Harris, "The Appearance of Justice: Court TV, Conventional Television, and Public Understanding of the Criminal Justice System," 35 *Ariz. L. Rev.* 785, 814 (1993) (citing Centers for Disease Control, U.S. Dep't. of Health and Human Services, No. 41, *Morbidity and Morality Weekly Report* 3 [May 29, 1992]).

87. *Id.*

88. Hodgkins, "Throwing Open a Window on the Nation's Courts by Lifting the Ban on Federal Courtroom Television," 4-*Spg Kan J. L. & Pub. Pol'y* 89, Spr. 1995.

89. Interview with Senior U.S. District Judge Laughlin E. Waters.

90. Serrano, "McVeigh Trial Begins Amid Tight Security," *Los Angeles Times,* Apr. 1, 1997, p. A3.

91. Scott, "With No Cameras in Court, Trial Didn't Mesmerize," *New York Times,* Jun. 4, 1997, p. D23.

92. Gerbner, "Trial by Television: Are We at the Point of No Return?" 63 *Judicature* 416, 424 (1980) (citing White, "Cameras in the Courtroom: A U.S. Survey," 60 *Journalism Monographs* 26 [April 1979]).

93. See Remshak, "Truth, Justice, and the Media: An Analysis of the Public Criminal Trial," 6 *Seton Hall Const. L. J.* 1083, 1116, fns. 121–123 (1996)(extent of coverage); Alexander, "The Impact of *California v. Simpson* on Cameras in the Courtroom," 79 *Judicature* 169 (1996).

94. Roman, *supra* note 57.

95. Laurence, "A Night of Decisions for TV Execs, Viewers—Big News Events Anguished Networks, Channel Surfers," *San Diego Union-Tribune,* Feb. 5 1997, p. A11.

96. Gabler, "Where Entertainment Rules," *Los Angeles Times,* Feb. 9, 1997, p. M1.

97. King, "A Long, Slow Trip in the Process of Justice," *Los Angeles Times,* Feb. 5, 1997, p. A1.

98. Gabler, *supra* note 96.

99. Power, "Television in the Courtroom: Von Bulow and the Jazz Singer," 25 *St. Louis Univ. L. J. 813–820* (1928), quoted in Barber, *News Cameras in the Courtroom: A Free Press-Fair Trial Debate,* Ablex (N.J., 1989), p. 114.

100. Krikorian, "Committee Hearing a Trial by Fire for the Jury System." *Los Angeles Times,* July 28, 1995, p. B3.

101. Abramson, *supra* note 40, at 281.

102. Hernandez, "Courtroom Cameras Debated," 2/17/96 *Editpub* 11.

103. Scott, *supra* note 91.

104. *Richmond Newspapers,* 448 U.S. at 572 (citations omitted).

105. Clark (with Carpenter), *Without a Doubt,* Viking (N.Y., 1997), p. 486.

106. 448 U.S. at 571.

Chapter Five

1. Justice Huffman, addressing the Psychological Law Society, San Diego, Apr. 26, 1997.

2. Ernest H. Short & Associates, Inc., *Evaluation of California's Experiment with Extended Media Coverage of Courts* (1981).

3. Hoyt, "Courtroom Coverage: The Effects of Being Televised," 21 *J. of Broadcasting* 487 (1977).

4. Borgida, DeBono and Buckman, "Cameras in the Courtroom: The Effects of Media Coverage on Witness Testimony and Juror Perceptions," 14 *Law and Human Behavior,* 489 (1990).

5. *Estes v. Texas,* 381 U. S. 532, 547 (1965).
6. *Id.* at 570.
7. Memorandum from D. M. F., Law Clerk for Chief Justice Warren, Chief Justice Earl Warren 1 (Apr. 12, 1965) (Earl Warren Papers, Library of Congress).
8. Clark (with Carpenter), *Without a Doubt,* Viking (N.Y., 1997), p. 485.
9. Uelmen, *Lessons from the Trial,* Andrews and McMeel (K.C., 1996), p. 97. Interviewed by the authors, Attorney Kelli Sager, who represented several media outlets, questioned Uelmen's assessment, noting that camera-related hearings consumed a matter of hours in a trial that lasted eight and a half months and the longest of the hearings, on November 7, 1994, occurred before the trial began.
10. *Id.* at 92.
11. Ruby, a Dallas nightclub owner, shot and killed Lee Harvey Oswald, the accused assassin of President John F. Kennedy, as he was being transferred between jail facilities on November 24, 1963. A large contingent of news cameramen captured the attack on film.
12. Darden, *In Contempt,* Harpercollins (N.Y., 1996), p. 260.
13. Administrative Order—Cameras in the Courtroom, West Maine's Rules of Court, Administrative Orders of the Supreme Judicial Court, 1996.
14. Panel discussion, Psychological Law Society, San Diego, Apr. 26, 1997.
15. Shartel, "Cameras in the Courts: Early Returns Show Few Side Effects," 7 No. 4 *INLIT.* 1, 23, Apr. 1993.
16. *Commonwealth v. Woodward,* No. 97-0433, Memorandum and Order, Nov. 10, 1997, p.l.
17. See CALJIC No. 5.17; *People v. McKelvy,* 194 Cal. App. 3d 694, 703 (1987).
18. Judge Weisberg declined to be interviewed since an appeal was pending.
19. Thaler, *The Watchful Eye: American Justice in the Age of the Television Trial,* Praeger (Conn., 1994), pp. 16–17.
20. Arenella, "Foreword: O. J. Lessons," 69 *S. Cal. L. Rev.* 4, May 1996, pp. 1254–1255.
21. *Id.* at 1256.
22. *Id.* at 1257.

Chapter Six

1. Shogren, "Clinton 'Troubled' by Racial Gulf Over Simpson Verdicts," *Los Angeles Times,* Feb. 12, 1997, A26.
2. "Courts and the Mass Media: The Ethical Issues," Markkula Center for Applied Ethics, Santa Clara University School of Law, Jan. 24, 1997.
3. 360 U.S. 310–312.
4. *Sheppard v. Maxwell,* 384 U.S. 333, 335, 338–340 (1966).
5. *Id.* at 340–344.
6. *Id.* at 345.
7. *Id.* at 362–363.
8. Moran and Cutler, "The Prejudicial Impact of Pretrial Publicity," 52 *Guild Practitioner* 1 (1995).
9. Roman, "O.J.'s Defense Banks on Cameras in Court—High Profile Trials Ended in Acquittals," *The Washington Times,* Nov. 7, 1994, p. A3.
10. "TV Issue Delays Kennedy Smith Jury Selection," *Star-Tribune* (Mpls.-St.Paul), Oct. 30, 1991, p. 16A, from *Washington Post.*

11. Shartel, "Cameras in the Courts: Early Returns Show Few Side Effects," 7 No. 4 *INLIT.* 1, Apr. 1993.

12. Roberts, "Judges Still Touchy on TV in Court," *Los Angeles Daily Journal*, Apr. 30, 1996, p.8.

13. Kolkey, "Should Cameras Be Banned from California's Courts?" Point Counter Point, *Cal. Bar Jour.*, Feb. 1996, p. 12.

14. *United States v. Oliver L. North*, 910 F. 2d 843, 851–852, 855, 872 (1990).

15. Transcript, 980 Hearing, *People v. Orenthal James Simpson*, No. BAO97211 (Cal. Super. Ct., Nov. 7, 1994).

16. The rule in effect at that time already prohibited camera shots that identified individual jurors.

17. See Associated Press, "Judge Refuses to Remove Wall Shielding Bombing Jury," *Los Angeles Times*, Apr. 27, 1997, p. A14.

18. Transcript, 980 Hearing, *People v. Simpson, supra* note 15.

19. *Id.*

20. Alexander, "The Impact of *California v. Simpson* on Cameras in the Courtroom," 79 *Judicature* 169, 172 (1996).

21. Halpert, "Court-Jester TV. Trials Work Better If They're Not Media Circuses," *Los Angeles Daily Journal*, Jun. 17, 1997, p. 6.

22. See Tarlow, "Robert Shapiro Recalls the 'Trial of the Century,'" 23 *CACJ Forum* 146–147 (1996).

23. Wilson, *Headline Justice Inside the Courtroom: The Country's Most Controversial Trials*, Thunder's Mouth Press (N.Y., 1997), p. 13.

24. Arenella, "Foreword: O.J. Lessons," People v. Simpson: Perspectives on the Implications for the Criminal Justice System, 69 *S.Cal.L.Rev.* 1233, 1265, fn. 58 (1996).

25. "Courts and the Mass Media: The Ethical Issues," *supra* note 2.

26. Arenella, "Televising High Profile Trials: Are We Better Off Pulling the Plug?" 37 *Santa Clara L. Rev.* 894 (1997).

27. Litman, "Show Trials? Cameras in the Courtroom Can Easily Prejudice the Rights of the Accused," *Los Angeles Daily Journal*, Feb. 22, 1996, p. 26.

28. 90 *Nw. U. L. Rev.* 863, 888, 891 (1996).

29. Dershowitz, *Reasonable Doubts: The Criminal Justice System and the O.J. Simpson Case*, Touchstone (N.Y., 1997), pp. 140, 142.

30. Shapiro, "Using the Media to Your Advantage," NACDL *The Champion*, Jan.-Feb. 1993, pp. 7–12.

31. Arenella, *supra* note 24, at 1265.

32. See McLuhan, *Understanding Media: The Extensions of Man*, McGraw-Hill (N.Y., 1964), chapter 1.

33. Uelmen, *Lessons from the Trial*, Andrews & McMeel (K.C.: 1996), p. 95.

34. 37 *Santa Clara L. Rev.* 913 (1997).

35. Panel on Cameras in the Courtroom, San Diego Chapter, Society of Professional Journalists, San Diego, May 11, 1996.

36. "Courts and the Mass Media: The Ethical Issues," *supra* note 2.

37. Arenella, *supra* note 24, at 1257.

38. Arenella, *supra* note 26, at 894.

39. *Id.* at fn. 39.

40. Gewirtz, *supra* note 28, at 888.

41. *Id.* at 887.

42. *Id.*

43. Arenella, *supra* note 24, at 1256–1257.

44. "Courts and the Mass Media: The Ethical Issues," *supra* note 2.

45. Howard, "We Pursue Different Objectives … They Aren't Always Compatible," Cameras in the Courtroom, *Quill*, Oct. 1996, p. 25.

46. Arenella, *supra* note 37.

Chapter Seven

1. *Chandler v. Florida*, 449 U.S. 560, 579 (1981), citing *New State Ice Co. v. Liebmann*, 285 U.S. 262, 311 (1932) (Brandeis, J., dissenting)(emphasis added).

2. 381 U.S. 532 (1965).

3. 449 U.S. at 560.

4. Geis, "A Lively Public Issue: Canon 35 in the Light of Recent Events," 43 *A.B.A.J.* 419, 420 (1957).

5. Strickland and Moore, "Cameras in State Courts: A Comparative Examination of Experimental Versus Permanent Usage by State," paper presented at the 1994 Annual Meeting of the American Political Science Association, The New York Hilton, Sep. 1–4, 1994, p. 5.

6. *Estes*, 381 U.S. at 535.

7. *Id.* at 551–552.

8. See "News Media Coverage of Judicial Proceedings with Cameras and Microphones: A Survey of the States," Radio-Television News Directors Association (RTNDA), Jan. 1997, pp. A-5—A-89.

9. Dyer and Hauserman, "Electronic Coverage of the Courts: Exceptions of Exposure," 75 *Geo. L. J.* 1633, 1643 (1987).

10. Strickland & Moore, *supra* note 5, at 7.

11. Rule 18c, Texas Rules of Civil Procedure, Texas Rules of Court-State, 1996, p. 15; Rule 21, West's Texas Rules of Court, Texas Rules of Appellate Procedure, Sec. 2, West 1997; Slover, "Return of Cameras to Texas Courts Hailed as a Success," *The Dallas Morning News*, Dec. 4, 1990, p. 24A.

12. Slover, *id.*

13. *Id.*

14. Hanna, "Camera Coverage of Griffin Trial Could Open Door for More," *The Fort Worth Star-Telegram*, Apr. 20, 1991, p. 22.

15. *Id.*

16. *Id.*

17. "Cameras Banned in Hutchison Trial. Senator Didn't Want Foes Using Pictures in Campaign Ads," *The Dallas Morning News*, Feb. 2, 1994, p. 25A.

18. *Id.*

19. Associated Press, "Houston Prepares for Media Rush Before Trial in Selena Slaying. Official Juggles Courtroom-Access Requests from 80 News Organizations," *The Dallas Morning News*, Sep. 8, 1995, p. 27A.

20. Rule 18 c(b), *supra*, note 11.

21. Associated Press, *supra* note 19.

22. *Id.*

23. Associated Press, "Judge in Selena Trial Reconsiders Role of Cameras in Courtroom," *The Dallas Morning News*, Apr.14, 1996, p. 43A.

24. Korosec, "Cameras Banned in the Courtroom for Irvin Drug Trial. The Judge Presiding Over the Football Star's Case Takes Pre-emptive Measures to Curb Publicity, Although a Trial Date Has Not Been Set," *The Fort Worth Star-Telegram*, Apr. 10, 1996, p. 15; "Dallas Cowboys Football Star Sentenced to Probation on Drug Charges," *Agence France-Press*, Jul. 16, 1996.

25. Korosec, *id.*

26. *Id.*

27. *Agence France-Press, supra* note 24.

28. Brokaw (anchor), Newscast: "Drug Trial for Dallas Cowboy Star Michael Irvin to Continue Despite Alleged Murder Attempt," NBC Nightly News, Jun. 28, 1996.

29. Dyer and Hauserman, *supra* note 9, at 1645.

30. *Id.* at 1643–1644.

31. *Petition of Post-Newsweek Stations, Florida, Inc. for Change in Code of Judicial Conduct,* 327 So. 2d 1 (1976).

32. *In re Petition of Post-Newsweek Stations, Florida, Inc. for Change in Code of Judicial Conduct,* 347 So. 2d 402 (1977).

33. *Id.*

34. Strickland and Moore, *supra* note 5, at 9.

35. *Zamora v. Florida,* 422 So. 2d 325, 326, 328 (1982).

36. Report of Judge Paul Baker to the Supreme Court of Florida Re: The Conduct of Audiovisual Trial Coverage in *Florida v. Zamora,* 1979, cited in Strickland and Moore, *supra* note 5, at 9–10.

37. Jopling & Jopling, "Perspective from the Bench," in Roschwalb and Stack, eds., *Litigation Public Relations: Courting Public Opinion,* Rothman & Co. (Cal., 1995) p. 165.

38. *Id.* at 166.

39. *Id.* at 166–167.

40. Kimberly's body was discovered in Live Oak, thirty miles from the even smaller town of Lake City, where she lived.

41. *Id.* at 167–168.

42. *Id.* at 169.

43. *Id.* at 170, quoting *Theodore Robert Bundy (Appellant) v. State of Florida (Appellee),* Vol. 72, pp. 16–17.

44. *Id.* at 171. (excerpt of letter written to the court by representatives of 18 press organizations).

45. *Petition of Post-Newsweek Stations, Florida, Inc.,* 370 So. 2d 764, 781 (1979).

46. *Id.* at 781.

47. *Id.* at 779.

48. Hoyt, "Prohibiting Courtroom Photography: It's Up to the Judge in Florida and Wisconsin," 63 *Judicature* 290, 293 (1980); *Chandler,* 449 U.S. at 562–577.

49. Gardner, "Cameras in the Courtroom: Guidelines for State Criminal Trials," 84 *Mich. L. Rev.* 475, 501 (1985).

50. *Estes,* 381 U.S. at 540.

51. *Chandler,* 449 U.S. at 567.

52. *Id.* at 562.

53. *Id.* at 568.

54. *Id.*

55. *Id.* at 572–575.

56. *Id.* at 575–576, fn. 11, 581.

57. *Id.* at 582–583.

58. See Gardner, at p. 478 and fn. 20 (*supra,* n.49).

59. *Chandler,* 449 U.S. at 564, fn. 6.

60. Richter, "Smith Attorneys Want TV Barred at Trial–Judiciary: They Argue That Coverage Will Influence Jurors, but Florida Law Permits Cameras in Courtroom. Data on Alleged Victim's Sex, Drug Histories Sought," *Los Angeles Times,* Jul. 30, 1991, p. 16.

61. Cauchon and Mauro, "Video Justice. Tonight, Real-life Courtroom Drama

Opens Its Case on TV. Viewers See 'L.A. Law' Isn't Real Law," *USA Today,* Jun. 21, 1991, p. 1A.

62. *Id;* Alexander, "Cameras in the Courtroom: A Case Study," 74 *Judicature* 307, 313 (1991).

63. Alexander, *id.*

64. Zeman, "Smith Pleads Not Guilty Amid Courtroom Salvos, Media Frenzy," *Houston Chronicle,* Jun. 1, 1991, p. 3.

65. Holbert, "Made for TV. William Kennedy Smith's Trial Cries Out for Coverage," *Chicago Sun-Times,* Aug. 8, 1991, p. 55.

66. Rosenberg, "T.V.'s Smith Trial: Welcome to Law 101," *Los Angeles Times,* Dec. 4, 1991, p. F-1; Wire Reports, "Names of Smith Jurors to Be Kept Secret," *The Ft. Worth Star-Telegram,* Nov. 7, 1991, p. 10.

67. *Id.*

68. *Id.*

69. Hutcheson, "Video Coverage Makes Rape Trial Larger Than Life," *The Ft. Worth Star-Telegram,* Dec. 13, 1991, p. 1.

70. *Id.*

71. Kogan, "Dahmer Case Comes to Cable's Court TV," *The Baltimore Evening Sun,* Jan. 28, 1992, p. C6.

72. Roman, "O.J.'s Defense Banks on Cameras in Court—High Profile Trials Ended in Acquittals," *The Washington Times,* Nov. 7, 1994, p. A3.

73. Temporary Rule 981; see Photographing, Recording, and Broadcasting in the Courtroom—Guidelines for Judicial Officers, Judicial Council of California, 1997, p. 1.

74. *Final Report of the Subcommittee on Free Press-Fair Trial,* 23 Assembly Interim Committee Reports 8 (1965–1966).

75. *Id.* at 9.

76. *Id.* at 24.

77. *Id.* at 1; *News Media Coverage of Judicial Proceedings with Cameras and Microphones: A Survey of the States* (as of January 1, 1997), Radio-Television News Directors Association (RTNDA), 1997, p. A-12; *Evaluation of California's Experiment with Extended Media Coverage of Courts,* Ernest H. Short and Associates, Inc. ("Short Report") Sep. 1981, pp. 1, 15.

78. Short Report, *id.* at 1.

79. Cameras in Court, California Judicial Council 1985 Report to the Governor and the Legislature, p. 24.

80. Short Report, *supra* note 77, at 6.

81. *Id.* at 218, 221–223, 225.

82. *Id.* at 43.

83. *Id.* at 224.

84. Rule 980, California Rules of Court, *West's Annotated California Codes,* 1995.

85. 221 Cal. App. 3d 1362 (1990).

86. *Id.* at 1367.

87. *Id.* at 1368–1369 (emphasis added).

88. Rule 980, *California Rules of Court* (effective Jan. 1, 1997), West Group, 1998, p. 173 (emphasis added).

89. See also, Weinstein, "More Judges Expected to Ban Cameras in Court," *Los Angeles Times,* Jul. 14, 1996, p. B-3.

90. *Id.*

91. The judge allowed each brother to be judged by a separate jury to avoid prejudice; some incriminating evidence against one brother would not be admissible against the other.

92. Pringle, "California Debates Pulling Cameras from Courts," *The Dallas Morning News*, Mar. 8, 1996, p. 43A.

93. Pringle, "Lights Out for TV in Courts? State Eyes Judicial Ban—O.J. Trial 'Trauma' Stokes Battle Over Camera Prohibition," *The San Diego Union-Tribune*, Feb. 5, 1996, p. A3.

94. Sweeney, "No Acquittal for Justice System. Case May Influence Future of Courts," *The Press Democrat* (Santa Rossa, CA), Oct. 4, 1995, p. A3.

95. Lewis, "Capitol Panel Rejects Ban on Court Cameras," *Los Angeles Daily Journal*, Apr. 11, 1996, p. 8.

96. "California Judge Recommends Limits on TV Coverage in Courts," *International Herald Tribune*, Feb. 26, 1996.

97. Associated Press, "Judges' Leaders Vote Narrowly to Keep Cameras," Feb. 13, 1996; Roberts, "CJA Rejects Banning TV from Courts—Proposed Revision to Give Guidance on Camera Access—Discretion Preserved," *Los Angeles Daily Journal*, Feb. 13, 1996, p. 1.

98. Editorial, "Judges Should Retain TV Option; They, Not Sacramento, Should Decide Court Issues," *Los Angeles Times*, Feb. 14, 1996, Part-B.

99. Weinstein, "TV Cameras in Court Gain State Bar's Backing—Trials: President Cites Public's Right to Know. Judges Would Still Have Discretion to Pull the Plug," *Los Angeles Times*, Apr. 21, 1996, p. A3; Ziegler, "Cameras in Courts Supported by Bar," *Los Angeles Daily Journal*, Apr. 23, 1996.

100. Weinstein, *id.* at p. A27.

101. Roberts, "Court Cameras a Touchy Issue to Some Jurists," *Los Angeles Daily Journal*, Apr. 30, 1996, pp. 1, 8.

102. Dolan, "State Task Force Urges Curbs on Camera Use in Courtroom," *Los Angeles Times*, Feb. 23, 1996, p. A3.

103. Dolan, "State Panel Puts Partial Ban on Court Cameras," *Los Angeles Times*, May 18, 1996, p. A19.

104. Lewis, "Panel Calls for Partial Ban on Use of Cameras," *Los Angeles Daily Journal*, Feb. 23, 1996, p. 1.

105. Dolan, "Courtroom Camera Plan Called Compromise—Law: Official Says Partial Ban Aims to Appease the News Media and the Judges Who Favor a Total Prohibition," *Los Angeles Times*, Feb. 24, 1996, p. A22.

106. Egelko, "Media, Wilson, Judges Clash Over Camera Access," Associated Press Political Service, Jan. 8, 1996; Cooper, "Pleas For, Against Cameras in Court," *The Sacramento Bee*, Jan. 9, 1996, p. B3.

107. "Judge Urges Ban on Courtroom Cameras," News—Bay Datelines, *San Francisco Examiner*, Jan. 9, 1996, p. A4.

108. Cooper, *supra* note 106.

109. Egelko, *supra* note 106.

110. Dolan, *supra* note 105.

111. Rule 980, *supra* note 88, at 173–175.

112. *Id.*

113. *Id.*

114. *Id.*

115. Willis, "Judicial Panel Rejects Ban on News Cameras in Court," *San Diego Union-Tribune*, May 18, 1996, p. A1.

116. Part of Judge Fujisaki's order was eventually relaxed by a higher court. Sketch artists were allowed in.

117. Transcript, *Sharon Rufo v. Orenthal James Simpson*, No. SCO31947 (Cal. Super. Ct., Aug. 23, 1996).

118. See, Alexander, "The Impact of *California v. Simpson* on Cameras in the Courtroom," 79 *Judicature* 169 (1996).
119. See e.g., Associated Press, "Jurist Calls for Cameras at Criminal Trials," *Times Union*, Jan. 9, 1997, p. B2; Stashenko, "Leaders Say O.J. Trial Has Affected Cameras-in-Courtroom View," Associated Press, Mar. 4, 1997; "Report of the Committee on Audio-Visual Coverage of Court Proceedings," May 1994, p. 104; Litman, "Minority Report of the Committee on Audio-Visual Coverage of Court Proceedings," Dec. 1994.
120. See "News Media Coverage of Judicial Proceedings with Cameras and Microphones: A Survey of the States (as of January 1, 1997)," Radio-Television News Directors Association (RTNDA), Jan. 1997.
121. Theobald, "Cameras Will Get a Shot in Court. State Supreme Court Only Will Be Opened on Experimental Basis, the Chief Justice Says," *The Indianapolis Star*, Sep. 1, 1996, p. B1.
122. See Supreme Court of Tennessee, in Re: Media Coverage—Supreme Court Rule 30, Dec. 30, 1996, West 1997; West's North Dakota Court Rules, North Dakota Supreme Court Administrative Rule 21, 1997; Administrative Rule 16, Supreme Court Administrative Rules, Missouri Court Rules, West 1997; West's Missouri Court Rules, 1997.
123. West's Idaho Rules of Court, Order in Re: Cameras in the Courtroom Committee, 1997.
124. See "Summary of Cameras in the State Courts," National Center for State Courts, Feb. 1, 1997.

Chapter Eight

1. "Souter Won't Allow Cameras in High Court," *Los Angeles Times*, Apr. 9, 1996, p. A6.
2. *Id.*
3. Biskupic, "Vote on Cameras Reveals Judges' Deep Concerns; Mistrust of Media Is Called a Factor in Decision Against Televising Federal Court Hearings," *The Washington Post*, Sept. 23, 1994, p. A3.
4. Murray, "Warren Burger Dies at Age 87; Served 17 Years as Chief Justice," *The Washington Times*, June 26, 1995, p. A1.
5. Savage, "Former Chief Justice Warren Burger Dies at 87. Judiciary: Conservative Nixon Appointee's Court Was Surprisingly Liberal. Clinton Hails Jurist's 'Tireless Service,'" *Los Angeles Times*, June 26, 1995, p. Al.
6. Briseno and Timothy Wind were acquitted. Laurence Powell and Stacey Koon were convicted of violating King's civil rights and served federal prison terms.
7. Federal Judicial Center, "Electronic Media Coverage of Federal Civil Proceedings—An Evaluation of the Pilot Program in Six District Courts and Two Courts of Appeals" (Wash. D.C., 1994) p. 3.
8. *Id.*
9. *Westmoreland v. Columbia Broadcasting System*, 752 F. 2d 16, 17 (1984).
10. Report of the Judicial Conference Ad Hoc Committee on Cameras in the Courtroom 7 (Sept. 6, 1984).
11. *United States v. Kerley*, 753 F. 2d 617, 622 (1985).
12. Jessell, "Courtroom Doors Begin to Open for TV, Radio," *Broadcasting & Cable*, Sep. 3, 1990, p. 25.
13. Federal Judicial Center, *supra* note 7, at 43.
14. *Id.* at 7.

15. Reske, "No More Cameras in Federal Courts: Judicial Conference Ends Experiment Despite Few Complaints from Judges," *80-NOV A.B.A. J.* 28 (1994).

16. *Id.*

17. Shartel, "Judicial Conference's Camera Ban Only Delays the Inevitable," *8 NO. 9 INLIT.* 2, Oct. 1994.

18. Federal Judicial Center, *supra* note 7, at 24.

19. *Marisol v. Guiliani*, 929 F. Supp. 660, 661 (S. D. N. Y. 1996).

20. Greenhouse, "Appeals Courts Get Permission to Use TV," *New York Times News Service*, Mar. 13, 1996.

21. Friendly, "On Judging the Judges, in State Courts: A Blueprint for the Future" 70, 72, National Center for State Courts (1978).

22. Mauro, "Justices Keep Out Cameras, Preserve Their Rite of Privacy," *Washington Journalism Review*, Nov. 1988, p. 24.

23. *Id.*

24. Goldfarb, "Cameras in the Courtroom Will Keep Justice in Balance," *Seattle Post-Intelligencer*, May 7, 1996, p. A15.

25. *Stanford Observer*, Fall 1995, p. 17.

26. Graham, "We Want Our Supreme Court TV. A Veteran Court Watcher Explains Why the Justices Won't Allow TV Coverage—and Why They Should," *TV Guide*, Apr. 2, 1994, pp. 34–36.

27. *Id.*

28. *Id.*

29. *Id.*

30. Miner, "Eye on Justice," lecture reprinted in 67 *New York State Bar Journal* 8, Feb. 1995.

31. Goldberg, "The 'L' Judge—Outspoken Jurist Carries Conscience of Court, Some Say," *Los Angeles Daily Journal*, Feb. 20, 1997, p. 1.

32. Mauro, "'Ancient Reluctance' Bids the Robed Ones," *USA Today*, Aug. 20, 1993, p. 2A.

33. Graham, *supra* note 26.

34. Santos, "Ginsburg Says VMI Work 'Exhilarating'—She Wrote Opinion Killing Men-only Rule," *Richmond Times-Dispatch*, Mar. 8, 1997, p. B4.

35. 492 U. S. 490 (1989).

36. Rosensteil, "Abortion Issue Quickly Segues into the TV Spotlight," *Los Angeles Times,* July 4, 1989, p. A27.

37. Slotnick, "Media Coverage of Supreme Court Decision Making: Problems and Prospects, 75 *Judicature* 128, 130 (1991).

38. Weinstein, "Scalia Defends 'Immovable' Constitution," *Los Angeles Times*, Jan. 24, 1997, p. B1.

39. 923 F. Supp. 580 (1966).

40. *Id.* at 588; see Pines, "TV Cameras Allowed in U.S. Court—'Presumptive Right' Seen in Constitution," *New York Law Journal*, May 1, 1996, p. 1.

41. 42 U.S.C.A. section 10608 (West 1996).

Chapter Nine

1. Court TV Viewer's Guide, p. 3, referring to the long-running NBC television courtroom-based drama series, *L. A. Law.*

2. Regular programming is augmented by "infomercials" during the early morning hours when viewership is sparse.

3. Castaeda, "In The Spotlight—O. J., Other High Profile Cases Benefit Court TV, but Controversy Over Televised Trials Is Renewed," *The Dallas Morning News*, Oct. 22, 1995, p. 1H.

4. "Court TV's Steve Brill: Witness for a Nation," interview by *Broadcasting & Cable*, Feb. 6, 1995, p 44.

5. Meisler, "Bochco Is Trying a Novel Idea with His 'Murder One,'" *Plain Dealer* (Cleveland), Oct. 8, 1995, p. 7K.

6. Harris, "The Appearance of Justice: Court TV, Conventional Television and Public Understanding of the Criminal Justice System," 35 *Ariz. L. Rev.* 785, 821 (1993).

7. *Id.* at 822.

8. "Facts and Opinions About Cameras in Courtrooms," Court TV informational publication, Appendix A, July 1995.

9. Transcript, 980 Hearing, *People v. Orenthal James Simpson*, No. BAO97211 (Cal. Super. Ct., Nov. 7, 1994).

10. Brill, addressing the San Diego Inns of Court, Jan. 17, 1996.

11. Brill, addressing the American Civil Liberties Union of Southern California, Los Angeles, May 24, 1995 (from transcript published in *Texas Lawyer*, June 12, 1995).

12. *Id.*

13. Aarons, "Time Warner Buys Out Brill's Share of Court TV, Publications," *Los Angeles Daily Journal*, Feb. 20, 1997, p. 1.

14. Strahinich, "Court TV's Rising Star," *The Boston Globe Magazine*, Mar. 19, 1995, p. 24.

15. Advertisement, *New York Times*, June 23, 1997.

16. Moore, "Trial by Wire: Court TV's Erik Sorenson Courts New Viewers," Associated Press, Aug. 18, 1997.

17. Abramson (with Flaste), *The Defense Is Ready: Life in the Trenches of Criminal Law*, Simon & Schuster (N.Y., 1997), p. 281.

18. See chapter 7, p. 105.

19. Harris, *supra* note 6, at 827.

20. Moore, *supra* note 16.

Chapter Ten

1. Uelmen, "*Leaks, Gags and Shields: Taking Responsibility,*" 37 *Santa Clara L. Rev.* 947 (1997).

2. Stephen, "Prejudicial Publicity Surrounding a Criminal Trial: What a Trial Court Can Do to Ensure a Fair Trial in the Face of a 'Media Circus,'" 26 *Suffolk U. L. Rev.* 1063, 1071 (1992).

3. *Sheppard v. Maxwell*, 384 U.S. 333, 342, 345 (1966).

4. *Id.* at 339.

5. *Id.* at 363.

6. Stephen, *supra* note 2, at 1074.

7. *United States v. DeLorean*, 729 F. 2d 1174, 1178–79 (citing district court opinion).

8. *Id.* at 1182.

9. Takasugi, "Jury Selection in a High-Profile Case: United States v. DeLorean," 40 *Am. U. L. Rev.* 837, 839, n. 84.

10. *Id* at 840.

11. Breheny and Kelly, "Maintaining Impartiality: Does Media Coverage of Trials Need to Be Curtailed?" 10 *St. John's J. Legal Comment* 371 (1995).

12. Uelmen, *supra* note 1, at 976, citing *Mu'Min v. Virginia*, 500 U.S. 415 (1991).

13. Whitebread & Contreras, "Free Press v. Fair Trial: Protecting the Criminal Defendant's Rights in a Highly-Publicized Trial by Applying the Sheppard-Mu'Min Remedy," 69 S. *Cal. L. Rev.* 1587, 1622 (1996).

14. *United States v. Simon*, 664 F. Supp. 780, 794 (S.D.N.Y, 1987).

15. Stabile, "Free Press-Fair Trial: Can They Be Reconciled in a Highly Publicized Criminal Case?" 79 *Geo. L. J.* 337, 344 (1990), citing *Gulf Oil v. Gilbert*, 330 U.S. 501, 508–9 (1947).

16. Weinstein and Rutten, "TV and Legal Wrangling Bog Down O. J. Trial," *Los Angeles Times*, April 16, 1995, p. A1.

17. Chiang, "Isolating a Jury Can Backfire—As Judge Ito Is Discovering," *San Francisco Chronicle*, May 3, 1995, p. A3.

18. Cossack, "What You See Is Not Always What You Get: Thoughts on the O. J. Trial," 14 *J. Marshall J. Computer & Info L.* 555, 557 (1996).

19. Bunting, "Jury in Penn Retrial Sequestered at Its Own Request," *Los Angeles Times*, July 14, 1987, p. B-2.

20. Transcript, 980 Hearing, *People v. Orenthal James Simpson*, No. BAO97211 (Cal. Super. Ct., Nov. 7, 1994).

21. Nietzel & Dillehay, "Psychologists as Consultants for Change of Venue, The Use of Public Opinion Surveys," 7 *Law and Human Behavior* 309 (1983).

22. O'Connell, "Pretrial Publicity, Change of Venue, Public Opinion Polls: A Theory of Procedural Justice," 65 *U. Det. L. Rev.* 171, 177 (1988).

23. *Irvin v. Dowd*, 366 U.S. 717 (1961).

24. Whitebread and Contreras, *supra* note 13 (emphasis added).

25. Judge Antolini, quoted by the Associated Press, *The San Diego Union-Tribune*, Sept. 19, 1995, p. A3.

26. Uelmen, *supra* note 1 at 976–77.

27. Stabile, *supra* note 15 at 344, citing *Gulf Oil v. Gilbert*, 330 U.S. 501, 508–09 (1947).

28. *Rideau v. Louisiana*, 373 U.S. 723 (1963).

29. *Nebraska Press Association v. Stuart*, 427 U.S. 539, 559 (1976).

30. *Id.* at 553–54 (quoting *Sheppard*, 384 U.S. at 362–63).

31. Transcript, *Sharon Rufo et al. v. Orenthal James Simpson*, No. SCO31947 (Cal. Super. Ct., Aug. 23, 1996).

32. Serrano, "Lawyer Seeks to Soften McVeigh's Public Image," *Los Angeles Times*, Sept. 9, 1996, p. A10.

33. *United States v. Salameh*, 992 F. 2d, 445, 446 (2d Cir. 1993) (quoting April 1, 1993 trial court ruling).

34. *Id.* at 447.

35. Snyder, "Rhetoric, Evidence, and Bar Agency Restrictions on Speech by Attorneys," 28 *Creighton L. Rev.* 357, 406 (Feb. 1995).

36. Transcript, *Rufo v. Simpson*, *supra* note 31.

37. Wilson, *Headline Justice: Inside the Courtroom: The Country's Most Controversial Trials*, Thunder's Mouth Press (N.Y., 1996) p. 85.

38. McCall, "Cameras in the Criminal Courtroom: A Sixth Amendment Analysis," 85 *Colum L. Rev.* 1546, 1572 (1985).

39. "TV in the Courtroom: Are We on the Air or Up in the Air"? American Inns of Court—Enright Chapter, San Diego, California, Sept. 7, 1995.

40. *Sheppard*, 384 U.S. at 362–363.

41. Uelmen, *supra* note 1, at 974–975.

42. *Dawud Majid Mu'Min v. Virginia*, 500 U.S. 415 (1991).

43. Uelmen, *supra* note 1, at 978.

Chapter Eleven

1. Brazaitis, "What the Nation Needs Is Supreme Court TV," *The Plain Dealer*, Jan. 12, 1997, p. 1D.

2. Burney, "Judge Bars Cameras from Testimony in 'Megan's Law' trial," Associated Press, Mar. 7, 1997.

3. Pugsley, "This Courtroom Is Not a Television Studio: Why Judge Fujisaki Made the Correct Call in Gagging the Lawyers and Parties, and Banning the Cameras from the O.J. Simpson Civil Case," Symposium—The Sound of Silence: Reflections on the Use of the Gag Order, 17 *Loy. L.A. Ent. L.J.* 369, 379 (1997).

4. Bell, "Let the Light in on Federal Trials. Judiciary: Paranoia Thrives in Darkness; Cameras in the Courts Can Help People Understand the Sometimes Inexplicable," *Las Vegas Review-Journal*, Jan. 21, 1996, p. 1C.

5. Simon, "Dramatic Reform Proposed for California Jury System. Courts: System Would Allow Less Than Unanimous Verdicts. But Overhaul May Be Too Extreme, Critics Say," *Los Angeles Times*, Apr. 30, 1996, p. A14.

6. California Rules of Professional Conduct, rule 5-120 (1995).

7. Cal. Evid. Code, sec. 1370.

8. Elias, "Simpson Case Spurs New Laws," *Newsday*, May 19, 1997, p. A29.

9. Larson, "Tuesday's Decisions Offered a Verdict on the State of the Networks," *The Fresno Bee*, Feb. 7, 1997, p. E6.

10. Chemerinsky and Levenson, "The Ethics of Being a Commentator," 69 *S. Cal. L. Rev.* 1303, 1322 (1996).

11. *Id.*, quoting Caplan, "Why Play-by-Play Coverage Strikes Out for Lawyers," 82 *A.B.A.J.* 62, 65 (1966).

12. Abramovsky & Edelstein, "Cameras in the Jury Room: An Unnecessary and Dangerous Precedent," 28 *Ariz. St. L. J.* 865, 885 (1996).

13. Holdsworth, *A History of English Law* 317 , Sweet & Maxwell (7th ed. 1956).

14. *Clark v. United States*, 289 U.S. 1, 13 (1933).

15. Abramovsky & Edelstein, *supra* note 12, at 883.

16. *Id.* at 868.

17. *Id.* at 874.

18. Scheflin & Van Dyke, "Merciful Juries: The Resilience of Jury Nullification," 53 *Guild Practitioner* 71 (1996).

19. Transcript, "CBS Reports: Enter the Jury Room," CBS, Apr. 16, 1997, Burrelle's Information Service, p. 39.

20. *Id.* at 33–36, 43, 49. The defense was allowed to tell the jury about the reduced penalty the co-defendant faced when he testified against Solano, to impeach his credibility.

21. *Id.* at 37, 39, 43.

22. *Id.* at 49–50.

23. *Id.* at 57.

24. *Id.* at 1–31 and 59–70.

25. *Id.* at 1, 4

26. *Id.* at 5.

27. *Id.* at 4.

28. Abramovsky & Edelstein, *supra* note 12, at 870–71.

29. As noted in chapter 8, some new federal court facilities feature an array of electronic equipment, although it is primarily designed to assist lawyers in presenting their cases and to provide a record of the proceedings.

30. See 49 *So. Car. L. Rev.* 1–82 (1997), for a debate over former U.S. Attorney

(Dist. of No. Dak.) Stephen Easton's proposal to assess broadcasters who televise trials; the funds would be used to assist crime victims. Opponents include South Carolina judge William Howard (Susan Smith trial), who contends Easton's idea would violate the First Amendment and the Equal Protection Clause.

31. Halpert, "Court-Jester TV. Trials Work Better If They're Not Media Circuses," *Los Angeles Daily Journal*, Jun. 17, 1996, p. 6.

32. Brill, letter to *ABA Journal*, Jul. 1994, p. 10.

33. Strahinic, "Court TV's Rising Star," *The Boston Globe Magazine*, Mar. 19, 1995, p. 24.

34. Uelmen, "The Five Hardest Lessons of the O.J. Trial," 7 *Issues in Ethics* 16, Markkula Center for Applied Ethics, Santa Clara University (1996).

35. Uelmen, *Lessons from the Trial*, Andrews & McMeel (K.C., 1996), pp. 100–101.

36. Bell, *supra* note 4.

Index

About the Authors

Marjorie Cohn is an associate professor at Thomas Jefferson School of Law in San Diego. A criminal defense attorney and legal analyst, she provides commentary on high profile trials and criminal justice issues for newspaper, television and radio. The Stanford University and Santa Clara University School of Law graduate is editor of *Guild Practitioner*. Cohn lives in San Diego with her husband, attorney Jerry Wallingford, and her young son.

David Dow is a retired CBS News correspondent and has covered many of the epic trials of the era—both O. J. Simpson trials, the Rodney King beating cases, the McMartin preschool molestation saga and the "Twilight Zone" trial. The Emmy Award-winning journalist has witnessed justice as it's carried out in more than two dozen nations of the Americas and Asia. A native of California's Gold Rush country and graduate of Stanford University, Dow now lives in the Los Angeles suburbs with wife Nancy Edwards, M.D.